WOMEN AND THE PIANO

WOMEN AND THE PIANO

A History in 50 Lives

Susan Tomes

YALE UNIVERSITY PRESS
NEW HAVEN AND LONDON

Copyright © 2024 Susan Tomes

All rights reserved. This book may not be reproduced in whole or in part, in any form (beyond that copying permitted by Sections 107 and 108 of the U.S. Copyright Law and except by reviewers for the public press) without written permission from the publishers.

All reasonable efforts have been made to provide accurate sources for all images that appear in this book. Any discrepancies or omissions will be rectified in future editions.

For information about this and other Yale University Press publications, please contact:
U.S. Office: sales.press@yale.edu   yalebooks.com
Europe Office: sales@yaleup.co.uk   yalebooks.co.uk

Set in Adobe Caslon Pro by IDSUK (DataConnection) Ltd
Printed in Great Britain by TJ Books, Padstow, Cornwall

Library of Congress Control Number: 2023946542

ISBN 978-0-300-26657-3

A catalogue record for this book is available from the British Library.

10 9 8 7 6 5 4 3 2 1

CONTENTS

List of Illustrations   viii

Introduction   1
From harpsichord to piano   5
From the eighteenth to the nineteenth centuries: Women and the rise of the piano   9

FIFTY WOMEN PIANISTS

The dawn of the piano era   23
   Anne-Louise Boyvin d'Hardancourt Brillon de Jouy   23
   Maria Theresia von Paradis   26
   Josepha von Auernhammer   30
   Marianna Martines   34
   Therese Jansen Bartolozzi   37
   Sara Levy   40
   Hélène de Montgeroult   43
Women in the age of the concert pianist   48
   Maria Szymanowska   51
   Lucy Anderson   54
   Louise Farrenc   56
   Fanny Mendelssohn   59
   Louise Dulcken   64
   Marie Pleyel   68

CONTENTS

Clara Schumann	72
Wilhelmine Clauss-Szarvady	79
Arabella Goddard	82
Amy Fay	85
Sophie Menter	88
Marie Jaëll	91
Leopoldine Wittgenstein	93
Teresa Carreño	96
Cécile Chaminade	102
Adele aus der Ohe	107
Fannie Bloomfield Zeisler	110
Winnaretta Singer	113
Amy Beach	117
Marguerite Long	121
Wanda Landowska	125
Olga Samaroff	129
Nadia Boulanger	132
Myra Hess	137
Guiomar Novaes	141
Clara Haskil	144
Maria Yudina	147
Lili Kraus	150
Eileen Joyce	155
Margaret Bonds	157
Annie Fischer	160
Nancy Weir	162
Alicia de Larrocha	165
Tatiana Nikolayeva	169
Yvonne Loriod	172
Philippa Schuyler	174
Zhu Xiao-Mei	178
Jazz and light-music pianists	181
Lovie Austin	181

Raie da Costa	185
Mary Lou Williams	187
Winifred Atwell	191
Hazel Scott	194
Nina Simone	196
Further perspectives	201
Where are we now?	209
Coda	239
Endnotes	*243*
Further reading	*253*
Acknowledgements	*256*
Index	*257*

ILLUSTRATIONS

Anne-Louise Brillon de Jouy depicted in Fragonard's *L'Étude*, 1769.	24
Hélène de Montgeroult by Louis-Philippe-Joseph Girod de Vienney, nineteenth century.	45
Maria Szymanowska by Aleksander Kokular, 1825. The Picture Art Collection / Alamy.	52
Fanny Mendelssohn by Wilhelm Hensel, 1847. Pictorial Press Ltd / Alamy.	61
Louise Dulcken by Richard James Lane, 1836. © National Portrait Gallery, London.	67
Clara Schumann by Franz Hanfstaengl, *c.* 1850. The Picture Art Collection / Alamy.	76
Wilhelmine Clauss-Szarvady, nineteenth century. Interfoto / Alamy.	80
Sophie Menter by Ilya Repin, 1887.	90
Teresa Carreño by Mathew Brady, *c.* 1862. National Portrait Gallery, Smithsonian Institution; Frederick Hill Meserve Collection.	97
Cécile Chaminade, *c.* 1880. Chronicle / Alamy.	105
Winnaretta Singer, 1926. Album / Alamy.	116
Amy Beach, nineteenth century. Library of Congress (LC-USZ62-65092).	119
Wanda Landowska.	126

Nadia Boulanger, 1962. Associated Press / Alamy.	136
Clara Haskil, 1929. Lebrecht Music & Arts / Alamy.	145
Nancy Weir by David Franklin, 1992. Creative Commons CC BY 2.5.	164
Tatiana Nikolayeva by Peter Rae, 1993. Fairfax Media Archives via Getty Images.	171
Philippa Schuyler by Fred Palumbo, 1959. Library of Congress (LC-USZ62-109640).	176
Mary Lou Williams by William P. Gottlieb, 1946. Library of Congress (LC-GLB13-0923).	190
Nina Simone by Ron Kroon, 1965. National Archive of the Netherlands, Fotocollectie Anefo (918-5601).	200

INTRODUCTION

This is a book about the history of women pianists, from the development of the piano in the eighteenth century to our own day. Why single out women for this history? The piano is an instrument that anyone can play, irrespective of gender, and today's world is full of both men and women pianists of every level of accomplishment, from beginners to celebrity concert pianists. But as with so many other fields, women pianists have long had to struggle against disparagement, neglect and collective amnesia. Even those who were famous in their own time have often been quickly forgotten.

When I was a child learning the piano, I took it for granted that eminent pianists were men, or, more accurately, I picked up that message from the opinions and conversations of those around me. Male celebrity pianists came to my home city of Edinburgh to play concertos with orchestra; their names were on LP records. When my piano teachers suggested I go and buy a record of piano music, to familiarise myself with great playing, the recommended artists were always male – I don't recall ever being pointed towards a recording by a woman pianist.

As a budding pianist I was taught to admire Cortot, Schnabel, Backhaus, Paderewski, Horowitz, Rubinstein, Richter, Gieseking,

Kempff, Solomon, Gilels, Curzon, Moiseiwitsch, Arrau, Michelangeli, Katchen – names that kept coming up in debates about who was best at which repertoire. And of course the repertoire they played was by the great male pianist-composers of the past, from Mozart to Rachmaninoff. When I went to orchestral concerts with a piano concerto on the programme, I was more impressed if the soloist was a famous man – though I do remember liking Annie Fischer, perhaps the only female pianist I recall from my early concert-going. For a while I kept a little autograph book in which I collected the signatures of famous visiting pianists, but I remember those pink, green and yellow pages as a parade of male names. I regret now that nobody tried to hold up women pianists as role models for me, and how little I thought to ask about them. Why were they not as famous as the men? I did not know how many obstacles society had put in women's way, or how consistently women pianists, no matter how talented, have been registered as less important simply because they were female.

I knew a few names from history books, of course – the small cast of female characters such as Clara Schumann, often the token woman at board meetings of history's famous pianists. Such women often have walk-on parts in the biographies of famous men who taught them, wrote for them, loved them, helped them, were inspired by them and depended on them in various ways. But when I delved deeper, I became aware of many *more* female pianists who had achieved a lot in their own day. They were every bit as interesting as their better-known male contemporaries, and when it came to the era of recordings, their playing sometimes seemed more distinctive. I knew the men's names – indeed I had known them for ages, had memorised them and their dates for music exams. Yet some of the women I had never even *heard of*.

What was going on? Why had they slipped through the net? I could only conclude that there had been some sort of deeply ingrained, tacit collective agreement that we could safely forget about them simply because they *were women*. They were what modern scholars might call 'a norm violation', a departure from the expected and therefore a source of discomfort. Proper concert pianists are men, aren't they? Making that magnificent instrument do one's bidding in front of an adoring crowd is a heroic, larger-than-life endeavour better suited to men. The few women pianists we read about were really just imitating men – weren't they?

In fact, these women were pioneers in a number of ways – studying abroad, travelling independently, playing from memory, giving lecture-recitals, performing 'cycles' of complete works and premieres of new works, reviving historical works, raising money for their own debut concerts, commissioning music, recording, broadcasting, fronting their own TV shows, devising educational initiatives, and carving out respected places for themselves in male-dominated fields – all against a background of often half-hearted support. Sometimes they were pioneers on behalf of their sex, and sometimes on behalf of the whole profession. There were too many to write about in detail, but I decided to highlight fifty enterprising women whose stories illustrate a range of issues that female pianists had to confront. These women helped to enlarge and diversify the profession. Between them, they demonstrated to the public that the male view of piano repertoire was not all-encompassing and the male approach to a career was not the only way of doing things. They showed that women were not merely imitating men but had their own artistic authority.

Many of those women pianists also composed their own music. As part of my research, I looked out some of their music and learned to play it. It was a pleasure to discover many fine pieces I had never heard of before, but as the tally mounted up, I also felt increasingly aware of previous ignorance: not just my own, but a widespread ignorance relating to high-quality piano music composed by women over the last 250 years.

Some of their names will be familiar, but many won't. I became painfully aware that there was really no justice in the way their achievements had been forgotten. To a large extent their fate was determined by the fact that most historians were male and chose to give priority to men's achievements, often discounting women's. In overlooking women's contributions, these male historians were only reflecting the social attitudes of their day, but unfortunately their neglect of women set an enduring pattern.

As Simone de Beauvoir pointed out in 1949 in *The Second Sex*, 'Representation of the world, like the world itself, is the work of men; they describe it from their own point of view, which they confuse with absolute truth.'[1] Historians of music joined the dots between high-achieving men of different generations, constructing lineages of piano-playing in which the Great X taught Y, who taught Z, who influenced Mr A, B and C. Perhaps this seemed a reasonable way to do it when men, once launched on their careers, remained in the public eye for decades at a time whereas women often had to drop out, either occasionally or permanently, in order to attend to caring responsibilities. As the novelist Anne Tyler observes in *Redhead by the Side of the Road*, 'Women kept the world running, really. (There was a definite difference between "running the world" and "keeping it running").'[2]

FROM HARPSICHORD TO PIANO

Since antiquity across Europe and Asia there have been images and descriptions of women playing psalteries, harps, lyres, citharas, zithers and dulcimers – multi-stringed instruments, one note per string, which were forerunners of our familiar keyboard instruments. We know that in ancient times these instruments were used for music of a gentler character and often to accompany singing; indeed dulcimers, which are mentioned in the Bible, derive their name from the Latin *dulce*, sweet, and Greek *mélos*, melody. The strings of the dulcimer were struck with little hammers or slender sticks with rounded heads a bit like teaspoons, making the instrument the ancestor of the piano. These instruments did not have the power of sustaining notes loudly or for a long time, as wind and bowed instruments could; they could not 'call to arms' in the way that brass or the more piercing wind instruments did. In short, they fulfilled the vision of the Greek philosopher Plato, who wrote in his *Laws* that women should make music that was 'orderly and moderate'.[1]

The idea of attaching a keyboard to a string instrument was put into practice in medieval times, and the arrangement of keys we have come to regard as classic – with seven 'naturals' and five raised keys in each octave – seems to have arisen in the fifteenth century. In Europe, psalteries, citharas and zithers were supplanted in the sixteenth century by harpsichords, their strings plucked by plectra operated from the keyboard, and by clavichords, in which the strings are struck by a metal tangent. Pianos, which were developed in the eighteenth century, were in effect dulcimers with keyboards, their strings struck with little mechanical hammers set in motion by pressing down the piano keys. There was no definitive moment when the piano supplanted the earlier instruments; rather, they coexisted for decades, with keyboard players accustomed to playing whatever instrument was available. Many homes appear to have had a larger keyboard instrument in the drawing room, to entertain family and guests, while perhaps a little clavichord would be found in the private room of a keen keyboard player.

In this period there were several distinguished female harpsichordists who played in artistic salons, and in court circles. Two of them, Marie-Françoise Certain (1661–1711) and Élisabeth Jacquet de la Guerre (1665–1729), were contemporaries at the court of Louis XIV in Paris. Certain, who had her own salon in the rue du Hasard, was known to encourage female composers to perform their works for her discerning audience. Her playing was praised in verse by Jean de la Fontaine, author of the *Fables*: 'The playing of this unique child touches me more than Isis and all her music.'[2] Jacquet de la Guerre, from a family of keyboard players, was dubbed 'the wonder of the universe' by the journal *Mercure galant* when she was only twelve.[3] In her salon in the rue Guillaume, she was renowned for her ability to improvise extensively. Somewhat later in London, the harpsichordist Elisabetta Gambarini (1730–65) was only eighteen when she became the first female composer in Britain to publish a collection of her own keyboard music, printed in a deluxe edition paid for by an impressively long list of subscribers including fellow composers Handel and Geminiani. In her twenties she performed frequently in London as harpsichordist, organist and singer.

Not known as a performer, but known to history because her husband J.S. Bach dedicated two *Kleine Notenbüchlein* (*Little*

Notebooks) of music to her in the 1720s, is Anna Magdalena Bach, who was clearly a prolific harpsichordist, collecting and copying many pieces by her husband and other composers.

As the eighteenth century progressed, harpsichord and clavichord shared the honours with the developing fortepiano/pianoforte/piano. These terms are interchangeable: Bartolomeo Cristofori's invention of around 1700 was initially referred to as a *gravicembalo col piano e forte*, or harpsichord with soft and loud, and its strings were struck with hammers rather than being plucked as on the harpsichord.

On the *gravicembalo col piano e forte*, unlike on the harpsichord, players could control the speed with which the hammers hit the string, so as to create variety of tone and volume. This gave them greater ability to reflect ever-changing feelings and to copy the phrasing of musical partners (voice, stringed or wind instruments). The first pianos were no louder than harpsichords, but as the mechanism developed and the frame was strengthened, the power of the piano's tone increased, making it more suitable than harpsichords and clavichords for being played in halls where listeners might be seated some distance away. As public concerts became more and more important in cultural life, this was a crucial advantage.

The piano started to overtake the harpsichord at different times in different cities of Europe. The German piano-maker Johannes Zumpe settled in London around 1760 and soon started to make square pianos (not in reality square, but rectangular). In 1766, J.S. Bach's son Johann Christian Bach, who had also settled in London, published *Six Sonatas for Harpsichord or Piano-Forte* (opus 5); these were probably in acknowledgement of Zumpe's pianos appearing on the scene. It was in this same year that Sir Joshua Reynolds painted the portrait of the beautiful Mrs Luther, a skilled amateur keyboard player whose salon illustrated the transition from the harpsichord to the piano. Initially Mrs Luther was a customer of Burkhart Shudi, the famous harpsichord-maker in London, but she later became a customer of the Scottish cabinet-maker John Broadwood, who became a partner in Shudi's firm in 1770 and went on to make the full-toned pianos that Haydn and Beethoven admired.

In 1767, an advert for a benefit concert on 16 May at the Covent Garden Theatre announced that the composer Charles Dibdin would be accompanying Miss Brickler in a song from Thomas Arne's oratorio *Judith*, 'on a new instrument called piano-forte'.[4] This event was the first known instance of the piano being played in a public concert in England.

It's intriguing to think that at this time, even Wolfgang Amadeus Mozart may not have encountered the piano. It was not until the winter of 1774–5 that Mozart was first reported to have played 'an excellent fortepiano' at the home of a Mr Albert in Munich.[5]

FROM THE EIGHTEENTH TO THE NINETEENTH CENTURIES: WOMEN AND THE RISE OF THE PIANO

As the piano improved and became popular, players of keyboard instruments were increasingly associated with the piano, and the notion of the 'pianist' took hold. At first, as in the days of the harpsichord and clavichord, the emphasis was on private music-making, in which women were encouraged to participate. In that era, playing the piano was not considered quite suitable for the manly man. In December 1829 the London *Morning Post* put it rather strongly: 'There is, we know, a common and *very natural prejudice* against men becoming musicians, and ardently as we are attached to the art, and impressed with its importance, we confess that we cannot see a man sit down to the piano, or take a guitar in his hand, without an involuntary feeling of degradation.'[1] Playing the piano was seen as passive, and while passivity may be a charming quality in a woman, it was not fitting for men.

All that began to change with the rise of the public concert and the piano recital. In the nineteenth century, when piano recitals became public events and pianists became exalted figures, men spearheaded that charge, as they did in so many fields, when the skill became professionalised and a matter of public *performance* rather than unassuming skill. Men made sure to let women know that the professional sphere was no place for ladies.

In the field of literature, there is an excellent example of this attitude in a letter written on 12 March 1837 by the poet laureate, Robert Southey, to the young Charlotte Brontë, who had sent him some of her poems along with a letter explaining that she intended to be 'forever known'. His reply? 'Literature cannot be the business of a woman's life, and it ought not to be. The more she is engaged in her proper duties, the less leisure she will have for it, even as an accomplishment and a recreation. To those duties you have not yet been called, and when you are you will be less eager for celebrity.'[2] Yet writing poems or novels was a private activity, unseen by readers. How much more improper then for a woman to want to be 'forever known' through her performances on the public stage!

Against this background, women who had ambitions to perform outside the domestic sphere needed exceptional determination, and even then they could succeed only with social and financial support, from their families and from promoters in high positions. Many great talents must have been lost to these conventional barriers. A poignant example is the sister of Wolfgang Amadeus Mozart, Maria Anna, known as Nannerl. She was four years older than Wolfgang, and when she was eleven, she and her brother were taken by their father, Leopold, on a three-year tour of European cities, playing to the nobility. At first it was Nannerl who was more highly praised, playing on the harpsichord 'the longest and most difficult pieces with impressive precision'.[3] As time went on, however, Wolfgang's development was so startling that he became the sensation of the tour. By the time Nannerl was a teenager she had been eclipsed. Her father decreed that she was no longer to tour with her brother. She continued to play and compose in private, married, raised three children and five stepchildren, and lived to the age of seventy-eight. But not a note of her compositions survives, and she never played the piano in public. Wolfgang, who died at the age of thirty-five, was one of the first composer-pianists to exploit the expressive possibilities of the instrument and rose to be one of the great names in European music. Wolfgang praised one of Nannerl's early songs, urging her to 'try this more often'.[4] But we don't know what her song was like, and we are left to wonder what she could have achieved as a performer and composer over her long life if she had had the opportunity.

Clearly, the great majority of women who played the piano did so at home. However talented they were, the conventions of their time encouraged them to restrict themselves to their domestic circle. Most of these women are unknown, unrecorded by writers and historians. But they nevertheless laid the foundation of women's piano-playing, and it is important to acknowledge them before we embark on the careers of the celebrated performers.

The association between keyboard instruments and women in private situations goes back a long way. One could even make a link with angels in Renaissance paintings. Renaissance artists considered keyboard instruments 'apt' for angels, who, as Christmas cards remind us each year, often play little 'portative' or portable pipe organs. Angels are traditionally neither male nor female, but Renaissance artists portrayed them with flowing locks and robes, enhancing the impression that playing keyboard instruments makes one look angelic. The patron saint of music, St Cecilia, is often portrayed as playing an organ.

Later, many seventeenth-century Dutch artists painted young ladies standing or sitting at a small, rectangular harpsichord appropriately named the 'virginal(s)': for example, Johannes Vermeer's beautiful *Lady Standing at a Virginal* (1672), *A Young Lady Seated at a Virginal* (1672) and *Lady at the Virginal with a Gentleman* (1674).

Among eighteenth-century commentators, John Essex, a dancing master and author of a 1721 treatise on correct conduct for young ladies, wrote that 'The *Harpsichord, Spinet, Lute* and *Base Violin* are Instruments most agreeable to the Ladies: There are some others that really are unbecoming the Fair Sex: as the *Flute, Violin* and *Hautboy*

[oboe]; the last of which is too Manlike, and would look indecent in a Woman's Mouth.'[5]

Essex's views on the unsuitability of many instruments for ladies were echoed by other writers later in the eighteenth century. By contrast, a keyboard instrument does not require the player to hold or support it in the air. There is no physical exertion involved in basic playing. And as the player's head is not involved in sound production, they might hope to retain control over their facial expression. Playing the harpsichord or piano did not look like *work*, which allowed listeners to enjoy it without being troubled by questions of propriety.

From the late eighteenth century onwards, when pianos became available and many European families acquired them for the home, playing the piano became one of the 'accomplishments' a well-brought-up young lady was expected to master. Along with drawing, painting, sewing and embroidery, playing cards, dancing and singing, having a nice posture and writing with an elegant hand, the ability to play the piano was prized when there was no recorded music to use as entertainment.

Domestic scenes in paintings continue to feature women at the keyboard right through the nineteenth to the twentieth centuries, echoing the theme set by Vermeer's player of the virginals back in the seventeenth century. Renoir, Matisse, Cézanne, Van Gogh, Picasso, Carl Larsson, Vilhelm Hammershøi and a host of lesser-known contemporaries evoked the rapt, private world of the female pianist. There are women alone at the piano, sometimes with their backs turned to us. Women looking graceful and lovely, turning to smile at us as they play the piano in their finest gowns. Women showing their daughters the piano. Women playing for singers or in chamber-music groups. Women sitting side by side playing piano duets. Women being given a piano lesson. Women sitting by a piano with their children grouped around it as though the piano were an emblem of wellbeing.

Knowing how to play simple tunes and chords on the piano enabled a young lady to accompany songs, and she could also provide music for dancing – an important social activity. For musical evenings, women could play piano duets, sharing the piano stool with another person (perhaps a man!) in unusual proximity – at least during periods when ladies' skirts were not so wide that they made it tricky for a duet partner to share the piano bench. If she became very skilled, a woman might aim to hold the attention of the room with the performance of solo music. This must have been quite thrilling for a pianist in any era when women were supposed to be seen more than heard, for, with the exception of reading aloud to the family circle, performing music was one of the only ways that a woman could command prolonged respectful silence from mixed company.

There was another reason why keyboard instruments – especially the larger ones – were 'apt' for women: because of the size and weight of the instruments, they remained at home. As pianos became larger and heavier, they tended to be placed in one carefully chosen spot in the house and left there permanently like any other item of heavy furniture. By the time piano frames were being made of cast iron (a development that began in 1825), there was no question of casually moving the instrument in and out of the house. Guaranteed to remain in the home, the piano was somehow a perfect partner for women.

Until the mid-nineteenth century, pianos were expensive, affordable only for affluent families. The later spread of pianos into lower levels of society was linked to the Industrial Revolution, the rise of factories and the increasing affordability of instruments. Until then, ladies' skill in piano-playing was in part a tribute to the financial standing (earned or unearned) of the male head of the family, able to support his wife and daughters in a life of leisure. Playing the piano for hours on end was proof of leisure time, the prerogative of certain social classes. Many women took their piano-playing very seriously, but the opportunity to do so was dependent on their family's affluence.

One reason that the piano became a popular domestic instrument is that first steps in learning to play it usually bring gratifying success. There is no physical effort involved in forming notes, and after even a single piano lesson a beginner can play a tune with a pleasing sound. Moreover, a novice cannot offend anyone by playing the piano out of tune by placing the finger in the wrong position, as on a violin. But although progress on the piano comes easily at first, sustained effort is needed to get past the stage of picking out a tune or accompanying yourself with a few basic chords, and there's a steep gradient between beginner's luck and the next levels.

Playing the piano nicely was an important calling card for a young lady in search of a husband, in the days when women's opportunities for economic independence were so limited. There was nothing new about this, of course. In the seventeenth century, Robert Burton in *The Anatomy of Melancholy* commented that young women were made to learn musical instruments as a way of attracting husbands, but often gave up their music once their aim of marrying had been achieved. 'We see this daily verified in our young women and wives, they that being maids took so much pains to sing, play, and dance, with such cost and charge to their parents, to get those graceful qualities, now being married will scarce touch an instrument, they care not for it.'[6] Almost two centuries later, an American newspaper, the *Star*, was more specific about the instrument: it claimed that in 1810 it was only necessary for a young lady to be able to play the *piano* to get a husband.[7] In Jane Austen's *Sense and Sensibility* (1811) we learn of a locked piano in Lady Middleton's drawing room and are dryly informed that upon her ladyship's marriage, she 'had celebrated that event by giving up music'.[8]

It is surprising to read how much effort sometimes went into practising this social skill. A striking example, from real life, is described in Elizabeth Grant of Rothiemurchus's *Memoirs of a Highland Lady*, in which she describes how she and her sister Mary got up to do their piano practice during the winter of 1812. They were from a well-to-do family, living in an elegant country house at the heart of the Cairngorm mountains.

> In winter we rose half an hour later [i.e. at 6.30 a.m.], without candle, or fire, or warm water. Our clothes were all laid on a chair overnight in readiness for being taken up in proper order. My Mother would not give us candles, and Miss Elphick [the children's governess] insisted we should get up. We were not allowed hot water, and really in the highland winters, when the breath froze on the sheets, and the water in the jugs became cakes of ice, washing was a cruel necessity, the fingers were pinched enough. As we could play our scales well in the dark, the two pianofortes and the harp began the day's work. How very near crying was the one whose turn set her at the harp I will not speak of; the strings cut the poor cold fingers so that the blisters often bled. Martyr the first decidedly sat in the dining room at the harp. Martyr the second put her poor blue hands on the keys of the grand pianoforte in the drawing room, for in these two rooms the fires were never lighted till near nine o'clock.[9]

Anyone reading Elizabeth Grant's recollection of piano practice might assume that hers was an extreme case. But the social reformer Hannah More recounts in *Strictures on the Modern System of Female Education* (1799) what 'a person of great eminence' had told her when discussing the long hours put in at the piano by young women:

> Suppose your pupil to have begun at six years of age and to continue at the average of four hours a day *only*; Sunday excepted, and thirteen days allowed for travelling annually, till she is eighteen, the state stands thus: 300 days multiplied by four, the number of hours stands at 1200; that number multiplied by twelve, which is the number of years, amounts to 14,400 hours.[10]

This exceeds by a wide margin the 10,000 hours which Malcolm Gladwell, in his book *Outliers: The Story of Success* (2008), tells us is necessary to achieve world-class expertise in any subject, but Hannah More remarks that the number of hours 'will perhaps be found to be far from exaggerated'.

In April 1786 Maria Josepha Holroyd, a fifteen-year-old English girl, wrote to her friend Serena describing a typical day, which saw her playing the harpsichord for an hour or more in the morning, and then, after drinking tea at 7 p.m., playing the piano until 10 p.m., 'when we have our little bit of supper'. These three or four daily hours spent at a keyboard are mentioned quite casually, as though they were an expected part of life, and it is also interesting to note that in 1786 the family possessed both a harpsichord and a piano, representing the old and new wave of domestic keyboard instruments.[11]

If a young lady was restricted in her social opportunities or unlucky in her search for a husband to support her, she still had the option of making some money by teaching the piano to carefully chosen pupils or as part of the duties of a governess to children of a well-to-do family. In Jane Austen's *Emma* (1815), Jane Fairfax is a talented pianist but a girl apparently without marriage prospects or money of her own. A conversation between Emma and her friend Harriet about Jane Fairfax's excellent piano-playing concludes with the dismissive remark, 'Besides, if she does play so very well, you know, it is no more than she is obliged to do, because she will have to teach.'[12] 'Having to teach' was a fate reserved for young ladies without inherited wealth, but teaching the piano was considered more genteel than lowlier occupations such as dressmaking or taking in laundry.

Music teachers would have been conscious of their role in supplying 'accomplishment' to female pupils. There were many notions of correct posture at the piano to pass on before one even embarked on questions of expression or musical interpretation. Elbows were to be held close to the body. The chair should be high enough to let the forearms slope down towards the keyboard. Hands were to move laterally, close to the keys, not jumping up and down or being raised so high that the result would be a hitting motion. The pupil should sit up, head and neck held nice and straight, without raising the shoulders.

As male pianists became increasingly famous, they were eagerly sought as teachers by wealthy families with talented daughters. Generally speaking, teachers came to the house, rather than the student going to them. Having piano lessons was fashionable, but parents were alert to the possibility that a male music teacher might take improper advantage of his physical closeness to the pupil during a piano lesson to prey upon a young lady's feelings. This had to be guarded against; consequently there might have been other people present in the room or within earshot during a lesson, and this would naturally have limited the scope of conversation. Piano lessons tended to be concentrated in the winter months because well-to-do families would decamp to summer residences for months at a time, interrupting the children's regular tuition (except in those cases where wealthy families took the tutors with them), and because the tutor, if he was a well-known performer, arranged his concert tours for the summer when travel was easier.

Many of the better-known teachers charged a hefty 'entrance fee' up front to guard against the danger that the student would vanish before the course of lessons had ended. In Haydn's London notebook he wrote that:

> If a singing, clavier or dancing master charges half a guinea a lesson, he requires an entrance fee of six guineas at the first lesson. This is because many Scotch and Irish in the winter proudly wish their children given lessons by the best masters and then at the end cannot pay. The entrance fee is waived if the master charges a guinea a lesson, but the guinea must be paid at each lesson.[13]

Haydn discovered that he could charge ten times as much for a lesson in London as he could in Vienna, while the entrepreneurial

Clementi was well known for having the highest fees of all, and he would sometimes teach high-paying 'society pupils' for as much as sixteen hours a day. In the 1830s, Chopin charged twenty francs for an hour's lesson in Paris at a time when a skilled French workman was earning no more than four francs a day, making Chopin's fee extraordinarily high. Moreover, Chopin made his pupils come to him, explaining that he taught better on his own piano in his own apartment. If his aristocratic lady pupils requested him to come to their home to teach them, he would charge a higher fee and make them send a carriage to fetch him.

Composers famous and not so famous wrote copious amounts of piano music for the domestic market, and many music publishing firms sprang up to deliver these new compositions to the public. Young ladies often collected single pieces of music and bound them together into folders of their own devising; in the family home of Jane Austen, who was fond of playing the piano, there were seventeen such home-made volumes of music amassed gradually over the years. These collections must have had a delightfully personal character, almost like diaries.

Although playing the piano was a valued occupation for a woman, there were plenty of doctors in the eighteenth and nineteenth centuries who worried about the effect of all this music on young ladies' health.[14]

In 1837 the Irish doctor James Johnson wrote that for young ladies, 'whose sensitive nerves, susceptible feelings, exquisite sympathies, tender affections, and delicate organization, are excited, stimulated, electrified' by too much music, the result could be disastrous for 'the countenance, the complexion, the gait – the whole physical and moral constitution of the female'.[15] This kind of view gathered pace throughout the nineteenth century. In 1877 the Scottish gynaecologist Lawson Tait wrote in *The Economy of Health* that music lessons 'were the cause of a great deal of menstrual mischief',[16] while in 1903 the psychiatrist Richard Krafft-Ebing pronounced that 'in cases of limited talent studying the piano is an inadequate achievement which makes heavy demands on the physical and mental strength of the player and often creates nervousness and in the case of untalented girls, if practiced too intensively or unwillingly, can become the cause of serious nervous diseases'.[17]

As a female reader from a later generation, one can sense an underlying, probably unconscious fear in these medical men that music would cause women to depart from their proper sphere – that of domesticity, childrearing and the care of husbands – and make inroads into spheres of activity that belonged to men. Music was all very well if limited to prettiness, but music had also long been recognised as a powerful force, capable of changing moods and behaviour. *What would happen if women actually took possession of its powers?* The biographies that follow give us some answers to this question.

FIFTY WOMEN PIANISTS

THE DAWN OF THE PIANO ERA

ANNE-LOUISE BOYVIN D'HARDANCOURT BRILLON DE JOUY

'La Brillante' was the nickname of the French keyboard player Anne-Louise Boyvin d'Hardancourt Brillon de Jouy (1744–1824), who presided over an artistic salon at her marital home in Passy on the outskirts of Paris. Her father, a royal treasurer, had grown up in India and was known for his devotion to culture. He made sure that his daughter received a thorough musical education. In due course, Anne-Louise married a man who was also a financial officer of the royal court and they moved to a beautiful estate with an extensive garden in Passy. Initially a harpsichordist, Anne-Louise became an early adopter of the piano when the new instrument appeared on the scene. In fact, she had Johann Christian Bach (J.S. Bach's youngest son, 'the London Bach') send her an English piano from London, and she also acquired a German piano.

She never performed outside her domestic circle, but was well known among musical connoisseurs as a fine keyboard player and composer. Each Wednesday and Saturday in her private salon she presided over a remarkable circle of guests, which included famous musicians and artists passing through Paris at the time. Her regular guests included Tartini's best pupil, the French violinist André-Noël Pagin, and the Italian composer Luigi Boccherini. Anne-Louise often played at these salons and accompanied others, for example her two daughters, the wonderfully named Cunégonde and Aldegonde, who were good singers. A delightful painting by Fragonard (a family friend), previously known as *L'Étude*, is thought to be a portrait of the young Anne-Louise Brillon de Jouy in about 1769. In 1767, having heard Brillon de Jouy playing her piano, the Italian composer Boccherini wrote a set of six sonatas for piano and violin for her, telling her that he had never before composed for the keyboard, but 'you inspired them, and you embellish them'.[1] Interestingly, Boccherini added dynamic markings of *piano*, *forte* and *fortissimo* to the piano parts, an innovation that identifies them as having been conceived for the new piano rather than the harpsichord, where

because of the plucking mechanism the player has no control over the tone of individual notes.

A number of other composers of the time also dedicated works to Anne-Louise. She herself composed extensively for keyboard, voice and chamber ensembles of various kinds, but never attempted to publish any of her works, for at the time it was not considered fitting for women to publish their own compositions, especially if they were from the aristocracy. The English historian Charles Burney was a guest at her salon and reported that she had played him some of her own music, first on the harpsichord and then on the piano. He said she played with great ease, taste and feeling, and described her as 'an excellent sightswoman', or sight-reader – which shows that she felt confident and comfortable enough to play something at sight in front of a distinguished visitor.[2] Around 1775 she composed two works for the probably unique combination of English piano, German piano and harpsichord (the three instruments she had in her salon), surely an indication that both harpsichords and pianos were to be found together in people's homes in the 1770s.[3]

In 1777 she acquired a new neighbour, the seventy-year-old American ambassador Benjamin Franklin, who came to live in a house in the same street in Passy. Franklin, one of the Founding Fathers of the United States, lived in France until 1785, charged with the task of securing French support for American independence. He soon became a regular guest at Anne-Louise's musical salons, which he described charmingly as 'my Opéra'.[4] He must have converted her to the cause of American independence, for in the year that Franklin came to live in her street she wrote what was to become her only well-known composition, the *Marche des insurgents*, to celebrate the surrender of the British Lieutenant-General John Burgoyne at Saratoga, New York, on 17 October 1777. This simple, fanfare-like piece is not, however, representative of her musical style; her sonatas for keyboard are bold and virtuosic. Some of them have been recorded in recent years and give the impression of lively, episodic improvisations that were written down as soon as possible after playing them, as if to capture and preserve their sense of fantasy and physical enjoyment of playing the piano.

The many letters between Benjamin Franklin and Anne-Louise make it clear that their friendship rapidly developed into a deep attachment; she told him that 'nobody in the four quarters of the world loves you as I do' and hoped to see him 'every Wednesday and Saturday for the rest of my life'.[5] Her husband was twenty-two years older than her, and it seems that their marriage was not always happy. Benjamin Franklin led an intensely active life in Paris as diplomat, scientist, intellectual, freemason and socialite; he was not available for the kind of settled relationship that Brillon de Jouy might have hoped for, but after some painful exchanges they came to an agreement in 1778 that she would consider him her 'Papa' and he would think of her in the light of a daughter. They corresponded warmly for the whole of Franklin's almost nine-year stay in France.

Her salons were brought to a halt by the French Revolution of 1789–94. The revolution had multiple causes, but ironically one of them was the near-bankrupting of the French government by its generous support of the American Revolution. Aristocrats in Paris were in considerable danger, and Brillon de Jouy retreated to the safety of relatives' homes in the French countryside, eventually settling in Normandy and following the upheaval in Paris from a distance.

MARIA THERESIA VON PARADIS

The delightfully named Maria Theresia von Paradis (1759–1824), a contemporary of the Mozart siblings, was a remarkable young woman whose life has inspired modern-day playwrights, composers, filmmakers and novelists to explore the mysteries surrounding her career.

Maria Theresia, the daughter of an imperial secretary in Vienna, was named after the Empress Maria Theresa, who took an interest in her education. The young Maria Theresia went suddenly blind in early childhood. She was extremely musical, and through her social connections was furnished with music lessons from several distinguished musicians who held positions at court. She studied piano with the Czech pianist and composer Leopold Koželuch, singing with Vincenzo Righini and composition with Antonio Salieri, anti-hero of Peter Shaffer's 1979 play *Amadeus* (later made into a film by Miloš Forman). Salieri it is who, in a fictional scene in the play, tries to stop Mozart from getting a court appointment by telling the emperor (falsely) that Mozart molested Maria Theresia von Paradis at a keyboard lesson. It was probably known in court circles that Maria Theresia's blindness made her vulnerable to deception. Curiously, it was also an advantage to her in her musical ambitions, because she was less eligible as a wife and therefore freer to pursue her musical interests. Her blindness also conferred some financial advantage on her family, for it prompted the empress to grant them an annual pension, to assist with her education.

This was an important factor in the episode that has most attracted playwrights and filmmakers. Maria Theresia had submitted to all kinds of weird and wonderful treatments intended to alleviate her blindness – encasing her head in plaster for weeks, 'bleeding' her with leeches, administering mild electric shocks to her eyes – but these were ineffective. In 1776, when she was a teenager, she became a patient of the famous physician Franz Anton Mesmer, a music lover and a friend of Mozart and Haydn. Mesmer had devised a therapy in which magnetised fluids were dispensed through pipes and applied to diseased parts of a patient's body with the aim of 'drawing off' the illness. He intensified the treatment by putting his patients into a trance and touching them in various ways. It was suggested that he might be able to cure Maria's blindness. She attended sessions with Mesmer at his grand house from 1776 until halfway through 1777. In a contemporary painting of one of his clinics she is portrayed at a keyboard instrument at the very right of the picture, among a crowd of mesmerised patients.[6]

It seems that during her sessions with Mesmer she did experience some return of the vision she lost as a child. This suggests that her blindness may have had a psychogenic component. However, her treatment was discontinued rather abruptly. There were hints of scandal – had Mesmer 'touched' his blind patient with more than therapeutic zeal? Or did Maria's father suddenly realise that the return of her sight would mean the loss of her disability pension, an important contribution to family finances? At any rate, when she ceased to be Mesmer's patient Maria Theresia's blindness returned. For a while she was disoriented and found piano-playing difficult, but she came to terms with not being able to see. Mesmer's methods became the focus of a critical inquiry. His 'magnetic fluids' were not proven to be effective, but later scientists felt that his ability to mesmerise or hypnotise his patients probably enabled some of them to mobilise healing effects within their own bodies.

Blindness did not hold von Paradis back; she became an excellent keyboard player, and, as has been noted with other blind pianists (for example the twentieth-century jazz pianist Art Tatum), her touch was unusually clear and precise. She was renowned for having memorised a large repertoire, and was said to be able to play complicated piano pieces she had heard only once. To set down her own compositions, she had a system of pegs of various shapes and sizes, representing notes and durations, which she stuck into holes in a board. This system was clear enough for music copyists to follow when transcribing her music into conventional notation.

She was able to go on concert tours – accompanied by her mother – as far afield as Paris (where she played fourteen concerts, including a performance for Queen Marie Antoinette) and London (where she played to George III). On her way to Paris in 1783 she called upon Leopold Mozart in Salzburg and happened to coincide with Wolfgang, who had brought Constanze to visit in an attempt to reconcile his father to his choice of a wife. It seems that this meeting may have prompted Mozart to promise von Paradis a new piano concerto, because, in a letter to Nannerl, Leopold Mozart referred to the concerto Mozart had written for Paradis as 'for Paris'; this seems likely to have been the B flat piano concerto K456, which she premiered.

A critic wrote in the *Journal de Paris* after hearing her play in a *concert spirituel* in the Tuileries in March 1784, 'One must have heard her to form an idea of the touch, the precision, the fluency and vividness of her playing.' Interestingly, he added:

> Until now, one had thought that the piano wasn't capable of making an impact on a hall as large as this one. Mlle P. is the first who has drawn from it a sound which allowed us to hear every note of her concerto, and also to be surprised by the nuances of forte and piano which this instrument hadn't seemed able to produce. She was given an ovation, and the applause redoubled when after her concerto she appeared in one of the boxes; this young person, as interesting for herself as for her talent, comes from Vienna in Austria. She is a pupil of Monsieur Kozeluch.

The *Mercure de France* agreed: 'Her success was prodigious and deserved to be so; we think it's impossible to bring this instrument to a higher degree of perfection.'[7]

Her gift for invention went further than her music-notating system. She invented devices that aided blind people to play cards, or to write down words. She made 'contour maps' out of papier-mâché. In Paris, her ideas helped Valentin Haüy with plans for the first ever school for the blind, opened in 1785 (Louis Braille, inventor of the Braille reading system, became a pupil in 1819). In Vienna, she opened her own music school for the blind when still only in her thirties, and managed to finance it by building up a list of subscribers, as well as by putting on a series of Sunday concerts in which she and her students played. She managed her finances so well, in fact, that she was able to leave a large sum of money for the continuation of her music school. This was an exceptional achievement for a woman who had no wealthy husband to support her initiatives.

In later years she focused more on composition and wrote a number of operas and cantatas as well as keyboard works, but most of her compositions – like Nannerl Mozart's – are now listed as 'lost'. I have seen an early edition of some of her songs, charming compositions whose lucidity and melodic gift remind one of Schubert.

Today, von Paradis is known for one particular composition, which ironically is not by her at all. The *Sicilienne* played at the wedding of Prince Harry and Meghan Markle in 2018 first popped into the concert repertoire in 1960, when the American violinist Samuel Dushkin presented it as a piece 'by' von Paradis. It seems likely, however, that Dushkin was copying the violinist Fritz Kreisler's cheeky trick of composing charming little pieces 'in old style' and attributing them to little-known composers of a bygone age. In this case, the *Sicilienne* is actually a lightly tweaked version of the slow movement of Carl Maria von Weber's violin and piano sonata in F major (opus 10, no. 1). Sad to say, Maria Theresia von Paradis is a good candidate for such a ruse, for she has a lovely name, but nobody knows her music.

JOSEPHA VON AUERNHAMMER

Mozart's letters to his family are famously spicy, and he was often alarmingly frank about people he met on his travels. Take, for example, the way he wrote about his Viennese pupil Josepha von Auernhammer (1758–1820), who was just two years younger than him. This talented young pianist had the misfortune not to be conventionally beautiful. The first time Mozart mentions the Auernhammer family, in 1781, he casually refers to her as 'the fat daughter'.[8] Once he is going to her house several times a week to have lunch and give her a piano lesson, he elaborates: 'If a painter wanted to portray the devil as lifelike as possible, he would have to seek out her face – she is heavy like a peasant wench, sweats to make you sick, and walks around dressed so scantily that one can read the message plainly: *I beg you, look right here!*'⁹

But he was not insensible to her talent:

> Her playing, however, is enchanting . . . She let me in on a plan that she keeps a secret, namely that she wants to study hard for 2 or 3 more years and then go to Paris and make piano-playing her profession. She says: *I am not beautiful,* o [*sic*] contraire, I am ugly; and I don't want to marry some petty clerk in the chancellery . . . and I don't have a chance of getting anyone else; so I'd rather stay single and make a living off my talent.¹⁰

(It's interesting that although von Auernhammer lived in the music-loving city of Vienna, she considered Paris a more important place to make a career.) Mozart asked his father to get his piano-duet sonata K358 and two concertos for two pianos (K365 and K242, the latter being his own arrangement for two pianos of a triple concerto) copied out and sent from Salzburg so that he could play them with Josepha.

At first Josepha was clumsy in her behaviour towards Mozart, as one could easily imagine from a girl not accustomed to success. Although she probably sensed that he was not attracted to her, she had the courage to confide in him about her romantic hopes. Mozart was irritated. 'I was compelled, in order to keep her from making a fool of herself, to tell her the truth tactfully,' he wrote on 22 August 1781. 'She took my hand and said: *dear Mozart, don't be so angry – you may say what you please, I love you all the same.*'¹¹

Somehow she gradually won him over. Her infatuation probably faded and his irritation subsided; at any rate, they settled into friendship. He stopped complaining about her appearance and more often mentioned that he was going to play duets with her. He wrote a brilliant four-hand sonata (in D major, K448) for the two of them to perform, designating the 'primo' or treble part for Josepha. Together they played it, and the two-piano concerto, at a concert in November 1781. He dedicated six sonatas for piano and violin (K296 and K376–80) to her.

The following year, he invited her to perform keyboard duets with him at one of his public concerts, and that autumn he postponed a visit to Salzburg in order to keep a promise to play in a concert organised by her. The Abbé Stadler, who later tried to complete some of Mozart's unfinished compositions, reported that when the first printed copies of these duo sonatas were delivered, Mozart invited him to come and hear the music played by him and 'the Auernhammer'. Mozart could play the violin, but on that occasion there was no violin available, so Josepha played the piano part and Mozart, sitting beside her at a second fortepiano, played the violin part on it. The Abbé was enchanted by their rapport: 'I never heard such an incomparable performance in my life.' By 1789, Mozart reported that on a visit to Dresden he had been invited to hear a local celebrity play the fortepiano, but 'I must say, Mademoiselle Auerhammer is just as good'.[12]

Von Auernhammer herself composed lots of piano music, particularly in variation style. Her six variations on Papageno's song from Mozart's *Magic Flute*, 'Der Vogelfänger bin ich ja' ('I am the bird-catcher'), show a confident array of techniques from rushing scales to crossed hands, cheeky grace notes, alternating hands and rhythmical jokes – all useful teaching material for her own school of piano students. Her early remark about not wanting to marry a petty clerk showed a touching foresight of what was to happen to her, for four years after meeting Mozart she married Johann Bessenig, a city clerk, with whom she had four children. She was, however, allowed to go on playing public concerts under her maiden name, which she did for many years. She never did go to Paris, but she was well regarded in Vienna. Faithful to Mozart, she often performed his piano concertos into the early years of the nineteenth century, and was one of the first pianists to perform Beethoven's C major piano concerto.

Auernhammer was one of several women pianists associated with Mozart. Two others were Rosa Cannabich (1764–1839) and Barbara Ployer (1765–1811). Rosa Cannabich's father was concertmaster of the Mannheim Court Orchestra. Mozart met the Cannabichs in 1777 when he was in Mannheim trying to secure himself a court appointment, and was invited to spend evenings at their home. He gave piano lessons to thirteen-year-old Rosa, and before long was telling his father that the Andante of his new piano sonata (in C major, K309) was a portrait of her: 'Wie das Andante, so ist sie' ('She's just like the Andante'). He stayed in Mannheim long enough to hear Rosa perform his piano concerto in B flat K238 in February 1778. A few years later Rosa was mentioned in Carl Ludwig Juncker's *Musikalischer und Künstler Almanach* as one of the most eminent pianists of the day, though she was only nineteen.

Barbara Ployer (1765–1811) was described by the Abbé Stadler (who later completed some of Mozart's unfinished compositions) as Mozart's 'most excellent pupil'. She studied counterpoint with Mozart, and the Austrian National Library has her exercise book from 1784, containing Mozart's light-hearted criticisms of her counterpoint, such as, 'I have the honour to tell you that you have made a nonsense.'[13] Mozart, however, had a high opinion of her playing and wrote two concertos for her, the E flat K449 and the G major K453. She premiered the G major concerto in June 1784 with Mozart playing in the string quintet accompanying the soloist, and in the same concert she and Mozart played his 'grand sonata for two claviers'. It was not only Mozart who had a high regard for her playing; in 1793, Joseph Haydn wrote his magnificent Variations in F minor ('Un piccolo divertimento') for Barbara Ployer.

MARIANNA MARTINES

When one reads about artistic life in Vienna at this period, one begins to realise what a small world it was. The story of Marianna Martines (or Martinez) (1744–1812) is a delightful illustration of how the music-loving Viennese got to know one another.

Marianna's father, Nicolò, was an Italian soldier from Naples who had come to Vienna on military duties but stayed on to take a post as chamberlain to the papal nuncio. The Martines family lived near the cathedral at 11 Kohlmarkt, in the 'Altes Michaelerhaus', a grand building that contained a number of apartments. (Visitors to Vienna today will know the Kohlmarkt as the location of the famous café-bakery Demel.) As a young man in Naples, Nicolò Martines had been a friend of the poet Antonio Trapassi, later to become famous as the opera librettist Metastasio. Some years after Nicolò had moved to Vienna, Metastasio was invited to take up a post there as court poet. He contacted his old friend Martines to ask for help in finding accommodation, and was offered a room in the spacious third-floor apartment. Metastasio was quickly taken into the heart of the family and remained living in the Kohlmarkt until his death in 1782.

When Marianna was just seven, the eighteen-year-old Joseph Haydn was expelled from the cathedral choir and from the choir director's home where he lived; his naughty pranks had annoyed the authorities, and as his voice had broken and he was no longer of use as a boy chorister they took the opportunity to get rid of him. He came to live in the attic of 11 Kohlmarkt, where for several years he gave Marianna Martines keyboard lessons in lieu of paying rent, and learned some Italian from Metastasio. During this time, both Haydn and Marianna Martines studied composition with Nicola Porpora (another Neapolitan), who was also living in the building. A further coincidence was that the widowed Countess Esterházy was living in an apartment on the first floor. In later years her sons Prince Paul Anton and Prince Nikolaus Esterházy became Haydn's principal employers, but it was presumably at 11 Kohlmarkt that the Esterházy family first took notice of Haydn. If the Michaelerhaus was a microcosm of artistic life in Vienna, it is easy to imagine how interesting it must have been to be a musician living there at the time.

Marianna Martines' parents died when she was in her early twenties, whereupon she and her siblings came into the care of Metastasio. He was elderly by this time, no longer so busy with writing poetry and drama. He became fond of Marianna and her brothers and tried to help them. Through his influence, the young Marianna was invited to play for the Empress Maria Theresa, who took a liking to her and often asked her to come and play or sing for her. On these occasions, the Emperor Joseph II would often sit beside Marianna at the keyboard to turn pages for her. When the music historian Charles Burney visited Metastasio in 1772, Marianna was summoned to play and sing for him; Burney reported that she had exceeded his expectations, singing two arias of her own composition and accompanying herself on the keyboard in a masterly manner.

A decade later, when Metastasio died, he left Marianna's older brother the bulk of his estate, but he also made sure that Marianna was independently wealthy. He left her an income of 1,000 florins a year, more than Haydn was making as director of music for Prince Esterházy. Marianna was now able to devote more resources to her own salon, which many well-known musicians of the time attended on Saturday evenings. Mozart was said to attend her salon at least once a week from 1781, and the Irish singer Michael Kelly, who became a friend of Mozart's when he was singing operatic roles in Vienna, said in his *Reminiscences* that 'Mozart was an almost constant attendant at her parties, and I have heard him play duets on the piano-forte with her, of his own composition. She was a great favourite of his.'[14] Haydn and Salieri also attended Marianna's artistic evenings, which were an important gathering point for Austrian and visiting musicians throughout the 1780s and 1790s. By this time, Marianna's own compositions had become known as far afield as Italy. She wrote at least sixty-five substantial pieces – masses, motets and cantatas (many of them premiered at the Michaelerkirche next door to the apartment) – and composed at least three piano concertos as well as numerous sonatas. Her keyboard style was rather like Haydn's: elegant, charming and decorative, with flashes of playful wit.

Today in Vienna one can still see the 'Michaelerhaus' where all this activity took place. On its walls are two plaques, one commemorating Metastasio and the other recording the fact that the young Haydn lived there for some years, but unsurprisingly there is no plaque for Marianna Martines.

Marianna Martines' life overlapped with Beethoven's. As the Romantic style took hold of everyone's imaginations, Martines' piano pieces came to be seen as conservative, and they faded from the scene. We may wonder why she did not adopt the punchy, dramatic style of Beethoven, but we must remember that women at the time were powerfully enjoined to make sure their behaviour and their accomplishments were always graceful and modest.

At the same time in Vienna there were two other fine female pianists named Maria Anna (or Marianna or Marianne). Marianne von Genzinger (1754–93) was a fine pianist for whom Haydn wrote his piano sonata in E flat Hob XVI:49. She and her husband hosted Sunday-evening salons which Haydn attended when he was in Vienna. Marianne started writing to Haydn about music, but their correspondence became gradually more personal. When Haydn was in Esterházy he confided to her his feelings of loneliness and isolation. From London, he told her that 'I don't hate London, but I would not be capable of spending the rest of my life there, even if I could amass millions. I shall tell Your Grace the reason when I see you.'[15] Is it too fanciful to imagine that she was 'the reason'? When she died in 1793, just after Haydn got back to Vienna, Haydn's friends noticed that his mood had darkened. This was the period when he wrote his finest single piece for piano, the Variations in F minor, whose cry of pain in the final pages may have been written in tribute to Marianne von Genzinger.

Then there was Marianna von Auenbrugger (1759–82), the younger of two sisters whose playing was much admired. Marianna was a fragile girl who only lived to the age of twenty-three, but after studying composition with Antonio Salieri she wrote a keyboard sonata whose three movements show a fertile imagination and a lightness of touch that might make one think she had been Mozart's composition pupil rather than Salieri's. Haydn dedicated six keyboard sonatas, Hob XVI:20 and Hob XVI:35–9, to the two sisters. He told his publisher Artaria that 'the approval of the Auenbrugger ladies is extremely important to me, because their way of playing and their true insight into the art of music is equal to that of the greatest masters; both deserve to be made known by public reports all over Europe'.[16]

THERESE JANSEN BARTOLOZZI

Therese Jansen Bartolozzi (1770–1843) was an excellent pianist who rarely performed in public. Her musicianship might not have been noted by posterity were it not that Haydn dedicated two great piano sonatas (Hob XVI:50 and 52) and three wonderful piano trios (Hob XV:27–9) to her. The complex piano parts of these works suggest that Therese was a very fine pianist.

It wasn't only Haydn who thought so highly of her – her teacher Clementi also dedicated three sonatas (opus 33) to her, and she was spoken of as 'Clementi's favourite scholar'. Yet another three sonatas were dedicated to her by the virtuoso composer-pianist Jan Ladislav Dussek, a lion of the London musical scene at the time. It was Dussek, incidentally, who first had the idea of turning the piano on the concert stage such that he was sitting sideways on to the audience, with his profile showing – an innovation that was adopted by most pianists, and 250 years later is still the most usual way of positioning a grand piano on stage. Prior to Dussek's era, when pianos were more usually played in private salons and the audience was not seated in strict rows, the piano could be positioned in whatever way best suited the situation; the pianist might face the audience, or, if playing with other musicians, might face into the instrumental group with their back to the listeners.

Therese Jansen was the daughter of a German dancing master who had moved to London to take advantage of the craze for dancing, which was so popular in Britain that dancing masters could hope to make a lot of money, firstly by teaching pupils and secondly by putting on dances where the cream of society would meet under the watchful eye of society matrons, who would allocate partners for specific dances throughout the evening. Therese's father founded a successful dancing school in London, and in due course Therese and her brother Louis also taught there. Is it too fanciful to imagine that the 'skipping' passages in the first movement of Haydn's last E flat sonata (dedicated to Therese) are jokey allusions to Therese's little pupils as they skipped across the floor in their dancing lessons?

The story of how she met Haydn is intriguing. According to the *London Chronicle* of 23 November 1786, when Haydn was coming to the end of his employment in Esterházy he was visited by a young Italian violinist and artist called Gaetano Bartolozzi, who discussed with him the idea of visiting London and subsequently handed over to the Hanover-Concert Society in London to firm up negotiations. This same Bartolozzi later became engaged to Therese Jansen. So when Haydn came to London, he already had a social connection to Bartolozzi and his circle. And let us not forget that Therese Jansen could speak German; no doubt it made Haydn's life easier when he was first in London to have some German-speaking friends.

At the time, there was a great fashion in London for clubs, sociable semi-private gatherings that organised entertainments of various kinds. The Anacreontic Society was a members-only club which from 1766 to 1793 put on twelve concerts of a high standard each year at the Crown and Anchor Tavern in the Strand. Each concert was followed by an elegant supper and after-dinner singing, humorous turns, puppet shows and other entertainments that went on late into the night.

Haydn was warmly welcomed to a meeting of the Anacreontic Society shortly after his arrival in London in 1791. The members were all men, but women were sometimes permitted as guests. Clementi and Louis Jansen both performed Haydn piano sonatas for the Anacreontic Society and it is tempting to imagine that in this semi-private setting Therese did too, but this is only speculation.[17]

Therese Jansen's husband became an art dealer, and for business reasons the family spent a period of time in northern Italy. On their return to London, Jansen, now thirty-six, took part in her only known public concert, in the concert room of the King's Theatre in 1806. She started publishing some of her own piano compositions: waltzes, variations and quadrilles, but also a virtuosic grand sonata in A major, one of the few grand sonatas known to have been written by a woman at this period. Her style, modelled on Clementi's and incorporating brilliant cadenzas, makes particular use of the upper part of the keyboard, known to have a particularly ringing tone on English pianos of the time.

Albert Dies, a biographer who interviewed Haydn in Vienna a number of times in his last years, reports that Haydn and Therese Jansen once shared a joke about a mutual friend who fancied himself a virtuoso violinist. Haydn wrote a piece called 'Jacob's Dream' for violin and piano, virtuosic for both players but with some extra-high and rapid passages liable to trip up the unwary violinist. (The piece was inspired by the biblical story of Jacob, who dreamed that he saw a ladder stretching from earth to heaven, with God's angels ascending and descending the steps.) Haydn sent the parts anonymously to the Jansens' house. Therese tried it through with the said violinist, saw him scrambling among the high notes and could not restrain her laughter when she realised that the 'anonymous' composer had depicted poor Jacob struggling to keep his footing on the ladder to heaven. Haydn later expanded the piece to become the piano trio in E flat minor, Hob XV:31; its finale is still a challenge.

Therese Jansen was not the only female pianist in London who became a close friend of Haydn's. Rebecca Schroeter (1751–1826) was the widow of Johann Samuel Schroeter, a German composer and pianist who was a protégé of J.C. Bach ('the London Bach'). Schroeter became Queen Charlotte's music master, but heavy drinking caused his early death. Three years later, when Haydn came to London, Rebecca Schroeter asked him for music lessons. Their friendship developed very fast. Soon he was dining regularly with her, and when they were apart they exchanged passionate letters. Haydn kept her letters, and in his old age he told a biographer that they were written by 'an English widow, who loved me ... a beautiful and charming woman and I would have married her very easily if I had been free at the time'.[18] He dedicated to Rebecca three wonderful piano trios (Hob XV:24–6), which include his most popular trio in G major with its 'Gypsy Rondo' finale.

SARA LEVY

Sara Levy (1761–1854) was a highly educated woman whose musical interests had a great influence on those around her – particularly her great-nephew, Felix Mendelssohn – yet who is virtually unknown today. Sara was the tenth child of Daniel Itzig, a wealthy Jewish banker in Berlin. Daniel and Mariane Itzig were very keen on the arts and their children were taught by Berlin's best musicians. Several of the girls became excellent keyboard players and it was said that their parents actually retained a salaried piano teacher because so many of the children were learning the piano. Sara's older sisters, Bella and Hanna, were taught by Johann Philipp Kirnberger, a student of J.S. Bach. Sara herself was the only known piano student of Wilhelm Friedemann Bach, who taught her for ten years. Unsurprisingly everyone was devoted to the Bach family, a loyalty Sara extended in later years by commissioning works from C.P.E. Bach.

The Itzigs were accustomed to hosting distinguished artists in their home, and when Sara married the banker Salomon Levy in 1783, she continued the tradition by opening her Berlin salon to visiting musicians and writers, including Schumann's beloved author E.T.A. Hoffmann. Sara herself often performed at her salons, to which she made a point of welcoming both Jewish and Christian guests.

In Sara Levy's day, concerts generally focused on the music of living composers; unearthing and performing the music of earlier masters was not the fashion that it later became. However, in the 1790s the Berlin Sing-Akademie was founded to revive and spread awareness of the music of older composers. Sara Levy's family was used to honouring the music of J.S. Bach and his circle, and it must have seemed quite natural to her to get involved in the Sing-Akademie. It began as a choral group, but in 1807 it added an orchestra to enable a wider repertoire to be played. This gave Sara the chance to perform as keyboard soloist in many concertos of J.S. Bach's day: his D minor harpsichord concerto, the fifth Brandenburg concerto (for keyboard, flute and violin) and other works of his contemporaries. Works of the great Viennese masters such as Mozart and Haydn were not performed at the Akademie – theirs was a cult of 'the olden days'.

Eventually it was decided that the Sing-Akademie needed a building of its own, and in 1827 a beautiful concert hall was built in the splendid avenue Unter den Linden (Under the Lime Trees) in central Berlin. Two years later, the young Felix Mendelssohn organised and conducted his famous revival of Bach's *St Matthew Passion* there. The general public had almost forgotten about J.S. Bach, but this performance revived his fortunes. Mendelssohn has always been praised for exceptional initiative in putting on this ground-breaking concert, but it sprang naturally from his family's love of all things Bach. His grandmother (Sara Levy's sister Bella) had commissioned a copy of the manuscript of Bach's *St Matthew Passion* as a gift for Felix when he was fifteen; his father had bought an important collection of Bach manuscripts at auction in 1805; his grandmother and several of his great-aunts had been taught by a pupil of Bach. His great-aunt

Fanny Arnstein kept the Bach family flame alive with performances in her influential salon in Vienna; his great-aunt Sara was constantly practising and performing works by J.S. Bach and his sons. So it is worth remembering that the groundwork for 'Mendelssohn's Bach revival' was laid by the women of his family.

In the last ten years of Wilhelm Friedemann Bach's life, Levy supported her old teacher financially. After his death, she took up contact with the elderly C.P.E. Bach and commissioned a number of works from him, including a double concerto for the unusual pairing of harpsichord and piano (perhaps intended for a particular room where those two instruments resided) and a set of quartets for the unusual combination of flute, viola, keyboard and a bass-enhancing instrument such as a cello. She collected manuscript scores of the Bach family and their contemporaries, which she left to the Berlin Sing-Akademie. This collection had a strange fate: in the Second World War it was looted from Berlin by the Red Army, taken to Russia and eventually lodged in a library in Kyiv, Ukraine. For decades, no music historian knew where it was, but in 1999 the Bach scholar Christoph Wolff managed to track it down and arrange for the scores to be returned to Berlin.

Sara Levy was a pianist, collector, patron, commissioner of music and host of an influential salon. She was interested in social justice and supported several Berlin orphanages financially. As far as we know, she did not compose, but she may well have known that her family wouldn't condone it; after all, her great-niece Fanny found little support in the Mendelssohn family for her composing, and that was two generations later. Levy did go on performing piano music into her old age, a bold move for a woman at that time. Many of her family converted from Judaism to Christianity, in accordance with the perceived need to 'assimilate' into German society, but Levy remained true to her Jewish faith. She saw no contradiction in immersing herself in music of the Christian Lutheran tradition, a testament to her open mind.

HÉLÈNE DE MONTGEROULT

Though many of the women in this book could easily be the heroines of novels or plays, the life of Hélène de Montgeroult (1764–1836) seems to call out for dramatisation. As a musically gifted child she was brought to Paris by her family to be educated by the best teachers, among them Hüllmandel (whose work was admired by Mozart), Clementi and Dussek. She played frequently in private circles in Paris. At twenty she married an older aristocrat, the Marquis de Montgeroult; together they frequented artistic salons, for example that of the painter Madame Vigée-Lebrun, who remembered being astonished by Hélène's playing: 'She made the keys speak. Already then she was a pianist of the first rank.'[19] In these salons Hélène got to know the Italian violinist Viotti, who had a high regard for her talent. She partnered him in duo repertoire and was known to improvise music with him for hours at a time.

In 1793, during the French Revolution, Montgeroult and her husband formed part of a diplomatic delegation (representing the concerns of aristocrats) to the Grand Duchy of Tuscany. The delegation was intercepted en route by the Austrian authorities, the diplomats were imprisoned, and the Marquis de Montgeroult died in prison a few months later. When Hélène was released and returned to France, she was arrested by the revolutionaries as a member of the hated nobility and condemned to the guillotine. It was now that the most colourful but not reliably documented incident in her life occurred: in 1794 she was made to appear in court, before the dreaded Committee of Public Safety. Allegedly she turned them in her favour by improvising variations on their revolutionary song 'La Marseillaise' (or, according to some accounts, simply playing 'La Marseillaise') on a piano. But it seems unlikely that there was a piano in the courtroom, or that she would have had been able to bring one.

It is more likely that Bernard Sarette, founder of the free music school that was to become the Paris Conservatoire, pleaded with the

Committee to spare her on the grounds that such a brilliant pianist would be an ornament to the new, egalitarian music school. The Committee agreed to spare her and when the new Conservatoire opened in 1795, Montgeroult became professor of the advanced piano class (though it was only open to male students). According to some reports it was she who brought the harpsichord music of J.S. Bach into the curriculum. It's pleasing to think about the line of influence: two of Montgeroult's own piano teachers, Hüllmandel and Dussek, were pupils of C.P.E. Bach, one of Johann Sebastian's sons.

Since 1788, Montgeroult had been composing her own course of piano studies, prompted by a request for new exercises from the teenage Johann Baptist Cramer, who studied piano with her in Paris. Over the years, Hélène continued writing her *Cours complet*, which eventually blossomed into an enormous collection of 972 exercises and 114 studies. When she joined the staff of the Paris Conservatoire in 1795 she probably hoped that the studies on which she'd already been working for eight years would be welcomed into the piano curriculum, but the task of creating an official course of piano studies was given to her male colleague, Jean-Louis Adam. Being overlooked like this may have been the reason that she became disillusioned with the institution; at any rate, she left her professorship in 1798. But there may also have been personal complications: in the year she started teaching at the Conservatoire, she gave birth to a son whose father she did not marry until 1797 (they divorced a few years later).

For some years, Montgeroult was a close friend and probably a romantic connection of Louis, Baron de Trémont, who visited Beethoven in 1809 and in his memoirs left us a vivid picture of the disorderly room, the unemptied chamber pot under the piano and the chairs festooned with plates bearing the remains of old suppers.

At the age of fifty-six, Montgeroult married for a third time, this time to Edouard Dunod, Comte de Charnage, nineteen years younger than her. This marriage too was short-lived: the count died six years later. Hélène went on teaching the piano until her health began to fail and she moved with her son to Florence, where she spent the rest of her life. In addition to her études she wrote piano sonatas and some chamber music for piano and violin.

Montgeroult was born eight years after Mozart and six years before Beethoven, but her style of piano writing – flowing virtuosity combined with graceful chromaticism – seems to point the way towards Chopin and Mendelssohn rather than marking her out as a contemporary of Beethoven's. She wrote sonatas and chamber music, but her collection of études is truly extraordinary. So many studies, written with such confident expression in so many different styles – why were they forgotten? Each study is prefaced by an explanation of what technique it aims to teach, and her remarks shine a wonderful light on how people played at the time. For example, in her preface to étude 51, a study for the left hand, she writes that it:

offers a nuance which is difficult to grasp. If one makes the notes of the right hand march in step too precisely with those of the left, the melody will become a little dry; on the other hand, if one separates the hands too much, the result will be an affected type of expression, which will deprive the piece of its unity and intention. We consider this study, then, a good way of testing the student's musical talent.[20]

The art of layering musical lines in this way was well known in Montgeroult's day, and indeed right through the nineteenth century and into the age of recording, where one can still hear pianists using this effect into the 1920s. Today, it is the custom to play with the hands precisely coordinated, but this custom arose in the age of recording, when 'untidiness' or 'randomness' started to be frowned upon, and when recording artists wished to play in a way that would stand the test of time without ever seeming dated. The older style of letting the two hands drift apart – for example, playing the bass chord in the left hand a fraction of a second before the melody note in the right hand, or 'spreading a chord' so that the listener hears one note after another in a rapid spray rather than in a single chunk – can sound old-fashioned or affected to our ears, but it is important to remember that in previous eras it was considered an expressive art, an art that is sometimes revived for repertoire from those eras.

Montgeroult's are no dry exercises – the pleasure of music-making shines through them. As one leafs through the pages, one finds oneself thinking, 'But this could be a "Song without Words" by Mendelssohn! This one could be a Chopin étude! This one reminds me of a Schubert impromptu! This is surely like one of Brahms's late intermezzi! This is like a Handel aria for the piano!' Yet Montgeroult's studies were written between 1788 and 1812, long before Mendelssohn (born 1809), Chopin (1810), Schumann (1810) or Brahms (1833) were writing anything at all. Chopin knew them, as we can deduce by comparing her étude no. 107 with Chopin's famous 'revolutionary' study (opus 10, no. 12) written twenty years later. He may turn her river into a torrent, but the river was mapped by her.

It may indeed turn out that Montgeroult's piano music was an inspiration for many composers of the next generation. The French musician and scholar Jérôme Dorival, who has written and lectured on Montgeroult, has pointed out that in her day it was all too easy for male composers to belittle or overlook the achievements of their female counterparts, and hard for men to acknowledge – even to themselves – that women composers influenced their work.[21] It was the fate of Montgeroult's studies to be eclipsed by those of her pupil Johann Baptist Cramer, the very person who asked her to write him some new studies and who probably built on her work when he wrote his own in 1810 and 1814. His are still practised by budding pianists, whereas hers were forgotten – for no other reason, perhaps, than that she was a woman and therefore not an official member of the composers' club. In recent years there have been some pioneering recordings of her music, and we can hope for more. Cramer's studies are good, but Montgeroult's are extraordinary, especially for the time when she wrote them.

WOMEN IN THE AGE OF THE CONCERT PIANIST

It was only in the nineteenth century – when public concerts became important, when orchestras were founded, railways were built, composers started writing heroic piano concertos and a large concert-going public was built up – that male pianists (initially from mainland European countries) seized the moment and created that icon of the music world: the *concert pianist*. Now the audience didn't need to be socially elevated enough to be invited to a drawing room in a private house to hear them – you could buy a ticket and go to hear them when they came to your town.

These men were able to use their greater freedom of action to travel independently. Some intrepid female pianists also went on concert tours, but had to negotiate all kinds of practical and domestic difficulties. (In 1825 one enterprising Russian amateur pianist, Princess Maria Volkonskaya, travelled 4,000 miles from St Petersburg to Siberia with a clavichord strapped to the sledge when she went to join her husband in political exile.) Their concert appearances elicited complicated reactions from the public, unsure whether to admire or censure them. Ironically, these pioneering women must have relied on female servants, maids and nannies to hold the fort for them at home while they were away, but of course the same is true of men – the difference in their case being that their wives were usually part of that home-based array of female support. Men could undertake concert tours without people raising their eyebrows at the spectacle of a man travelling on his own, or casting aspersions on his character because his children were being cared for by someone other than him while he was away.

From the mid-nineteenth century, male pianists dominated the public perception of what pianists should be. Franz Liszt and fellow virtuosi such as Sigismond Thalberg built up their reputations through carefully stage-managed solo recitals. Once the careers of Liszt and co were in full flood, historians of pianism (themselves male) became obsessed with male pianists, their careers and their respective strengths, and arguably it has remained largely that way despite the achievements of female pianists. The notion that piano-playing was 'degrading' for men was swiftly forgotten when titans of European pianism such as Liszt and Chopin as well as virtuosi like Thalberg and Tausig came on the scene in the mid-nineteenth century. The fostering of personality cults, shrewdly managed by their chief exponents, trained the public to see male pianists in a wholly positive, indeed heroic, light. The rise of the public concert, with tickets available to all and sundry as long as they could pay, seemed to push the piano and pianism into a public realm where it was obvious that men would hold sway (and 'sway' is quite a good word for those who made ladies in the audience swoon). In a sense, piano recitals started to become 'professionalised', with concerts advertised far ahead of time, ticket money taken and substantial fees being earned. The great virtuosi attracted large audiences, made lots of money and kept the public amused with gossip about their love affairs.

There was an element of competition about public recitals. Who got a bigger audience than whom? Who played faster and louder? Whose improvisations were more dazzling? Who got a better write-up in the coffee-house journals? There were supplementary dramas such as pianistic 'duels' where they vied to out-perform one another with difficult piano pieces and compositions or transcriptions of their own (a famous 'duel' took place between Liszt and Thalberg in 1837 in the Paris salon of Countess Cristina Belgiojoso, who is said to have pronounced the magnificently tactful judgement, 'Thalberg is the first pianist in the world, but Liszt is unique').[1] These competitive sessions might be regarded as forerunners of the 'cutting competitions' – displays of instrumental prowess also dominated by men – which became popular in the jazz world early in the twentieth century.

Many of the famous virtuosi were writing new music for their own concerts, so there was the added fascination of seeing the repertoire grow in front of one's eyes. All these elements made the solo recital more of a male sport than a female one. The piano in the home had been associated primarily with women, but a grand piano on the stage of a prestigious concert hall was seen as the preserve of men. A network of public concert opportunities sprang up to support them, creating what performers know as 'the circuit'. After that, if women pianists wanted to join men in having public performing careers they had not only to be at least as good at their craft, but also to negotiate the whole minefield of public life, with all its opportunities for rebuffs.

Between the private drawing room and the public concert stage there was a halfway house that offered women some performing opportunities without going so far as to put them on entirely public display. Cities such as London, Paris and Vienna hosted many gatherings of music lovers in semi-private societies as well as larger drawing rooms. We have already seen in the biographies of Martines, Levy and de Montgeroult that such private gatherings were enjoyed in major centres in the late eighteenth century. By the mid-nineteenth century, performances at these 'salons' amounted to a circuit of their own. Performers were not paid directly, but women who sang or played to those appreciative audiences might also hope that they would acquire some pupils, and therefore some income, as a result. Many of the salons were presided over by high-ranking women, some of whom were distinguished pianists themselves. Even those who avoided the public realm could be immensely influential. And as we'll see from the biographies that follow, there were some exceptional women from the early nineteenth century onwards who succeeded in breaking through the usual conventions, leading public lives and equalling the men at their own game.

MARIA SZYMANOWSKA

Maria Szymanowska (1789–1831), born Maria Wołowska, was ahead of her time in insisting on her right to be a professional performer, supporting herself and her family with the income from her concerts. She was born in Warsaw, where her affluent Jewish parents hosted a circle of artistic and intellectual friends. Maria began piano and composition lessons at the age of nine and was soon playing in private salons. Like Josepha von Auernhammer, she considered Paris the crucial place for an ambitious pianist to be heard. At the age of twenty-one, Szymanowska gave her debut concert in Warsaw and then left for Paris, where she succeeded in meeting the influential Cherubini, director of the Paris Conservatoire, as well as other leading musicians, who dedicated pieces to her and wrote complimentary things in her guestbook. From the very start of her career she understood the importance of 'networking', and pianists who might have been her rivals actually became her friends.

That same year, 1810, she took the somewhat puzzling decision to marry a Polish landowner, Józef Szymanowski. He had no understanding of her musical vocation and disapproved of women appearing on the public stage. Off she went to her husband's rural estate in Poland, where over the next few years she had three children. Concerts were few and far between, but she had plenty of time to compose. In 1820, her *Twenty Exercises and Preludes* (later admired by Robert Schumann) were published by Breitkopf and Härtel. This may have strengthened her resolve to do more with her music. Her hopes and ambitions were not compatible with her husband's idea of what she should be doing, and their marriage was dissolved in 1820.

With remarkable resourcefulness, Szymanowska now began to organise extensive concert tours. Her parents took care of the children in Warsaw while her brother and sister went on tour with her to keep track of money and take care of the practicalities involved in putting on concerts, leaving her free to practise. Portraits of her around this time suggest that she was a beautiful, soulful-looking woman with an eye for stylish clothing.

By 1822 she was playing in St Petersburg, where the tsarina, Maria Feodorovna, took a liking to her and gave her a salaried appointment as 'first pianist to the royal court', which opened many doors for her. With the help of the Irish composer-pianist John Field, who was living in St Petersburg, Szymanowska toured Russia. After one of those concerts, a Russian critic described her as a 'virtuoz', probably the first use of that musical description in the Russian press.[2] It appears that she sometimes performed from memory – if so, she was one of the first pianists to do so, well in advance of Liszt and Clara Schumann, who are more often credited with this innovation. It seems likely that the works she played from memory were her own compositions. To John Field she dedicated her *Caprice on the Romance of Joconde*, a technically demanding set of variations on a theme from the opera *Joconde* by Nicolo Isouard. In it, she evokes the brilliant runs of an opera singer's 'coloratura' aria, taking full advantage of the piano's ability to produce faster and more dramatically leaping intervals than the human voice can easily produce. In 1823 she played it from memory in a recital in Poznań, Poland, causing a flurry of excitement because playing 'by heart' was still rare.

By 1823 she had found her way to Germany, where she met and probably had a love affair with the great German poet Goethe, who dedicated the poem 'Aussöhnung' ('Reconciliation') to her. Every day she went to play to him in his house in Weimar; Goethe invited guests to come and hear her, enthusiastically encouraging the applause himself. The following year Szymanowska was in London, where she was a toast of the town and a sought-after piano teacher despite the competing activities of many eminent musicians. In 1827 she went back to Warsaw – arranging for an English Broadwood piano to be sent there too – where she played to an audience of 1,200 people in the National Theatre. We know from a letter of Chopin's that he intended to go to this concert, though it is not proven that he did. He certainly knew all about Szymanowska, who was a frequent topic of conversation in Warsaw at the time.

In 1827 Szymanowska decided to return for good to St Petersburg, where as 'first pianist to the royal court' she could command high fees for teaching and performing. Royalties from her compositions added to her income. She established a salon whose visitors included the writer Pushkin, the composers Glinka and Field, and Chopin's favourite poet Adam Mickiewicz, who had married Szymanowska's daughter. Continuing her early custom of asking her listeners and visitors to write in her 'album', Szymanowska kept scrapbooks in which her distinguished guests drew little pictures and wrote lines of music and poetry, a testimony to her enduring charm. She shone in the cultural life of St Petersburg until the cholera epidemic of 1831 claimed her as one of its victims.

Despite Szymanowska's musical and social success, she and her music faded rapidly from the public's memory, partly because Chopin had so thoroughly displaced her with his brilliant playing and compositions. But it is notable that Szymanowska preceded Chopin in writing music in many of the forms which he made famous: études, preludes, ballades, polonaises, mazurkas, nocturnes and waltzes. Some of her études, indeed, can be regarded as having given specific inspiration to Chopin. He never mentioned her music, but it was not his way to acknowledge his sources. A comparison of her pieces with his suggests that he knew her work and found it stimulating. Her achievements – her tours, her compositions, her skilful cultivation of people who could help her in her quest – are remarkable in themselves, and probably also served as a model for Chopin to follow.

LUCY ANDERSON

Lucy Anderson (1797–1878), like Maria Szymanowska, rose to the heights of a royal court appointment – in fact two appointments, for in 1832 she became court pianist to Queen Adelaide (wife of King William IV of Great Britain), and in 1837 she became court pianist to Queen Victoria. She taught Queen Victoria at Kensington Palace when the future queen was a child, and continued her association with the royal family so long that she was able to teach Queen Victoria's own children. In 1840 she was granted a Civil List pension, meaning a pension from the government fund that pays the salaries of the royal staff. All this was astonishing for a woman from a very ordinary background.

Born in the same year as Franz Schubert, Lucy Anderson (née Philpot) grew up in Bath, the setting for so many crucial scenes in Jane Austen's novels. Unlike most of Jane Austen's piano-playing ladies, however, Lucy did not hesitate to pursue a career in music. This was not easy at a time when the leading pianists of the day were male foreigners, their path to fame in England laid open by the prevailing view that music was no profession for a respectable Englishman. Her father was a music seller and teacher, and he and her cousin taught her the piano. Despite poor eyesight Lucy made rapid progress and was soon playing in concerts. She moved to London in 1818 and two years later married violinist George Frederick Anderson, who later became master of the queen's music. In 1822 Lucy was the first woman to perform at the Philharmonic Society, playing a virtuosic piano concerto by Hummel; altogether she performed nineteen times at the Philharmonic Society over the course of her long career.

Anderson performed a huge repertoire of piano music, ranging from Mozart and Beethoven to Mendelssohn, Hummel, Ries and Czerny, but was particularly known for her performances of Beethoven's fourth and fifth piano concertos, which she played in London more often than any other pianist up until 1850. In fact she was the first person to play Beethoven's 'Emperor' concerto at the Philharmonic Society in 1830. That same year she was introduced at court by Sir George Smart, organist of the Chapel Royal, and became Princess Victoria's piano tutor in 1834. In 1837 she and her husband had quite a coup when George Anderson gave the publisher Novello an interest-free loan to enable him to publish Mendelssohn's brilliant second piano concerto; in return for this loan, Novello granted Lucy Anderson the exclusive right to perform the concerto in England for six months after its publication. She also taught at the Royal Academy of Music and had private pupils, among them Kate Loder and Arabella Goddard, who became leading pianists in their turn. Making use of her illustrious social connections, Anderson put on a charity concert each year, inviting famous performers such as Hummel to join her, in a series that became an important event in the London season.

Lucy Anderson had to contend with what might now be termed 'gender-specific criticism': her playing was described in a way that would not be applied to male performers. For example, in 1835 the (male) London correspondent of the *Allgemeine musikalische Zeitung* felt free to say that 'Mrs Anderson, whom I would like to call a piano-playing Amazon because she attacks the piano with her wiry arms, is the teacher of Princess Victoria, who through her presence at concerts helps her to fill the halls year-round'.[3] Conversely, another German critic (also male) wrote in the *Neue Zeitschrift für Musik* that Anderson 'did not have the physical strength to perform' Beethoven's 'Emperor' concerto.[4] Such remarks, however, did not prevent her establishing herself as one of the most eminent English pianists of her day.

LOUISE FARRENC

Louise Farrenc (1804–75) was a pianist, prize-winning composer, piano professor, compiler of historical piano music and early fighter for equal pay. She was born into the Dumont family living in an artists' community on the Left Bank in Paris; many of her relatives were painters and sculptors. Her parents made sure she received a wide education, and unlike many of her female contemporaries she was not trained to accept limited horizons. From the age of six she learned piano from Cécile Soria, a student of Clementi, and later she had some lessons with pianist-composers Hummel and Moscheles as well. Unusually for the time, Louise was encouraged not just to learn composition but also to perform her own music. She studied counterpoint, fugue, harmony and orchestration with Anton Reicha at a time when women were not even allowed to enrol in a composition class at the Paris Conservatoire (this didn't become possible until 1870).

At the age of seventeen, Louise was also lucky in her choice of a husband: flute player Aristide Farrenc, ten years her senior, was very supportive of her musical ambitions and set up Éditions Farrenc so that he could publish her compositions. In 1830 Louise gave a concert in which she played her own works, earning praise from a French critic who observed that she had managed to resist the frivolous habit of treating the piano as a machine for rapid fingerwork, and had taken a purer path.[5]

In 1842 Louise Farrenc was appointed a full professor of piano at the Paris Conservatoire, the only woman to achieve this distinction in the whole of the nineteenth century. (Hélène de Montgeroult had achieved it in 1795. And there were other women who preceded Farrenc in teaching at the Conservatoire but were not employed full-time or graced with the title 'professor'.) Three years later Farrenc's *Thirty Studies in All Major and Minor Keys* became a set work for pianists at the Conservatoire, and the conservatoires of Brussels and Bologna also adopted it as a set work. Her piano class became known for her rigorous and painstaking approach, avoiding musical 'effects' and prioritising serious expression.

Despite her success, Farrenc discovered she was not paid as much as her male colleague, piano professor Henri Herz. Farrenc's class was for female students, and she herself was a married woman; together, these facts seemed to the authorities to justify a lesser salary. However, this was a time of much debate in French society about the rights of workers and the rights of women. The 'February Revolution' of 1848 arose partly from widespread discontent about working conditions. Perhaps this motivated Farrenc to tackle the director of the Conservatoire about equal pay. Following a successful performance in 1850 of her nonet with the nineteen-year-old Joseph Joachim playing the first-violin part, Farrenc demanded that she be paid on the same level as her male colleagues, and she won her case. When we remember that women in France did not get the vote until 1944 and are still fighting for equal pay in many workplaces, Farrenc's stand in 1850 seems even more remarkable.

Louise and Aristide Farrenc had one child, Victorine, who studied in her mother's class at the Conservatoire, graduated with a first prize and went on to become a concert pianist. However, not long after her first concerto appearances, Victorine became ill and withdrew from concert life; she died in 1859. Louise stopped composing and performing. For the next decade she and Aristide devoted themselves to bringing out multiple volumes of historical piano music in a series called *Le Trésor des pianistes* (*The Pianists' Treasury*). Although she didn't perform in them herself, Louise organised a series of concerts in which her students presented these historical pieces to the public.

Farrenc's prolific output of piano pieces broadened out into chamber music and orchestral music. In the 1840s she composed several symphonies at a time when opera and popular music were all the rage and abstract orchestral music was somewhat out of fashion, yet her symphonies were appreciated by critics. In 1861 and again in 1879 she won the Prix Chartier for her chamber music, one of the few women ever to do so. Although she hardly toured outside France, her reputation spread internationally, as proven by the fact that when she died in 1875 the *New York Times* carried her obituary. Her chamber music, often built around a substantial piano part, continues the tradition of Hummel in highlighting the virtuosic powers of a good pianist. Sometimes she revels in the piano to the detriment of the other instrumental parts, which are plainly written by comparison. However, one could say the same about Hummel's chamber music, which is much better known. Farrenc's music has enjoyed something of a revival in recent years.

When Farrenc retired from her piano class at the Conservatoire, it was taken over in 1874 by another fine pianist, Louise-Aglaé Massart (1827–87). She and her husband, violinist Joseph Lambert Massart (teacher of Kreisler, Ysaÿe and Wieniawski), were close friends of Berlioz in his later years. The Massarts held a salon in their home, at which leading musicians performed and at which Berlioz gave readings of Shakespeare plays to the assembled company, taking all the parts himself. Louise-Aglaé was devoted to chamber music at a time when French taste lay elsewhere. From 1856 to 1867 she was the pianist of a piano-and-strings chamber group that performed quartets and quintets by Mozart, Beethoven, Schubert, Mendelssohn and Schumann. These works all have virtuosic piano parts, so she must have been a fine pianist.

FANNY MENDELSSOHN

Until recently, 'Mendelssohn' simply meant Felix Mendelssohn. Any mention of his sister Fanny (1805–47) probably amounted to no more than saying that she was 'also musical'.

As we saw in the story of Fanny Mendelssohn's great-aunt Sara Levy, the extended Mendelssohn family was cultured, affluent and devoted to music, in particular the music of J.S. Bach. In the family home in Berlin where Fanny was brought up there was a Silbermann clavichord (C.P.E. Bach's preferred make), a grand piano and from 1816 a Broadwood grand, a type of English piano Fanny particularly liked. Later still they acquired an Erard grand piano. It was a rich environment for budding keyboard players like Fanny and her younger brother Felix (Fanny was four years older than Felix).

The family was Jewish, but following the principles of Moses Mendelssohn, Fanny's parents decided to assimilate and were baptised into the Christian church when she was a teenager. They added Bartholdy to their surname, to dilute the impression of Jewishness given by the name Mendelssohn. Fanny Mendelssohn Bartholdy was able to study piano with the best teachers of the day: Marie Bigot in Paris; Ludwig Berger, Hummel and Moscheles in Berlin. By the age of thirteen she could play the first book of Bach's *Well-Tempered Clavier* by heart.

The Mendelssohns were friendly with the composer Carl Zelter, who ran the Berlin Sing-Akademie. When Fanny was just eleven, Zelter wrote to Goethe, introducing her father Abraham to the great poet. Zelter wrote: 'He [Abraham] has adorable children and his oldest daughter could give you something of Sebastian Bach. This child is really something special.'[6] This elevation of Fanny above her brother is an echo of what happened to Mozart's sister Nannerl: admired as much or more than him when the siblings were little, she was expected to step quietly aside in her teenage years. Correspondence between Zelter and Goethe mentioned Fanny once more in 1839, when Zelter told Goethe that Fanny 'plays like a man' (this was intended as a compliment).[7] Even Felix, whose piano-playing was much praised, admitted that Fanny played the piano better than he did. Both siblings showed precocious talent in composing and piano-playing, but a career in music was only open to the boy. Famously, Abraham Mendelssohn told his daughter when she was fifteen, 'Music will perhaps become his profession, while for *you* it can only be an ornament; never can or should it become the foundation of your existence and daily life ...'[8] Her brother agreed. 'Fanny is too much all that a woman ought to be for this,' he wrote to his mother. 'She regulates her house, and neither thinks of the public nor of the musical world, nor even of music at all, until her first duties are fulfilled.'[9] Was this true? Fanny herself seems to have accepted her fate. She was very fond of her younger brother and proud of his talent. How many girls have found themselves in her position – having to derive vicarious satisfaction from their brothers' achievements?

Felix looked up to her tremendously and asked her advice about his own work, even nicknaming her 'Minerva' (Roman goddess of wisdom) because she was so discerning. While Felix's youthful compositions were startling the musical world, Fanny's remained unpublished. She went on composing, particularly songs and piano music in the 'song without words' genre made famous by Felix. In 1826, with her consent, some of her songs were published under her brother's name in his opus 8 and opus 9 collections. When Mendelssohn visited Queen Victoria in London in 1842, the queen suggested she should sing a favourite song from this collection, with Mendelssohn at the piano. The queen's choice turned out to be Fanny's 'Italien'. (To his credit, Mendelssohn admitted that the song was actually by his sister.)

By a happy chance, in 1829 Fanny married Wilhelm Hensel, a court painter, who not only approved of her composing but also thought she should publish her compositions. They had a son, Sebastian (his name a homage to Bach, perhaps). Two years later Fanny (now Fanny Hensel) took over the running of the well-regarded Sunday concert series her mother had initiated. The *Sonntagsmusiken* were held in the spacious garden room of the family home; here Fanny could play for an invited audience and put on performances of some of her compositions. In time she even organised a choir, which expanded the range of music she could present. Her *Sonntagsmusiken* were attended by many well-known figures: Liszt, Heinrich Heine, Robert and Clara Schumann, Goethe. That same year, a cholera epidemic struck Berlin and raged in various parts of Europe into 1832. Fanny kept track of the epidemic in her diary and commemorated the end of the painful year by composing a cantata in honour of those who had died; her *Choleramusik* was performed by the choir in the Sunday series.

In 1839–40 the Hensels visited Italy and spent some time in Rome, where on Sunday evenings Fanny often played the piano (including Beethoven sonatas from memory) for artists gathered in the Villa Medici. One of the listeners was the French composer Charles Gounod, who remembered:

> Madame Hensel would sit down at the piano with the readiness and simplicity of one who played because she loved it. Thanks to her great gifts and wonderful memory, I made the acquaintance of some masterpieces of German music which I have never heard before, among them a number of the works of Sebastian Bach – sonatas, fugues, preludes and concertos – and many of [Felix] Mendelssohn's compositions, which were a glimpse of a new world for me.[10]

Fanny's touching piano piece *Abschied von Rom* (*Farewell to Rome*) conveys her regret at being parted from this congenial company.

'Leaving Rome is costing us both a heavy struggle,' she wrote in her diary.

> I would never have thought that it could make such an impression on me. I will not conceal it from myself, that the atmosphere of admiration and respect with which I am surrounded has partly contributed to it. In my early youth I have never been so courted as now, and who can deny that this is very pleasant and gratifying.[11]

In 1841, energised by her Italian journey, Fanny composed *Das Jahr* (*The Year*), a wide-ranging cycle of piano pieces depicting the seasons and moods of the year, with little illustrations by her painter husband at the top of each piece. After Fanny's death, the manuscript was lost and only rediscovered in the late 1980s, since when Fanny's reputation has grown as pianists belatedly discover the scope of this ambitious work.

In 1846 she finally decided – without consulting her brother – to publish six songs as her opus 1, but told her friend Angelika von Woringen, 'I can truthfully say that I let it happen more than made it happen ... If they want more from me, it should act as a stimulus to achieve. If the matter comes to an end then, I won't grieve, for I'm not ambitious.'[12] Perhaps not, but she worked enthusiastically at many new pieces, including a large-scale piano trio (for violin, cello and piano) full of confidence and high spirits. Seeing the score, which assumes a high degree of virtuosity and has much in common with Felix's piano chamber music, makes one wonder which of the siblings in fact influenced the other.

Alas, Fanny's sudden death from a stroke at the age of forty-two brought an end to further endeavour. Her brother's acute distress at her death surely indicated his complex feelings about what had been lost. He set about gathering up Fanny's manuscripts with the intention of getting them published, but six months later he too succumbed to a stroke at the age of only thirty-seven. In recent years, more of Fanny's works have seen the light of day; an ambitious *Easter Sonata* from 1828, depicting the Passion of Christ, surfaced in the 1970s and was thought to be by Felix until more recent scholarship attributed it to Fanny. In 2018 a small Mendelssohn museum opened in Hamburg, in the house where the family lived until 1811; pleasingly, it is called the 'Fanny and Felix Mendelssohn Museum'.

LOUISE DULCKEN

Louise Dulcken (1811–50), born Marie Louise David, was a German-born pianist who settled in London after her marriage and gave the English premieres of Chopin's F minor piano concerto (opus 21) and Mendelssohn's D minor piano concerto (opus 40).

She was fortunate to come from a very musical family and to marry into a family that could already boast generations of women musicians. She was the sister of the renowned violinist Ferdinand David, for whom Felix Mendelssohn composed his celebrated violin concerto. The David family was very cultured, and in addition to being tutored in piano and composition during her youth in Hamburg, Louise mastered English, French and Italian. At the age of ten she performed a Hummel piano concerto for a Hamburg audience, and often partnered her brother in chamber music, of which she was very fond.

When she was only seventeen, she married Theobald Augustus Dulcken, from an old family of Flemish harpsichord-makers. Over time the Dulckens had made the transition to making pianos, and Theobald's father was a court piano-maker in Munich. Theobald's mother was the German pianist and composer Sophie Lebrun, herself from a family of musicians – in fact Sophie Lebrun was born in London while her mother Francesca was on tour as an opera singer!

Louise David, now Dulcken, converted from Judaism to Protestantism on her marriage and moved with her husband to London in 1828. They must have been affluent, for they lived at prestigious addresses: Portman Square and later Harley Street. Louise lost no time in making her presence known. Her admired German training gave her an entrée to the London musical scene, and she became known as a witty person who could be humorous in several languages. Months after arriving in London she performed in a mixed programme of solo and chamber-music works in the Argyll Rooms, drawing praise from *The Times*: 'Madame Dulcken is a pianoforte player of great ability. She has evidently studied in the very best school, namely, that of Hummel and other contemporary German pianists.'[13] The following year she was the soloist in a performance of a piano concerto by Henri Herz in the Philharmonic Concerts at the King's Theatre.

She was also appointed a piano tutor to Princess Victoria, whose mother, the Duchess of Kent, gave Dulcken the title of 'pianist of the Duchess of Kent'. After Victoria became queen in 1837, this title was upgraded to 'pianist of Her Majesty'. The patronage of the duchess and her daughter the queen ensured that Dulcken could command a large and faithful audience for the concert series she put on annually with an orchestra from 1836, inviting other leading musicians and singers to perform in it. Although she was still only twenty-five, *The Times* said that 'This lady is unquestionably the first pianist of the day, Moscheles excepted. We know no performer of the other sex who is superior to her in certain qualities. Indeed, her touch and style altogether resemble those of Moscheles in spirit and energy.'[14]

Over the next decade she played regularly as a soloist at the Philharmonic Concerts and in April 1843 she gave the English premiere of Chopin's piano concerto in F minor. At this premiere it was she rather than Chopin who pleased the public: 'To Madame Dulcken's playing it would be almost impossible to give too high praise, the brilliancy of the player compensating in a great measure for the comparative inefficiency of the composition, and the applause that was bestowed being certainly awarded to the pianiste rather than to the composer.'¹⁵ The following year she invited Mendelssohn to perform with her at one of her mixed programmes:

> Of the performances of Madame Dulcken the most striking were the concerto in E flat of Weber, and the duet of Mozart for two pianos, of which one was played by Mendelssohn. The latter was perhaps the greatest treat of the concert, both pianists vieing with each other in giving the most exquisite softness and elegance of expression to the graceful inspirations of Mozart.¹⁶

We are used to musicians 'vieing with each other' to be more brilliant, so it is charming to find that Madame Dulcken and Dr Mendelssohn vied with one another to be exquisitely soft.

In 1845 the *Musical World* praised her – 'the charming, the amiable, the accomplished, the brilliant Madame Dulcken' – for daring to play a serious Beethoven sonata to a society audience:

> We must, however, offer our warm praise to Madame Dulcken, first for introducing, second for playing so superbly, the magnificent Sonata Appassionata in F minor of the mighty Beethoven. Madame Dulcken is one of the few who, surrounded by an audience of aristocrats and fashionables, dare to regale them with a sonata – and such a sonata! Honour and glory to our charming pianist, whose soul is full to the brim of music, and who takes every occasion to uphold it in her career of artist!¹⁷

Dulcken didn't confine her playing to London – she performed all over England and also toured Germany, Latvia and Russia during the 1830s and 1840s, sometimes partnering her brother Ferdinand David in duo recitals, and travelling as far as St Petersburg, where the Russian royal family rewarded her performance with a gift of diamonds. In October 1846 she was the soloist in Mendelssohn's D minor piano concerto at the Leipzig Gewandhaus with Mendelssohn conducting. It seems he had written her a new cadenza for the concerto, but the cadenza is thought to be lost.

In the last decade of her life, Dulcken established a successful Academy for Young Pianoforte Players at her home, firstly in Portman Square and later in Harley Street. She advertised it in *The Times*: 'Madame Dulcken, pianiste to Her Majesty, begs to inform the nobility and gentry that her Academy for young pianoforte players has recommenced, and will be held on Tuesdays and Fridays, at 2 o'clock, at Madame Dulcken's residence.'[18] Her academy attracted so many pupils that she employed several other leading female pianists of the day, such as Kate Loder and Louise Bendixen, to share teaching duties. Dulcken taught there herself when she wasn't organising concerts or travelling to play abroad. Alas, she died at the age of only thirty-nine after complications from an abscess. George Grove's *Dictionary of Music and Musicians* in 1879 judged that 'in fact, she had overtaxed her strength',[19] but perhaps Grove would not have made the same comment about a man. Half a century later, because of her Jewish origins, Louise Dulcken was listed in several anti-Semitic German lexicons of prominent Jewish writers, poets, artists, bankers and so on who were judged 'enemies'.[20]

The National Portrait Gallery has a lithograph of Louise Dulcken by Richard James Lane, from 1836, in which the beautiful Louise surveys us with calm self-possession.

MARIE PLEYEL

Marie Pleyel (1811–75), born Camille Marie Louise (or Denyse) Moke, is another woman whose life would make a tremendous subject for a film. She had a huge performing career in Europe and was admired by all the leading musicians of the day. The influential critic Joseph Fétis wrote in his *Biographie universelle des musiciens* (Paris, 1860–8) that he had heard all the famous pianists, but none had given him the feeling of hearing perfection like Marie Pleyel.

Marie Pleyel is sometimes referred to as Camille Moke, but after she married a man whose first name was also Camille, she exclusively used the name Marie, and for simplicity that is what I call her here. Marie Moke was a very pretty girl who seems to have been fully aware of her charm from an early age. She was still at school when Berlioz came to teach there and fell madly in love with her. In his *Memoirs*, Berlioz alludes to her 'maddening beauty'[21] at eighteen:

> She is nearly as tall as me, figure slim and graceful, with magnificent black hair and large blue eyes which shine like stars but cloud over and become opaque like the eyes of a dying man when the

demon of music takes possession of her ... At times there's something a little childlike about her ... [but] at the piano she's a Corinne [the strong-minded heroine of a novel by Madame de Staël]. Nothing childlike about her then. It is almost too much to listen to her, and to *watch* her is positively so. Her talent has something miraculous about it.[22]

Marie and Berlioz were briefly engaged to be married, but while Berlioz was in Rome he received a letter from Marie's mother informing him that the engagement was broken and that Marie was going to marry Camille Pleyel, heir to the famous Pleyel pianomaking firm and son of composer Ignaz Pleyel. Berlioz considered and even planned a murderous revenge on Marie and her mother, but fortunately did not carry it through. He did, however, take revenge in his writings, dealing out gruesome imaginary fates for Camille under the easily decipherable name Ellimac in his novella *Euphonia* (serialised in *La Gazette musicale* in 1844) and in the twenty-fifth evening of his *Soirées dans l'orchestre*, where she is known as Mina.

Her fiancé Camille Pleyel was forty-two when he married the twenty-year-old Marie. Within a few years, he had repudiated her, supposedly because she was unfaithful to him. Undeterred by the shame of separation, Marie Pleyel embarked on a concert career that took her far afield: she played in St Petersburg (where she met and was much influenced by the playing of virtuoso Sigismond Thalberg), in Leipzig (where she played with Mendelssohn), in Vienna (where she met Liszt) and in Paris (where her alleged affair with Liszt led to the break-up of Liszt's friendship with Chopin). Chopin, Liszt and Kalkbrenner all dedicated piano pieces to her. However, she also withdrew from the concert scene for various periods when she felt she needed to work on her piano technique. She was not content to confine herself to 'pretty' or 'feminine' repertoire and made a point of performing pieces associated with famous male pianists – for her London debut in 1846 she chose the same Weber *Konzertstück* in

F minor for piano and orchestra which both Mendelssohn and Liszt had played at *their* London debuts.

Her platform manner was a fascinating mix of charm and control, as many reviewers noted. In 1845, critic Henri Blanchard wrote that:

> she is calm at the piano; her eyes are almost constantly fixed on the keyboard; and when she raises them, her look has an almost unbelievable expression of audacity, of Mephistophelian irony, of scorn for all the difficulties of the pieces she plays. She is not painfully affected, she does not flutter around to gain audience support; she conquers it, smiles imperceptibly to herself at such an easy victory, and her beautiful curved figure, immobile, impassive, does nothing to betray the prodigious work of her fingers: it is the highest musical poetry coming from a soul shaped by all the experiences of life, and which enjoys tossing the strangest seductions in your direction. Can the art of piano playing go any further?[23]

The critic of *Le Monde musical* said that:

> As bar by bar, Madame Pleyel let the piano keys speak, this expressive and inspired playing, so powerful and graceful by turns, this expansive and fine style gradually seduced every ear and every heart; before the end of the first piece, the whole hall had yielded to the irresistible power of this beautiful and charming woman who is at the same time one of our finest pianists.[24]

The way she raised her eyes from the piano keys also made quite an impression on Robert Schumann, who in November 1839 reported to his fiancée Clara: 'She also has a habit of sometimes shutting her left eye and looking upwards with the other in a most gorgeous manner, and this is so sweet it can take your breath away.'[25] Not surprisingly, Clara regarded Marie as a rival and followed her career with some envy, ruefully noting how often her charming platform manner was mentioned, until the two women finally met in 1851 and Clara too fell under Marie's spell: 'I was actually very surprised by her great amiability which seemed so perfectly natural.'[26]

In later years Marie Pleyel became piano professor at the Brussels Conservatoire, where she taught the 'ladies' class' with great success. Liszt commented that many pianists had made their reputation by being good at some particular aspect of piano music, but the only piano class he knew that embraced the whole art of piano-playing was that of Madame Pleyel.

Katharine Ellis describes Marie Pleyel as 'matchlessly combining masculine authority with feminine grace'.[27] She was 'an honorary man'. Her contemporary, the playwright and composer Henri Blanchard, said that 'at the piano she has no gender'.[28] Pleyel cultivated this androgynous image, sometimes referring to herself in letters in the masculine: *un ami* instead of *une amie*.[29] Many women pianists (for example Clara Schumann) have wanted to look serious and be taken seriously, but Pleyel was doing something more complicated – creating what we might now call a sort of cognitive dissonance in the observer, a deliberate ambiguity that gave her artistic persona a special piquancy.

When Pleyel was just over forty and performing in London, a young Dutch pianist, Edouard Silas, visited her for a lesson.

> When I got there, she came in and said, 'I must take off my bonnet, it interferes with my smoking.' I thought I had misunderstood her; but when she presently brought out a box of big strong cigars, her meaning became clear. She offered me one, took one herself, lay down on her sofa and said, 'Now play me something.' I soon found that I had found more than my match in the consumption of big and strong cigars. Madame Pleyel is a fine woman, an excellent pianiste, has led a rather wild life and has all sorts of scandals attached to her name, but – I liked her nevertheless.[30]

CLARA SCHUMANN

Clara Schumann, née Wieck (1819–96), is one of the most admired and best documented of women pianists. Until quite recently she was often one of the few representatives of her gender in books on the history of the piano. What can one add to the biography of a woman who was a child prodigy, a composer, protagonist in a famous struggle to marry Robert Schumann, mother of eight children, one of the nineteenth century's leading pianists, friend to many distinguished musicians, muse to Schumann and Brahms, editor and arranger of her husband's music, sole financial support of her family after her husband's death, teacher of a younger generation of concert pianists, and a pioneer in the inclusion of 'early music' in her concert programmes as well as one of the first recitalists to play from memory in public? Clara Schumann encountered many challenges in her long life, and overcame them with extraordinary strength of mind. A glimpse through a gallery of portraits and photos of Clara at various ages will illustrate the stages in the life of this serious young woman as she matured from a *Wunderkind* into a doyenne of European music.[31]

Clara was a child prodigy, the product of a thorough and systematic musical training invented by her father Friedrich Wieck, who paraded her through Europe in much the same manner as the young Mozart was exhibited through Europe by *his* father. Less well known perhaps is that Clara's mother Marianne was Friedrich Wieck's first piano pupil. Marianne was the daughter of a church music director so strict that he was known by his other students as 'the iron cantor'. Her father was her first teacher, but she later studied piano with Wieck and married him when she was nineteen. Three years later, Clara was born. When Clara was four and a half, Marianne scandalised local society by leaving her husband and going home to her parents' house in Plauen with little Clara and a newborn baby boy, Victor.

Caught between 'the iron cantor' and a domineering husband, Marianne's life cannot have been easy. German law at the time awarded custody of children to the father once the children had turned five. It was only a few months later, therefore, that Marianne had to hand Clara back to her father in Leipzig. They made a deal that Marianne could visit her little girl, but only as long as she was living in Leipzig. As it happened, Marianne was already romantically involved with a colleague of Wieck's, the pianist Adolph Bargiel. For work reasons, they moved to Berlin; Marianne lost her right to see her daughter, and more or less disappeared from Clara's story. In Berlin, we know that Marianne sang solo parts in the Sing-Akademie, and she must have known the Mendelssohns. She went on to have several more children, among them Woldemar Bargiel, who became a well-regarded composer.

It must have been a strange experience for Clara's mother to watch from a distance as Clara became the obsessive focus of her father's musical ambitions. Schooled intensively in piano, violin, theory and composition, Clara made rapid progress and gave her public debut as a pianist at the age of nine. Wieck arranged concert tours for her, his sights set on Paris, considered an essential city to win over. Clara duly won over the Parisians in 1831–2 and a few years later had huge success in Vienna, where she played Beethoven's 'Appassionata' sonata in F minor (opus 57), and was given the title of 'royal chamber virtuoso' by the emperor. At the age of eighteen she was rated as highly as Liszt, Thalberg and Pleyel. Her repertoire, initially based on charming virtuoso works, broadened and became more serious. Her father availed himself of publicity methods old and new; he published 'recommendations' from leading cultural figures, put adverts in the press with pictures of Clara, and offered signed portraits of Clara as souvenirs at concerts.

Clara was not her father's only piano student. Another was Robert Schumann, who gave up his thoughts of becoming a lawyer when he heard Clara play the piano and enrolled instead as a student of her father's. Despite Robert's dalliances with other women, he and Clara gradually fell in love. He helped her with the orchestration of her remarkable piano concerto in A minor when she was only sixteen (interestingly, he later chose the same key for his own piano concerto). Their courtship is one of music history's most well-known stories. Clara's father bitterly opposed their match to the point that the young couple had to go to court to obtain permission to marry. (Clara's mother made a rare appearance in her life at this point to give her written approval to the match – perhaps a welcome opportunity for her to assert herself against her domineering ex-husband.)

Clara and Robert did finally marry in 1840, and thus began Clara's life as Frau Schumann. They kept a joint diary describing their musical lives, noting what pieces they were studying or composing and leaving messages for one another to read. It turned out that while Clara was required to support Robert's composing, the converse was not true. The modern reader will wince at the assumptions made in an entry in Robert's diary in February 1843:

> Clara has written a number of smaller pieces which show a musicianship and a tenderness of invention such as she has never before attained. But children, and a husband who lives in the realm of the imagination, do not go well with composition. She cannot work at it regularly, and I am often disturbed to think how many nice ideas are lost because she cannot work them out.[32]

One might wonder why, if he was 'often disturbed' by Clara's lack of time to devote to composing, he did not take action to remedy the situation. Why did he assume that once his famous wife was married she would automatically give up her own creative work and make husband and children her priority? But he did assume it, and his attitude was typical of the time.

Clara too was assailed by doubts: 'I once believed that I possessed creative talent, but I have given up this idea; a woman must not desire to compose – there has never yet been one able to do it. Should I expect to be the one?' she had written in her diary in November 1839.[33] Nevertheless, she did go on composing – her early training in the art must have made it a familiar and even necessary exercise, and perhaps also an important escape valve for her during the years when Robert was suffering from nervous illness. Her compositions were mainly songs and short pieces for piano – romances, variations, impromptus, scherzos, *pièces fugitives*.

It is interesting to reflect that although Robert did not do much to encourage Clara's composing, he nevertheless often used little themes of hers as 'mottos' in his own work. Perhaps Robert imagined that his use of Clara's themes would remain his private secret, but once one knows some of her piano music one can find scraps of her melodies *en passant* in her husband's music. Was Robert's use of Clara's musical themes a kind of tribute, or was it rather a kind of possessiveness, subsuming her work into his?

Performing as Frau Schumann, Clara's repertoire broadened to include works by her husband. The general public took a keen interest in them as a 'power couple'; Clara's renown was enhanced yet more by the perception of her as muse to the gifted Robert Schumann. How she managed to combine concert tours with giving birth to eight children and supporting a depressive and increasingly unstable husband will remain a mystery, but it is clear that she possessed exceptional steadiness, both mental and physical. Throughout Schumann's illness, and despite being constantly pregnant or suffering miscarriages, she continued performing – motivated at least in part by the wish to earn money for her family's expenses and her husband's medical bills.

In 1846 she wrote a lovely four-movement piano trio (for piano, violin and cello) which has become part of standard repertoire. Compared with Robert Schumann's wildly imaginative piano trios (which came later), Clara's is conservative; it is charming, well crafted and demure. When I was the pianist in the Florestan Trio, we used

sometimes to include Clara's piece alongside one of her husband's trios, which we all loved. I remember feeling some frustration with Clara's trio, which though tuneful and pleasing had an air of submissiveness, as though she wanted to make it perfectly clear that she had no intention of trespassing on her husband's wildly creative domain. She herself was the first to be critical of her trio, writing in her diary after the first rehearsal in October 1846 that 'there are some pretty passages in the Trio, and I think it is fairly successful as far as form goes'. A month later she had cooled further towards it: 'This evening I played Robert's piano quartet and my own trio, which seems to me more harmless each time I play it.'[34] It is interesting that, although she was a revered virtuoso pianist herself, Clara wrote a restrained piano part for her trio, avoiding the torrents of notes which many other pianist-composers have been unable to resist.

A few years later she had attained a more personal voice in her compositions. By the early 1850s, Robert Schumann's mental health issues were causing problems, not just privately at home with the family, but in public too because of his unreliable behaviour when conducting orchestras and choirs. Can it be a coincidence that as Robert's creative life began to fade, Clara's attained a new conviction? In May and June 1853 she wrote an impressive set of variations (her opus 20) on a theme of Robert's, following them with her three romances (opus 21). The third and most intriguing of these, marked 'Agitato', evokes with its corkscrewing melodic line a ceaseless turning and twisting in a narrow space. These pieces marked more or less the end of Clara's composing career. Robert entered a mental asylum shortly afterwards and Clara stopped writing music. Perhaps she gave up composing in some kind of solidarity with him – but it is tantalising to reflect on what she might have written, had she felt able to put all her life experience into further compositions.

Robert Schumann died in 1856 after a few years in the asylum. Clara walked in the funeral procession: 'His dearest friends went in front, and I came (unnoticed) behind, and it was best thus; he would have liked it so.'[35] After his death, Clara did not retreat from public life but instead intensified her concert activities. It was hardly a matter of choice – she was now solely responsible for earning the family's income. Her programmes became thoughtful curations of serious works and her focus on interpretation (rather than display) was praised by critics. Frothy virtuosic pieces gave way to works by Bach, Scarlatti, Beethoven, Chopin, Mendelssohn, Schumann and Brahms; she propelled Schumann's piano concerto towards the popularity it still enjoys. In 1856, the year her husband died in an asylum, *The Times* declared that 'Madame Schumann is not merely an accomplished and admirable executant, but an intellectual player of the highest class, with a manner and expression of her own as original and unlike anything else'.[36] She performed Beethoven's 'Hammerklavier' sonata, still considered knotty and intractable, and earned praise for the way she illuminated it. Her friendship with Brahms, whom she and Robert had met when he was a 'young lion', continued and deepened. When she toured, she taught private lessons in the cities she visited, augmenting her income. In fact, she managed to improve the family's financial situation substantially, and her concert income supported not only her children but also some of her grandchildren.

Gradually she became a senior figure among pianists, respected for her long career and the courageous way she had faced personal hardship. Leading critic Eduard Hanslick had described her as 'the greatest living pianist rather than merely the greatest female pianist, were the range of her physical strength not limited by her sex ... To give a clear expression to each work in its characteristic musical style and, within this style, to its purely musical proportions and distinctions, is ever her main task. She seems to play rather to satisfy a single connoisseur than to excite a multitude of average listeners.'[37] She had outlived Chopin, Mendelssohn and Schumann; she was still active as a pianist after Liszt had quit the concert stage; and she continued performing until she was seventy-one, then considered a great age. Sometimes, in mixed programmes with other artists, she was seen knitting as she waited among the audience for her turn to play. The public knew her history, and no doubt found it endearing. She became a role model for a younger generation of concert pianists. Born when Beethoven and Schubert were still alive, and performing almost into the twentieth century, she made the difficult transition from child star to *grande dame* without faltering.

WILHELMINE CLAUSS-SZARVADY

Wilhelmine Clauss-Szarvady (1834–1907) was a contemporary and duet partner of Clara Schumann, with whom she was often compared. She was highly esteemed by Robert Schumann, Liszt, Louis Spohr, Berlioz and a host of admiring critics, who compared her playing to Chopin's. Not only did she have a glittering solo career across Europe, but her inclusion of the works of Bach and other Baroque composers in her recital programmes also had a significant influence on Parisian musical taste in the mid-nineteenth century. Her hugely successful Paris salon raised the profile of chamber music at a time when it was languishing in the shadow of opera.

Wilhelmine Clauss was born in Prague and her early signs of pianistic talent were encouraged by her parents. When she was only sixteen, her mother accompanied her on an extensive concert tour to Germany; in 1847 she performed at the court in Dresden, where she met the Schumanns and Robert noted in his Housekeeping Book: 'the little Clauss studying with Clara – very talented'.[38] Clara generously ceded a planned concert date of her own at the Leipzig Gewandhaus to 'the little Clauss', and also performed Schumann's piano duet *Andante and Variations* (opus 46) with Wilhelmine at a soirée. In Leipzig, Wilhelmine met Liszt, who dedicated two piano works to her. In Kassel, the composer Spohr was her page-turner: 'It was delightful to see the great master busying himself by turning the pages for the young lady,'[39] reported the German music magazine *Signale*, which also reported about Wilhelmine's playing that 'Chopin's genius is reborn in her'.[40]

The next year in Paris her performance of Beethoven's 'Appassionata' sonata 'increased the applause to a pitch which had not been heard since Liszt's appearance here'.[41] Sad to say, Wilhelmine's mother died while they were in Paris, and her concert tour was interrupted (this has a strange echo of Mozart's mother dying in Paris in 1778 in the middle of her child's concert tour). Wilhelmine played again in Paris in 1852, causing Berlioz to say, 'For me, this young lady, endowed with the deepest musical feeling and a perfectly pure taste, possessing a wonderful technique, an encyclopaedic memory and an incomparably elegant style, is the first among pianists.'[42] That same year she took part in the Paris premiere of Schumann's now-celebrated piano quintet. (Clara Schumann noted sadly in her diary that she rather felt the honour should have fallen to *her* instead.[43]) She also started including works of Bach in her recitals; this was unusual at the time, but the Parisians liked it. 'Fräulein Clauss has become a trendsetter in musical fashion: all of a sudden it is fashionable for concert performers, but even for the shallowest virtuosos, to play at least one piece by the old Sebastian Bach in their concerts,' reported the *Süddeutsche Musik-Zeitung*.[44] Her appearance was part of her charm: 'Her small childish hands, delicate arms, her slim, white, finely veined wrists have extraordinary strength,' said *Signale*.[45]

In London, Wilhelmine Clauss played to Queen Victoria and in 1853 was invited to play at the queen's recently built palatial holiday home, Osborne House on the Isle of Wight, where 'Miss Clauss played Beethoven's opus 53 Sonata with such perfection that the Queen requested another piece'.[46] She toured several European countries, revisiting her home city of Prague where she was made an honorary member of the Sophien-Akademie in recognition of her achievements. In Vienna, where her concerts were overcrowded, the piano manufacturer Pleyel sent her a new piano to use for the rest of her series.

In 1855, she married the Hungarian writer Frigyes (Frédéric) Szarvady, a compatriot and associate of Liszt. After the birth of their son, Wilhelmine reduced her concert activities, but when she announced that she would play in London in 1858, tickets were sold out days before she appeared in the city. That same year, Liszt's mother reported to him from Paris that 'it's only Madame Clauss, now Szarvady, who does good business. She gave four concerts in less than four weeks, with great success, and with good income, without orchestras.'[47]

In the 1860s she turned more towards chamber music. She performed piano duets with Clara Schumann on a number of occasions, including in Paris where Clara presented her with the autograph of Robert Schumann's *Faschingsschwank aus Wien* (*Carnival Jest from Vienna*) (opus 26). In 1865, Clara took over a concert date from Wilhelmine in Frankfurt, in a pleasing reversal of what happened in Leipzig almost twenty years earlier. Wilhelmine played sonatas with violinist Joseph Joachim and chamber music with leading string players. After her son died in 1871, she stepped back from the public concert hall, but instead cultivated an enormously successful salon; her husband was now first secretary at the Hungarian section of the Austrian embassy in Paris.

In their Paris home she put on regular concerts of chamber music, presenting new works but also pioneering programmes with historical keyboard music by Couperin, Rameau, Pergolesi and Scarlatti.

According to the journal *Neue Zeitschrift für Musik*, her salons contributed more to Paris musical life than the Paris Opéra did:

> She did not send out invitations, but awaited applications for admission. In the first session, she played a Beethoven trio, a Schumann piano quartet, and a Raff sonata with the most eminent quartet players. In a second session she added Bach and Mendelssohn. The crowds grew, the requests to attend became more and more pressing.[48]

With her salons and her championing of contemporary works and the music of *les clavecinistes*, Clauss-Szarvady had a big influence on French musical thinking and beyond. 'It is her unique gift to pour a lovely poetical, perfumed atmosphere over everything, revealing her as one of those special talents who don't just have a clear and proper understanding, but also know how to put the stamp of her personality on her art, so that piece and performance flow together into a poetic whole,' wrote *Signale* in 1863.[49]

ARABELLA GODDARD

Arabella Goddard (1836–1922) was the most prominent British concert pianist for decades of her long career. She was the first woman (and one of the first pianists) to perform Beethoven's 'Hammerklavier' sonata (opus 106) in England, and the first to perform a sequence of Beethoven's late piano sonatas at a time when they were still considered intimidating and, with their craggy masculinity, the rightful preserve of male pianists.

She was born to English parents living in France and gave her first recital at the age of four. At six she was taken to Paris to study with the renowned Kalkbrenner, who had great hopes of her. To avoid the dangers of the French Revolution of 1848, her family moved to London where she studied with Lucy Anderson and Sigismond Thalberg. Her early career was based on the showy virtuosic pieces she learned in her youth, but things changed when Thalberg introduced her to James W. Davison, founder of the journal *Musical Examiner* and from 1848 the chief music critic of *The Times*. Thalberg thought that Davison could be a useful mentor for Goddard, encouraging her to tackle more serious pieces.

This approach took immediate effect and at the age of only seventeen, Goddard made her solo London debut with Beethoven's 'Hammerklavier' sonata, most of which she played from memory. It is often said that Goddard was the first person to perform it in England, but it appears that the French pianist Alexandre Billet had got there three years ahead of her. In any case, her debut made a huge impression: 'So grand and masculine a conception of a work of such matchless profundity ... was little short of miraculous in a girl of seventeen,' said the *Musical World*: 'one of the most extraordinary achievements of this or any other season'.[50] Naturally the grandeur of her conception was deemed to be 'masculine' and the critic felt free to hint at 'unfeminine' qualities in her appearance: 'She is very tall for her years, and slight rather than thin, her arms exhibiting a tendency to muscular development rare in one so young. No doubt this is caused by frequent exercise at the piano.'[51]

Still only eighteen, Goddard embarked on a two-year tour of Germany, Austria and Italy, playing in major cities and in many spa towns, varying her repertoire according to her sense of the audience's appetite for serious works. She was much praised for her performances of Mendelssohn: 'It is high praise, but no more than just when we record our opinion that Miss Goddard's execution of this great work [Mendelssohn's piano concerto in D minor] is the finest that has ever been heard here, excepting, of course, the composer's own performance of it,' said the *Daily News*.[52] But the leading music journal, *Neue Zeitschrift für Musik*, found that her playing 'lacked intellectual stimulation. An unhealthy calm was poured over the picture.'[53] The virtuoso pianist Moscheles was at the same concert but judged it differently: 'Miss Goddard conquers enormous difficulties with consummate grace and ease; her touch is pure as a bell.'[54]

These contrasting opinions were repeated throughout Goddard's career. She was felt to have profited unfairly from being the protégée of *The Times*'s music critic, who managed her career and made sure that her concerts were glowingly reviewed. (Goddard and Davison married in 1859 and had two children, though the marriage was not to last.) Davison's promotion of his wife was so blatant that a French journal cheekily maintained that whenever a foreign pianist approached the English shore, J.W. Davison could be seen standing on the white cliffs, waving a banner with the legend, 'No pianists wanted here! We have Arabella Goddard!'[55] In 1868, the *Neue Zeitschrift* remarked that it was hardly surprising if *The Times* had failed to do justice to Clara Schumann's soulful playing since its chief critic was Arabella Goddard's husband – 'but', said the *Neue Zeitschrift* cuttingly, 'what Goddard lacks, Clara Schumann possesses in the highest degree'.[56]

After reigning over the London piano scene for some years, Arabella Goddard spotted the potential for travelling by steamship, a possibility just opening up to the public. She decided to go on a world tour in 1873. Her tour lasted for three years and took her to Australia, India, Hong Kong, Shanghai, Australia (again) and New Zealand, then Canada and the United States, which she crossed from west to east, starting in California and finishing in New York. Because of the unpredictability of pianos in far-flung venues, she arranged to have her favourite Broadwood grand piano transported alongside her, only shipping it back to England once she got to the US with its more reliable instruments. In the 1870s, Goddard's world tour was a pioneering musical (and organisational) achievement, and the English press followed her progress avidly. She had announced that she would retire on her return from the United States, but in fact she must have been buoyed up by her tour because she went on performing into the 1880s, and when the Royal College of Music was founded in 1882 she became one of its first professors, teaching female pianists for some years.

In 1899 the playwright George Bernard Shaw, a passionate music lover, made a telling comment about Arabella Goddard's playing:

> There was something almost heartless in the indifference with which she played whatever the occasion required – medleys, fantasias and potpourris for 'popular' audiences, sonatas for Monday Popular ones, concertos for classical ones; as if the execution of the most difficult pieces was too easy and certain to greatly interest her ... She was more like the Lady of Shalott working at her loom than a musician at a pianoforte. I can see her now as she played; but I confess I cannot hear her, though I can vouch for the fact of her wonderful manipulative skill.[57]

AMY FAY

Amy Fay (1844–1928) was an American pianist who crossed the Atlantic by steamship in 1869 to study in Germany with Liszt and other influential piano teachers. She chronicled her six years in Europe in a series of letters to her sister Melusina. These were first published in the *Atlantic Monthly* in 1874 while Amy was still in Germany, and were later turned into a book, *Music-Study in Germany* (1880).[58] Amy's delightful account of her travels, lessons, struggles to learn German and boundless enthusiasm for German musical life made her a celebrated figure in the United States; the book went through twenty-five editions during her lifetime and was often given as a leaving prize at girls' schools. It inspired many young American pianists to dream of following in her footsteps.

In her letters home, Amy described her lessons with Liszt, Theodor Kullak and finally Ludwig Deppe, whose pedagogical methods became the basis of her own teaching career. For most readers, the heart of the book is her description of getting to know Liszt, then in his sixties but as quick-witted and full of charm and spirit as ever. In her pages Liszt comes alive in anecdotes about, for example, how he tossed a hot potato across the room to Amy at a dinner, mischievously improvised a new ending to one of his own pieces which Amy had brought to a lesson, or sat with her in the twilight chatting about the time Chopin put on a blond wig and imitated Liszt to perfection.

Amy had many opportunities to hear Liszt play in Weimar. In June 1873 she described him astutely:

> In Liszt I can at last say that my ideal in something has been realised. He goes far beyond all that I expected. Anything so perfectly beautiful as he looks when he sits at the piano I never saw, and yet he is almost an old man now. I enjoy him as I would an exquisite work of art. His personal magnetism is immense, and I can scarcely bear it when he plays. He can make me cry all he chooses, and that is saying a good deal, because I have heard so much music, and *never* been affected by it. Even Joachim, whom I think divine, never moved me. When Liszt plays anything pathetic, it sounds as if he had been through everything, and opens all one's wounds afresh. All that one has ever suffered comes before one again ... Liszt knows well the influence that he has on people, for he always fixes his eyes on some one of us when he plays, and I believe he tries to wring our hearts. When he plays a passage and goes pearling down the keyboard, he often looks over at me and smiles, to see whether I am appreciating it. But I doubt if he is feeling any particular emotion himself, when he is piercing you through with his rendering. He is simply hearing every tone, knowing exactly what effect he wishes to produce and how to do it. In fact he is practically two persons in one – the listener and the performer. But what immense self-command that implies![59]

In 1875 Amy Fay returned to America, giving concerts in Boston and Chicago before settling in New York. Perhaps sensing that her German adventure had given her a certain authority on European piano classics, she began speaking to the audience before performing a piece, telling them a bit about the music and what the composer hoped to convey. She noticed that the audience responded more warmly to the performance when they had heard her speak about the music. This gave her the idea for a series of 'Piano Conversations', a format she used for the rest of her career. Thus she was a pioneer of the modern lecture-recital at a time when it was unusual for women to speak in concerts.

Fay came from a family of independent thinkers and was quick to use her platform to speak up about the inequalities she saw women musicians suffering. Joining in the debate about why there were few women composers, she pointed out in her lectures that women were not offered the 'mind training' routinely provided for men. She spoke up for female piano teachers, who often found it difficult to obtain payment in advance for lessons – a practice that was considered normal for male teachers – or sometimes to obtain payment at all. She was active in founding and running musical clubs for women, and from 1903 to 1914 she took over from her sister Melusina as president of the New York Women's Philharmonic Society.

Fay's German adventures in the 1870s offer a precious glimpse of a time when Germany, with its art, culture and old-world values, was a magnet for musical Americans, and when German musical values dominated the classical music scene in the United States. In the twentieth century, these attitudes changed along with political developments and naturally with two world wars; Germany was no longer viewed so benignly. However, it was not long before eminent musicians started emigrating from Europe to the United States, and German culture once again became available in American conservatoires in a new way.

SOPHIE MENTER

Sophie Menter (1846–1918) was a favourite of Liszt's, 'my only legitimate piano daughter' as he called her.[60] When she played in Paris, her charisma as a performer earned her the nickname 'the incarnation of Liszt'.

Sophie was born in Munich to musical parents. Her father died when she was nine, one of his last remarks to his wife being, 'Take care of Sophie – that girl has something in her.' Sophie enrolled in the Munich Conservatorium and made rapid progress, giving her debut with Weber's *Konzertstück* at age fifteen. She later studied with Carl Tausig, Liszt's best pupil, probably the first in a long line of Sophie's disappointed suitors, and she started to build up her repertoire of Liszt's piano music. In 1867 she was appointed court pianist to the Prince von Hohenzollern, at whose castle she met the cellist David Popper. They married, and Sophie gave birth to a daughter Celeste in 1872. During the 1870s, Menter and Popper toured as a cello–piano duo, but this ceased with their divorce in 1886.

In 1869, Menter met Liszt on the occasion of her performance of his E flat piano concerto in Vienna. She became a protégée of Liszt, a lifelong friend and possibly a lover (there has been conjecture that Celeste was Liszt's daughter rather than David Popper's). She was never officially a student of Liszt, but they often played music together and there is no doubt that he was a great influence on her. When Amy Fay asked Liszt if Menter had been his pupil, 'He said no, he could not take the credit of her artistic success to himself. I heard afterwards that he really had done ever so much for her, but he won't have it said that he teaches!'[61] It was Liszt who nicknamed Menter's cat 'Klecks' (or Smudge, as we might say in English) because of the mark on its nose. He and Menter performed his *Concerto pathétique* for two pianos at a private concert, and he said about her that 'Sophie Menter is the piano itself. Others play the piano – the piano plays Sophie Menter.'[62] Yet Menter did not take her rapport with the piano for granted: she was said to practise for ten hours a day and to be obsessed with the piano to the exclusion of all else except her beloved cats. Those who knew her well said she wasn't interested in literature, painting or even nature: her passion was piano music.

She undertook concert tours all over Europe and eventually answered an invitation to play and teach in St Petersburg, where enthusiasm for her playing became quite fanatical. In 1880, after she performed Wagner's *Tannhäuser* overture arranged for piano by Liszt, she was mobbed by so many admirers that the police had to come and control the crowd. At her Russian concerts, wealthy patrons allegedly threw jewels at her feet. The following year she triumphed in Spain, Portugal and Denmark. In Denmark, special trains had to be put on to convey her audiences to Copenhagen. After one of her concerts there, members of the audience unhitched the horses waiting outside and insisted on pulling her carriage themselves. In 1881 she visited England, where she was made an honorary member of the Royal Philharmonic Society. Interestingly, she never went to America, though she had invitations to do so; the journal *Signale* reported that she felt 'her health would not be up to the strains of American concert life'.[63]

In 1884 Menter bought Schloss Itter, a castle in Austria, where her menagerie of cats had free rein. Tchaikovsky came to visit her and in 1892 agreed to orchestrate a piano piece called *Ungarische Zigeunerweisen* (*Hungarian Gypsy Airs*), a potpourri of Hungarian themes very much akin to Liszt's Hungarian rhapsodies. Allegedly, Menter had composed the piece herself, but there are indications in letters between her and Liszt in the mid-1880s that he was writing such a piece for her. Whether composed by Liszt or Menter, the 'Hungarian' piece was a barnstorming success. When the American critic Edward Baxter Perry heard Menter play it in Stuttgart in 1899, he wrote in *Étude* magazine that 'at the close we were left dazed, confused, breathless and, may I add, nearly deafened, by this, undoubtedly the most brilliant and astounding concert number ever rendered upon any program'.[64] The same year, playwright George

Bernard Shaw heard her and observed that 'she produces an effect of magnificence which leaves Paderewski [the great Polish pianist and Chopin expert] far behind. Madame Menter seems to play with splendid swiftness, yet she never plays faster than the ear can follow, as many pianists can and do.'[65] This astute remark shows that sometimes the effect of swiftness is actually *increased* if one can hear every note at a fractionally more controlled tempo.

As may be surmised from the description of her enraptured audiences, Sophie Menter was not only a wonderful pianist but also very beautiful. Her loveliness is mentioned in review after review, even into her fifties. In that respect she was a good candidate for 'the incarnation of Liszt', for his physical appearance too had an overwhelming effect on his listeners. The Chilean pianist Claudio Arrau was taken to visit Menter at her final home in Stockdorf near Munich when she was around seventy, by then living a reclusive life with her fifty cats. He described her as 'a very impressive lady, still gorgeously beautiful. And still very elegant, with lots of marvellous jewellery.'[66] Despite protesting that she didn't play anymore, she played him some excerpts from Liszt's A major piano concerto.

MARIE JAËLL

Marie Jaëll, née Trautmann (1846–1925), was a French pianist from Alsace, renowned for feats of endurance in performances of 'cycles' such as the thirty-two Beethoven sonatas, the complete works of Liszt (performed in six concerts) and those of Schumann (in another six). There was no piano in her village and she did not see one until she was six, at which point she pestered her parents to buy her 'a music' (meaning a piano) until they gave in. After that, there was no stopping her: she would trudge through the snow to the next village every week to have a piano lesson. By the age of nine she was playing concerts, organised by her mother. At eleven she played to Queen Victoria, who described her as a 'Liliputian pianist'.[67] In her teens she met Liszt, who was to play a great part in her life. In 1861 she joined the ladies' piano class at the Paris Conservatoire, passing the final exam very quickly the same academic year and triumphing with a performance of a piano concerto by Moscheles, a set piece for all twenty-one women pianists that year. Marie was the twentieth to perform it, but did so with such freshness that the weary examiners were quite rejuvenated and were unanimous in awarding her the first prize.

At twenty she married Alfred Jaëll, a well-known pianist who had been a pupil of Chopin. Their home in rue Saint-Lazare in Paris became a popular meeting place for artists. The Jaëlls went on tours together throughout Europe, often playing duets, two-piano concertos and compositions of their own. Marie started to compose many works for piano. Alfred Jaëll generously used his connections to enhance his wife's career, introducing her to influential composers and promoters.

In 1868, Liszt described Marie as having 'the brains of a philosopher and the fingers of an artist'.[68] Gradually, critics started to say that Marie's playing outshone her husband's, and their duet appearances gave way to solo recitals for Marie. Marie was the first woman to perform the whole set of Beethoven's thirty-two piano sonatas in Paris.

After Alfred Jaëll died in 1882, Marie moved to Weimar, where she became part of Liszt's close circle, acting as a secretary to the great man but also taking part in his classes, where her playing was much admired. One of Liszt's final performances was given in Marie's salon in Paris. After Liszt died in 1886, Marie focused more on composing. She took lessons from César Franck and Saint-Saëns, both of whom rated her highly. It was through Saint-Saëns's intervention in 1887 that she became one of the first female members of the Société des Compositeurs.

Some of her piano works – concertos, sonatas, impromptus, pieces for children – have been recorded in recent years. They often make a rather curious impression, as of a fantastical creature composed of parts of different animals. On the one hand, her writing is often 'masculine' and heroic, as if she were at pains to show that she was not a 'weak and feeble woman'; on the other hand, her music can be strangely lacking in direction, as though she could not see her way out of the musical patterns she had set up. Altogether her work is a strange hybrid, like a cross between Saint-Saëns and Erik Satie, which is to say: either too many notes or too few.

She also started to turn her attention to pedagogy. It appears that she may have suffered from tendonitis, that scourge which so many modern pianists have had to contend with as a result of too much practice of an effortful kind. This was hardly surprising in one who had made a point of undertaking huge 'cycles' as Marie had done; the stiffness she experienced in her arm muscles may have been responsible for the 'banging' which critics complained about at this period.

Her ideas about the link between the mind and the hand were pioneering for the 1890s and preceded by a long way the better-known methods of male teachers such as Tobias Matthay. She advised that the student should spend more time thinking about the sound they wanted to make *before* they played the note (echoing Liszt's famous, though possibly apocryphal, advice to 'think ten times and play once'). She counselled playing with less weight and less force, and spending not more than two hours a day at the keyboard. She recommended slow practice, practice away from the keyboard (on a tabletop for example), and cultivating a deep connection to music rather than just to the piano. She thought that children should learn to play by ear before anyone showed them how to read music.

Marie's ideas were glowingly endorsed by one of her pupils, Albert Schweitzer, the German theologian, philosopher and musician who translated her book *Le Toucher* (*Touch*) into German in 1897. As time went on, Marie's ideas became more outlandish: colours were assigned to fingers, students' fingerprints were analysed, the piano had to be placed on a north–south axis to promote the right flow of energy. These ideas naturally fostered a reputation for eccentricity, even mental instability. But her earlier insights into how to play with a healthy technique were not only extremely wise, but also far ahead of her time. Even her later ideas might find an echo in 'alternative' philosophies of health and wellbeing today.

LEOPOLDINE WITTGENSTEIN

Leopoldine Wittgenstein (1850–1926) was an excellent pianist but did not perform publicly. She presided over an influential salon at her palatial home in Alleegasse 4 (now demolished) in Vienna, where there were seven pianos, a library of music manuscripts and an important art collection. The Wittgensteins had bought several paintings by Gustav Klimt and allegedly it was Leopoldine who had the idea of commissioning Klimt to paint a portrait of her daughter Margaret (now in the Neue Pinakothek, Munich). Brahms was a close friend of the family; Mahler, Schoenberg, Bruno Walter and Richard Strauss were frequent visitors to the salon; Joachim and Casals performed there. Leopoldine owned an important collection of music manuscripts, including works by Bach, Beethoven and Brahms. A jewel of her collection was the autograph manuscript of Beethoven's piano sonata in E major (opus 109); Otto Schenker managed to persuade her to let him come to the house in Vienna to study the manuscript when he was preparing his influential book on Beethoven piano sonatas in 1912.

I have included Leopoldine here because, although the achievements of the male members of the Wittgenstein family are well known, Leopoldine is a shadowy figure. Yet her obsession with the piano had a big influence on her children's lives.

Leopoldine, or 'Poldi' as she was known, was a talented young pianist, given to long hours of practice. She was courted by the industrialist Karl Wittgenstein through the medium of piano duets and chamber music, of which they were both devotees. A revealing glimpse into the power balance of their relationship is given by the gold bracelet Karl gave Poldi, its golden links engraved with the words 'Du musst immer gut sein': you must always be good. Husband and wife regularly played piano duets, which Karl found relaxing after a day of business. In later life, he developed cancer of the jaw and found himself facing a serious operation. He chose to spend the evening before it playing Brahms and Beethoven duets with Poldi, which must show how greatly he relied on music for peace of mind.

Nevertheless, Karl the industrial magnate was implacably opposed to any of his sons becoming musicians. There were five sons and three daughters, all of them sensitive, clever and artistic. They grew up listening to their mother playing the piano; several of them would have liked to pursue music as a career. Their father's ban on pursuing a career in the arts must have seemed cruel to his sons, three of whom came to a tragic end. The oldest son, Hans, a gifted pianist and violinist, committed suicide in America in 1903. The following year,

Rudi poisoned himself in a bar in Berlin, possibly on discovering that his homosexuality was about to be made public. Kurt, an Austrian officer, shot himself at the end of the First World War.

Then there was Paul, a talented pianist who was shot while on patrol duty in the Austrian army and suffered such serious injuries to his right arm that it had to be amputated. Held prisoner in Siberia immediately after the amputation, he managed to draw the outline of a piano keyboard on a wooden crate and set about working out how he would play the piano with his left hand alone. When the war was over, he built a much-admired career as a left-handed pianist for whom several leading composers wrote special pieces (for example, Ravel's *Piano Concerto for the Left Hand*). Clearly Paul's iron will was the equal of his father's. Nevertheless, when the Austrian currency collapsed in 1922 and Paul lost a chunk of money he had invested on behalf of the whole family, his siblings stopped speaking to him. Finally there was the austere Ludwig, mathematician, engineer and author of the celebrated *Tractatus Logico-Philosophicus* (written during his time in the Austrian army). Ludwig studied music in his youth and became so good at whistling that he could whistle the solo parts of entire concertos. Philosophy was his chosen field, but like the rest of his siblings he was very musical.

What of the mother of this extraordinary brood? Leopoldine was said to be very shy and averse to conflict.[69] Within the family there was frustration that she was so dominated by her husband. However, her love of the piano was indulged and even encouraged because it was 'only a hobby'. Never very comfortable in the presence of children (even her own), she seems to have sought escape from the family psychodramas by retreating into her music room and playing the piano for four or five hours a day, almost as if she were a professional concert pianist, which perhaps she was in a parallel fantasy life. In 1917 her daughter Hermine remarked in a letter to Ludwig that she wondered 'what would have become of Mama if she had married someone else ... She's really like a plant that's not withered, but constricted; that blossoms only when the big tree has gone.'[70] In this regard, Leopoldine shared the experience of many historical women, including some of the most significant figures in this book.

TERESA CARREÑO

Some years ago, the Simón Bolívar Youth Orchestra of Venezuela captured everyone's hearts with their fiery performances. In the world of classical music, they seemed like refreshing newcomers. But 150 years before they came on the scene, a young female pianist from Venezuela had swept all before her. After a splendid career as a child prodigy, by the 1890s Teresa Carreño (1853–1917) was regarded as the world's leading pianist, her pianistic gifts matched by her confidence and good looks. She herself was related to the 'Liberator' Simón Bolívar, her mother being a niece of Bolívar's wife and also a niece of one of his generals.

Teresa's father was the director of the Bank of Venezuela and the author of an etiquette guide that was required reading in government schools and colleges. In 1862, however, he had to leave Venezuela in a hurry when the political regime changed. He moved his family to New York, where they were fortunate to be able to afford a home on Second Avenue. Teresa took piano lessons from composer-pianist Louis Moreau Gottschalk. At the age of nine, Teresa burst onto the American musical scene with sold-out concerts – five performances in New York in December 1862, twelve in Boston in January 1863, playing virtuoso piano works and operatic transcriptions. As a result she was invited to perform for President Lincoln at the White House in the autumn of 1863.

Years later, Carreño recalled that at the White House she had embarrassed her father by refusing to play the Bach invention he wanted her to play and launching into Gottschalk's *Marche de nuit* instead. Then she complained that the White House piano was out of tune.

Mr Lincoln patted me on the cheek and asked if I would play *The Mocking Bird* with variations. The whim to do so seized me and I returned to the piano, gave out the tune and then went off into an impromptu series of variations that threatened to go on forever. Mr Lincoln declared that it was excellent, but my poor father thought I had disgraced myself, and continued to apologise in his broken English until we were out of hearing.[71]

This reminiscence is interesting because it shows that improvising was still a normal part of performance in 1863; though Lincoln's request did not surprise Teresa, it would surely have taken some boldness for a young pianist to improvise extensively in front of the president, especially if she had no advance notice of the tune. *The Mocking Bird* was an American Civil War marching song of which Lincoln was fond, and with regard to the present story it is intriguing that Lincoln once said the song was 'as sincere as the laughter of a little girl at play'.[72]

By 1866, still only twelve, Teresa and her family sailed across the Atlantic and arrived in France for her triumphant European debut. This brief but gushing report in May 1866 from the Parisian journal *L'Art musical* conveys the tone of her reception:

> A little wonder, a real prodigy arrived among us a few days ago. She comes from America. Her name is Teresa de Carreño; she is but twelve years of age and endowed with ideal beauty. This young and sympathetic child plays the piano in a manner that would surprise Liszt himself. It is incredible. In a few days, although the season is near its close, the name of Teresa de Carreño will be known in all our Parisian salons. She is accompanied by her mother and by her father. Señor de Carreño is a distinguished man: ex-minister of finances in Venezuela and now a political exile. These three travellers were nearly a month upon their ocean voyage. The steamship upon which they were passengers was wrecked, and by an unheard-of chance they were taken up by a passing ship.

In the next issue of *L'Art musical*, having heard a concert given by the young pianist, the reviewer declared that 'she has transported the audience ... Miss Carreño is simply a genius.'[73]

Furnished with an ecstatic letter of introduction from Rossini, they then travelled to London where critics noted the high-society audience at her concerts and admired Teresa's playing with characteristic English reserve: 'altogether a "taking player"', she was called.[74] The Carreños returned to Paris, where Teresa was not eligible to join the Paris Conservatoire because of her nationality but was able to study privately with Georges Matthias, a pupil of Chopin, and with Anton Rubinstein, who became a lifelong supporter. Sadly, a cholera epidemic struck Paris while the Carreños were there, and Teresa's mother caught it and died. (Thus, strangely, Señora Carreño is the third mother mentioned in this book to have died in Paris while accompanying her piano-playing child on a concert tour.)

Carreño's touring continued apace with successful appearances all over Europe in the 1870s. Extraordinarily, she turned out to be gifted as a singer as well – so much so that at one point she was able to step in for an indisposed opera soprano in a performance of Meyerbeer's *Les Huguenots* in Edinburgh in 1872. She also found time to marry the first of her four husbands, with whom she had six children in total. In the early 1880s she started to petition the president of Venezuela with her plans for a national music conservatoire, hoping she would be summoned back to South America to lead it. This petition did not have immediate results, though she was commissioned to write a song in honour of Bolívar; the result, *Himno a Bolívar*, is still known to all Venezuelans. A few years later, her world stature now established, she was invited to form and direct a national opera company in Venezuela. With great effort she used her New York contacts to put together an orchestra, chorus, dancers and opera stars, presenting a series of operas in Caracas in 1887 (and performing virtuoso piano pieces herself in between the acts), but political shenanigans interfered with the smooth running of the company and it folded at the end of the run.

Conscious that no really major career could be made without conquering Germany, she borrowed thousands of dollars from the Chicago industrialist N.K. Fairbank to pay the expenses of travelling to Germany and hiring a good orchestra and concert hall for her debut. (Such an undertaking showed exceptional administrative zeal.) The result was a spectacular success at the Berlin Sing-Akademie in November 1889, Carreño performing Grieg's piano concerto with the Berlin Philharmonic but also playing virtuoso piano works including Schumann's demanding *Études symphoniques*. The opportunities that opened up to her thereafter led her to base herself in Berlin from 1895 to 1916. She toured constantly, making a particular impact in Russia where critics praised her incomparable impetuosity and strength. 'Her Southern temperament is everywhere in evidence,' wrote critic Nikolai Feopemptovich Soloviev. 'Her technical equipment that knows no limits enables her to infuse everything she interprets with noble purity and loftiest idealism.'[75] She became a champion of Grieg's piano music and also that of her American pupil Edward MacDowell, performing these composers' piano concertos to great acclaim. A painful chapter of her personal life saw her married briefly to the concert pianist Eugen d'Albert, whose domineering personality made life difficult.

She also composed a quantity of piano and chamber music of her own. Her piano pieces give a vivid sense of her personality: confident, open, fun-loving. For example, *Un Bal en rêve* (opus 26) depicts alternating episodes of slumber and dreaming about a dance at a ball. Classical repertoire has many evocations of dances at balls, but they tend to be wistful, dreamy waltzes. By contrast, Carreño's remembered dance is a cheerful, vigorous affair with a strong hint of the merengue, a popular dance of her native South America. If, as we may assume, it is a young girl who is recalling the dance, she is clearly not a girl waiting to be swept off her feet by a handsome man, but rather a young woman with a healthy sense of her own powers.

In the early years of the twentieth century Carreño's tours took her to the United States, Australia, Mexico and South Africa as well as Europe. Everywhere she went she was admired for her strength and dynamism and passion for performing; she was often referred to as the 'Valkyrie of the Piano'. The great Polish pianist Paderewski (who was not only a renowned virtuoso but also a politician, eventually becoming prime minister of Poland) once said that her playing was 'perhaps too strong for a woman',[76] a comment that shows the prejudices with which women pianists had to contend. Her concerto repertoire expanded to include many pieces more often associated with men – Tchaikovsky, Liszt, Brahms, Rubinstein, Saint-Saëns, Beethoven's 'Emperor' – but she was also praised for her performances of Schumann, Mendelssohn and Chopin concertos. In 1916, fifty-three years after she played to President Lincoln, she was invited once more to the White House, this time to play to President Woodrow Wilson.

Sir Henry Wood, founder of the Proms, wrote in his memoirs that:

> It is difficult to express adequately what all musicians felt about this great woman who looked like a queen among pianists – and *played* like a goddess. The instant she walked onto the platform her steady dignity held her audience who watched with riveted attention while she arranged the long train she habitually wore. Her masculine vigour of tone and touch and her marvellous precision on executing octave passages carried everyone completely away.[77]

We may note that even 'a queen' and 'a goddess' were perceived as 'masculine' when she played with command.

Carreño has been publicly honoured more than almost any other female pianist. Today in Caracas there is a performance space named the Teresa Carreño Cultural Complex (where some of her concert gowns are displayed), and the Venezuelan youth orchestra is now called the Teresa Carreño Youth Orchestra. In Miami there is a piano competition named after her; in 1991 a crater on the planet Venus was named Carreno after her; and in 2018, on the 165th anniversary of her birth, a Google Doodle was created in her honour.

CÉCILE CHAMINADE

Cécile Chaminade (1857–1944) was the first woman composer to be awarded the Légion d'Honneur in her native France. She thought of herself as a composer rather than a pianist, but used her pianistic skills to advertise and convey her music to new audiences, particularly in the United States in the early years of the twentieth century.

Chaminade was born in Paris and privately tutored at home in piano, violin and composition. Her talent was noticed by her professors and by a neighbour, Georges Bizet (composer of *Carmen*). They advised that Cécile should join the class at the Paris Conservatoire, but her father refused to allow it, fearing that her morals might be compromised by encountering the bohemian atmosphere among the students. Cécile was allowed to continue private lessons, but, as musicologist Marcia Citron has astutely pointed out, 'As a result Cécile missed out on the full breadth of institutional education, which permits group socialization, individual contacts, and exposure to other ideas as much as it sharpens musical skills.'[78]

This is of course true of all the women who were not permitted to study at music conservatoires, but in relation to Chaminade it is worth mentioning because although she *was* given access to tuition, she was denied the valuable opportunity to rub shoulders with other budding composers. When one thinks of the fertile conversations and piquant social scene which her Parisian contemporaries Debussy, Ravel, Poulenc, Satie and other male composers enjoyed, it is easy to see that Chaminade was at a disadvantage in having to develop her style in isolation.

She became known for her charming piano pieces, evocatively titled, printed with beautiful pictures on the covers of the sheet music, cleverly written for the amateur market and more specifically for the *female* market. Her most famous piece was *Scarf Dance*, a pretty waltz just difficult enough in places to give amateur pianists a sense of achievement. It had sold over 5 million copies by the time of her death in 1944. Her charming song 'L'Anneau d'argent' for voice and piano was recorded and performed by countless artists including Clara Butt, John McCormack and more recently Anne Sofie von Otter.

Chaminade's style was elegant with a hint of exotic harmonies, a bit like early Debussy, the piano compositions of Enrique Granados or the style of her composition teacher Benjamin Godard, who was said to have proposed to her (without success). The playability of her shorter piano pieces was an important factor in their wide appeal. Indeed, it could be said that her approach to writing for amateur pianists was a refreshing change from that of some (male) composers who loftily ignored the practical difficulties of playing their music, especially for those with smaller hands. Many generations of amateur pianists have laboured under the near-unplayability of some wonderful music, so Chaminade is to be applauded for actively concentrating on the amateur pianist and her limited time for piano practice.

Chaminade was adept not only at miniatures. In the 1880s and 1890s she also wrote technically challenging concert studies, character pieces, a piano sonata, a concertino for piano and orchestra, and two large-scale piano trios (for piano, violin and cello), which deserve to be better known. Her concert pieces show a confident grasp of larger structures and a gift for melodic line that could be compared with Fauré's. *Automne* (opus 35), for example – a great favourite in her day – is a kind of ballade, with luscious harmonies in the peaceful sections and a stormy, rippling middle section evocative of Liszt. (Its main melody, incidentally, is very like a smoothed-out version of the melody in the finale of Brahms's horn trio, but this is probably pure coincidence.) *Guitare* (opus 32) is a spicy evocation of the folk music of Spain, in the fine tradition of French composers such as Bizet, Debussy, Chabrier and Ravel, who knew how to pay tribute to the sultry music of their Spanish neighbours.

Since it was easier for a woman to make a name as a pianist than as a composer, Chaminade first made headway with concert tours, and played well enough to be admired by Liszt. Her programmes were often exclusively made up of her own compositions, a very unusual strategy for a woman at that time and one that was perhaps prompted by the collapse of her father's finances after some unwise investments. Chaminade needed to make some money of her own and succeeded by selling copies of her sheet music in association with her concerts, in the process becoming probably the first professional female composer. In the 1890s she visited England several times and became popular in London. Queen Victoria liked her music, and in fact an organ prelude by Chaminade was played at the queen's funeral in 1901. Already in the 1890s Chaminade's music was becoming popular with women in the United States, where 'Chaminade Clubs' were springing up in tribute to her.

Being a woman, she was not immune from comments on her appearance, and male critics found her insufficiently pretty. In 1899 Edward Baxter Perry, an American critic, wrote in *Étude* magazine that:

> Except for a fine figure and a fine pair of dark eyes, she can boast no physical charms, while her face is unfortunately not in her favor, when seen in profile as she sits at the piano. An extremely retreating chin, that might be called no chin at all, gives it an expression of weakness bordering upon imbecility, which very much belies her mental and artistic powers.[79]

The same year, critic Ward Stephens described a visit to Chaminade, telling the reader, 'I have been told that Chaminade is over forty years of age. She does not look it. She is not married; neither is she beautiful; but in conversation her face lights up with animation and a smile which grows very fascinating.'[80] No physical charms; over forty; not married – were male pianists ever subjected to this kind of public disparagement? Probably not: it would have been an affront to male camaraderie.

Her female fans did not care about Chaminade's lack of appeal to male critics. Her direct appraising gaze, elegant no-fuss appearance, refusal to wear jewels and independent lifestyle made her a role model for many. In 1901 she married a much older man, with whom she never lived; theirs was said to be a platonic marriage. Chaminade liked to describe herself as 'music's nun'.[81]

In 1908 her popularity led to the creation of a perfume and a soap named after her by the newly formed Morny company of New Bond Street in London: 'Chaminade' was their first successful perfume, and the pretty boxes of soaps had a few bars of Chaminade's *Air de ballet* on them. When she wrote a new piece of piano music, she took care to commission attractive covers for the sheet music: delicate forest scenes of starlight, dancing birds and half-glimpsed boats in waving reeds, guaranteed to create a dreamy mood. The covers themselves became collectors' items.

After her husband died in 1907, Chaminade was freer to travel. She toured the United States, where in 1908 she experienced her greatest period of success and was even invited to lunch at the White House to meet President Theodore Roosevelt and his wife, Edith. Her sold-out Carnegie Hall debut was attended by many adoring members of Chaminade Clubs. Next day, her piano music was condescendingly described by a (male) *New York Times* critic as 'claiming immediate acceptance by those whose knowledge and taste in music are not erudite'.[82] Undeterred, Chaminade's fans flocked to buy the sheet music and try these attractive pieces for themselves.

At this time, American women were energised by the question of what their role in society should be. They didn't want only to accompany their husbands to social events; they wanted a social life of their own, and forums in which they could be comfortable. Women-only clubs were a welcome counterbalance to the many private clubs open only to men, and to have music as a focus gave extra legitimacy. Chaminade Clubs became even more popular; at one point there were more than 200, and some of them are in existence to this day. Their wider remit was (and is) to promote the performance and teaching of music, but naturally they were united by enthusiasm for the music of their favourite female composer. It is hard to think of any composer of piano music today, female or male, whose music would inspire fans to set up hundreds of clubs in their honour.

Chaminade's 'perfumed' style of writing was swept away as the First World War put an end to the salons of the belle époque and the music world was shaken by the innovations of Stravinsky, Schoenberg and their contemporaries. Chaminade's style did not evolve in the same radical way. Asked what she thought of Debussy's music, Chaminade bafflingly replied 'well, grey ... a little bit grey'.[83] She retreated from composition and lived in increasing seclusion. She never remarried; as the fierce heroines of her *symphonie dramatique Les Amazones* sang, 'Loin des hommes vivons en méprisant l'amour!' ('Far from men let us live, distrusting love!')

ADELE AUS DER OHE

Adele aus der Ohe (1861–1937) was the only child prodigy Liszt ever accepted as a pupil. She successfully made the transition from 'a little fairy of a scholar' (as recalled by Amy Fay when she was studying with Theodor Kullak) to a major international artist who performed big piano concertos like Tchaikovsky's first and Brahms's second at a time when few women were tackling them.[84]

Adele was the youngest child of German parents who were middle-aged when she was born. Her obvious musical gifts prompted her father to move the family to Berlin so that Adele could study piano with Theodor Kullak. She progressed so rapidly that at the age of twelve she was taken to Weimar to become a pupil of Liszt. She studied with Liszt for seven years, not only in Weimar but also in Rome when he moved to Italy for the summer months; she was probably his longest-serving student. Like all Liszt's students she was devoted to him and always included one of his virtuoso piano works in her recital programmes.

Aus der Ohe's mother died in 1884 and she decided to grasp the nettle and embark on a concert career. She persuaded her older sister Mathilde to become her companion/manager. Aged only twenty-five, Aus der Ohe made a far-reaching and somehow very modern decision: although she had not yet established herself in Europe, she would go straight to the United States and try to make her name there. This decision was spectacularly vindicated. The two sisters arrived in New York in 1886, days after the Statue of Liberty had been dedicated at a ceremony whose important guests included no women except for the wives of the architect and engineer. American suffragettes got as close as they could to Ellis Island in boats, making speeches through loudhailers about women's right to vote.

Just weeks after arriving in New York, Aus der Ohe performed Liszt's E flat piano concerto in Steinway Hall, earning rave reviews. 'Tremendous physical strength was allied to considerable sensitivity and intelligence ... and a breadth and freedom of style totally at variance with her youthful appearance ... She is of the stuff of which great artists are made,' said the *New York Times*.[85] Soon she was planning a major tour across the country. Over the years she undertook seventeen extensive tours, travelling thousands of miles by rail with her sister. She played a large repertoire from memory, and it was thought that she must have used the long hours aboard American trains to study her scores. Aus der Ohe was especially popular in the cities of the Midwest, where in 1893 she gave the inaugural recital for the Schubert Club of Saint Paul, Minnesota, a distinguished music club that is still thriving today.

In 1891 she was invited to play a very special concert as part of the opening festival of Carnegie Hall in New York. Tchaikovsky had been invited to the city, and Aus der Ohe was asked to perform his recently revised piano concerto no. 1. The concert was a triumph and Tchaikovsky wrote in his diary: 'My Concerto went magnificently, thanks to Aus der Ohe's brilliant interpretation. The enthusiasm was far greater than anything I have met with, even in Russia. I was recalled over and over again; handkerchiefs were waved, cheers resounded – in fact, it is easy to see that I have taken America by storm.'[86] They repeated the programme in Baltimore and Philadelphia, and Tchaikovsky invited Aus der Ohe to perform the concerto in his home city of St Petersburg. She travelled there in October 1893 and played the concerto at a concert which included the premiere of Tchaikovsky's symphony no. 6, 'Pathétique', but also a solo performance of Liszt's virtuoso *Spanish Rhapsody* played by Aus der Ohe. She was still in St Petersburg when, that same week, Tchaikovsky died, probably of cholera. So soon after having such success with Tchaikovsky's concerto, Adele found herself being asked to play at his memorial concert at the start of November, which she did, although 'I could hardly see the keys through tears. People felt that a great and noble man had gone.'[87]

Aus der Ohe performed an enormous repertoire with several features unusual at the time. She often included the works of the old harpsichordists and French *clavecinistes*. She played Bach 'straight' – that is to say, not in transcription or 'modernised' by adding octaves and other effects as was then fashionable. She played new music by her female contemporaries, the Austrian–German composer Grete von Zieritz and the American composer Amy Beach. She composed and performed her own pieces – mainly waltzes, 'character' dances and suites, though she also planned to write a piano concerto. Her short pieces such as *Melodie* and *Pastorale* are delicately drawn and immediately appealing, with a gentleness and restraint all the more admirable given that she was a favourite student of the mighty Liszt.

She publicly declared that she loved chamber music (sometimes considered a distraction for a soloist) and enjoyed performing with the Kneisel Quartet, whose members all belonged to the Boston Symphony Orchestra. She performed as concerto soloist with the Boston Symphony no fewer than fifty-one times, and a typical large-scale recital programme in her favourite Boston included Beethoven's 'Waldstein' sonata, Chopin's 'Funeral March' sonata, Schumann's *Fantasie in C* and Liszt's *Réminiscences de Don Juan* – a combination that even today would be thought demanding. Considering the huge repertoire she played, the amount of train travel she did and her lack of practice time, she must have had extraordinary stamina.

The death of her sister and travelling companion Mathilde in 1906 prompted her to return permanently to Berlin. This move was a sad counterpart to her decision to move to the United States as a young woman. Germany was entering a difficult period. Aus der Ohe lived through the First World War and the period of hyperinflation that followed. Her savings gone, she supported herself by teaching, and was active in societies for socially committed women. In the 1920s her supporters in the United States, including Rachmaninoff, sent her money and organised benefit concerts for her. Her German admirers were hardly in a position to join in. Her admirers felt that she would have been wiser to stay in the US, where the material conditions of life were easier. But she remained living quietly in Berlin, teaching and composing until arthritis intervened.

FANNIE BLOOMFIELD ZEISLER

Fannie Bloomfield Zeisler (1863–1927) was a leading American pianist whose powerful style helped to enlarge the public's concept of female concert pianists. Alert to the prevailing view that a woman's place was in the home, she was careful to craft an image of herself as a devoted wife and mother as well as a successful concert artist.

Fannie Blumenfeld (later Bloomfield) was born into a German-speaking family in the Austrian Silesian town of Bielitz (now in Poland). Her family immigrated to the United States when she was a small child. She made her debut as a pianist at the age of twelve, and at fourteen she played to the Russian pianist Annette Essipoff, who recommended her to go to Vienna to study with her own former teacher, the renowned Theodor Leschetizky. Fannie took her advice and studied with Leschetizky from 1889 to 1893. It seems that Leschetizky was concerned about her being physically frail and 'nervous', a quality often remarked upon during her career, but she countered any frailty with a remarkable work ethic.

The unlikelihood of any young woman making a lasting career as a pianist in that era is illustrated by an anecdote told in his memoirs by the pianist Harold Bauer. Leschetizky (Bauer said) watched a group of his female students leaving his house and remarked sardonically to the remaining men, 'Just think! Some fellow must be found for each of these girls, and his sole reason for existence will be to nullify their studies and ruin their careers.'[88] Fannie Bloomfield obviously knew that she was expected to desist from her career on marrying, but she had no intention of giving in to such expectations.

She was fortunate in her husband, the lawyer Sigmund Zeisler, who touchingly admitted that for a long time he hoped that Fanny would give up her playing career and settle down to be a wife and mother. 'But then I discovered the truth that wherever nature plants an outstanding artistic gift, it plants right next to it an intense desire for its recognition,' he said.

> I became convinced that Fannie's gift was quite out of the ordinary and that her ambition was a perfectly natural passion for self-expression. Having seen the light I not only ceased my opposition to her professional career, but began to further it in every way I could, realizing that this course was an essential condition to our continued happiness.[89]

The Zeislers must have come to an unusual understanding, because after the birth of their first child, Fannie (now Bloomfield Zeisler) went back to Europe for 'polishing' lessons from Leschetizky. She was right to feel optimistic about her chances of success. In 1887, American music critic James Huneker wrote, 'Here was something rare in pianism, particularly from a woman. Breadth, color, fire ... and an intensity of attack that was positively enthusing ... the vehemence of her attack is like a stealthy panther lying in wait for its prey.'[90] Fannie immediately laid claim to 'men's repertoire', playing works like Anton Rubinstein's piano concerto in D minor and forging lasting relationships with the great orchestras of New York, Chicago, Boston and Pittsburgh. In the 1890s she toured Europe and North America with great success, in 1896 undertaking a West Coast tour that featured seven different concert programmes in eighteen days, one of the many feats which led to her being called 'America's greatest virtuoso'. In 1901 the *New York Sun* described her as 'an electric dynamo with a human body and soul'.[91] Because of her powerful and expressive style, she was often dubbed 'the Sarah Bernhardt of the piano'.

To offset this alarmingly assertive image, Bloomfield Zeisler made sure the public knew that she was also a conscientious housewife. Goodness knows what she said to the *Detroit News* to make it come up with the headline, 'Noted Pianiste Likes to Darn Hubby's Sox'. In the article she was quoted as saying that she had sewed buttons on her husband's shirt 'just as carefully as if I could not play a note'.[92] Behind the scenes, it seems she was a little less selfless than such interviews implied, often opting out of domestic commitments if she felt she was behind with her preparations for a concert. She was very conscious of her status in the profession, and was known to refuse to appear in contexts where she was not the most important artist. For example, she was invited to play for the Roosevelts at the White House in January 1904, but withdrew when she discovered that she was to share the occasion with 'a vocalist, probably someone from the social circle'.[93] Informed of Mrs Bloomfield Zeisler's wish to have the occasion to herself, Mrs Roosevelt regretted that she did not 'feel that she could conveniently assent to this', which is interesting in light of the fact that the presidential couple hosted a solo concert that same month from (male) pianist Ferruccio Busoni.

With clever management of her time and her image, Bloomfield Zeisler struck many contemporary observers as 'combining modesty with genius and tranquil domesticity with fame', as the *Musical Courier* wrote in 1900.[94] Bloomfield Zeisler herself proudly claimed, 'I did not give up my art when I married, nor have I neglected my home.'[95] In that home, she and her husband always spoke German with their three boys.

She worked tirelessly to maintain her position through the first two decades of the twentieth century.[96] In 1920 she performed three piano concertos (Mozart, Chopin and Tchaikovsky) in a single evening at Chicago's Orchestra Hall, repeating the achievement at Carnegie Hall. For a woman once thought too fragile for a performing career, she had proved triumphantly strong. In 1925 she marked the fiftieth anniversary of her debut with the Chicago Symphony by performing the Schumann piano concerto and Chopin's F minor concerto with them.

Despite claims of having achieved an ideal work–life balance, she was ruefully aware of the unequal situations of male and female pianists. The female performer, she admitted, 'assumes additional heavy burdens and is obliged to lead two entirely full lives – that is if she does her duty. In the case of the man who carries on a public career it makes little difference. He acquires in his wife someone who surrounds him with all of the comforts of domesticity and often stands between him and the unreasonableness of the outside world.'[97]

WINNARETTA SINGER

Winnaretta Singer (1865–1943) was a fine pianist and organist, but performed mainly in the surroundings of her own salons in Paris and Venice, where she presided over and nurtured a formidable gathering of artistic talent. She was born in New York, the twentieth of twenty-two children (by five women) of Isaac Singer, founder of the famous American sewing-machine business. Her mother, the French model Isabella Boyer, was said to be the model for the Statue of Liberty in New York, though this has been disputed in recent years. Isaac Singer had numerous girlfriends, some of whom he married and some of whom he did not. His constant acquisition of new lovers caused him to be pursued by vengeful exes, necessitating moves from New York to Paris, to London and to Paignton in Devon where he built Oldway Mansion, a 115-room palace for his family with Isabella Boyer to live in.

Isaac Singer died in 1875, when Winnaretta was ten. Her mother moved the family back to Paris and shortly afterwards married a Dutch violinist, Victor Nicolas Reubsaet. Winnaretta's new stepfather took her to Bayreuth to experience Wagner operas and encouraged her love of music in general; the success of his endeavours may be seen in the fact that for her thirteenth birthday present she requested a performance of Beethoven's string quartet in C sharp minor (opus 131), a work still regarded as enigmatic and difficult for even seasoned musicians to understand. But relations between her mother and stepfather soured, and the atmosphere at home became fraught. When Winnaretta reached the age of twenty-one, she inherited $1 million from her father (equivalent to around $32 million today) and lost no time in leaving her family home and setting out on her own independent path. Her first purchase was a large building on the corner of avenue Henri-Martin and rue Cortambert, which became her new home.

Her wealth made her extremely eligible and she was courted by high-society suitors. First she married the Prince de Scey-Montbéliard, but this was not a success. Romantically she was more interested in women than in men, and her first husband could not come to terms with this. She had better luck with her second husband, Edmond, Prince de Polignac, whom she married in 1893 when she was twenty-eight and he was fifty-nine. His ideas about his private life mirrored hers, and they agreed to base their *mariage blanc* (chaste marriage) on shared interests in music and art, to which they were both devoted. Surprisingly, this worked very well. Singer became the Princesse de Polignac, and the couple set about building up the circle of artists, writers and musicians who frequented their salon at the avenue Henri-Martin. They also loved to spend time in Venice, where in 1900 Singer bought her husband a building he especially admired, the Palazzo Contarini on the Grand Canal.

After her husband's death in 1901, Singer flourished as a patron of the arts. Both in Paris and at the Palazzo Contarini Polignac in Venice she hosted an impressive array of artists, many of whom became friends and were regarded almost as 'house musicians'. The Italian conductor Arturo Toscanini, for example, would stay on after concerts in the palazzo to make spaghetti for Singer and her friends. The pianist Arthur Rubinstein spent his honeymoon at the palazzo, and the Russian pianist Vladimir Horowitz lived there for several years.

Numerous portraits and photos of Winnaretta as the Princesse de Polignac survive, showing that she was strikingly tall and slim, dressed of course in the most luxurious fabrics and couture styles, and with a direct, almost austere gaze. Over the years, she was known to conduct discreet affairs with quite a few well-known women: painter Romaine Brooks, Baroness Olga de Meyer, Italian pianist Renata Borgatti and several English lovers – the authors Violet Trefusis and Virginia Woolf, and composer Ethel Smyth, who was much smitten by her.

Winnaretta, known as Winnie or 'Tante Winnie', unselfishly used her fortune to support a large circle of artists and composers. For fifty years she actively commissioned new works: songs from Fauré, Erik Satie's *Socrate*, Poulenc's organ concerto and his concerto for two pianos, Kurt Weill's second symphony, Manuel de Falla's *El retablo de maese Pedro*, Milhaud's *Les Malheurs d'Orphée*, Germaine Tailleferre's first piano concerto, Stravinsky's *Renard* and *Persephone*. She sponsored Diaghilev's Ballets Russes on numerous occasions. She gave financial help and performance opportunities to several leading pianists: Clara Haskil, Arthur Rubinstein, Dinu Lipatti, Vladimir Horowitz. She supported the Paris Opéra and the Orchestre Symphonique.

She spared no expense in putting on elaborate concerts in her Paris salon – although 'salon' seems too modest a word for her grandiose drawing room with its splendid chandeliers and mirrors. Although there were already two grand pianos in the salon, she had two more delivered so that Stravinsky's *Les Noces* could be performed. The building was large enough that she had a second, smaller performance space on the rue Cortambert where she was able to present informal concerts. She played piano and organ at her house concerts. Performances of music by Debussy and Ravel were presented, and the young Ravel dedicated his celebrated *Pavane pour une infante défunte* to the Princesse de Polignac. Her salon was frequented by Cocteau, Monet and Colette. Each month, Singer hosted legendary gatherings where *le tout Paris* would enjoy a splendid dinner before moving to the huge drawing room to hear concerts by some of Europe's finest musicians. A regular guest from 1894 was the author

Marcel Proust, who based his famous descriptions of Madame Verdurin's salon in *Swann's Way*, the first part of *À la Recherche du temps perdu*, on the Princesse de Polignac's artistic evenings.

Musicians and artists were not the only beneficiaries of the Singer fortune. Winnaretta also funded developments in public housing in Paris, aiming to build homes for 'the working poor'. She commissioned the architect Le Corbusier to build a Salvation Army hostel. During the First World War, she helped to commission mobile radiology units to be used for the benefit of soldiers at the Front, and she persuaded her wealthy friends to donate limousines, which she paid to have converted into ambulances. After the war she helped to fund a new hospital, the Foch Hospital, which is still flourishing in Paris. Her concert series was continued, after her death, under the leadership of the composer Nadia Boulanger, and later still of the composer

Jean Françaix. Her Fondation Polignac still supports artistic and scientific projects and puts on regular concerts in the mansion where the artistic life of Paris swirled so happily under her patronage.

AMY BEACH

Amy Beach, née Cheney (1867–1944), was the first female composer in the United States to achieve recognition for her large-scale music. She was also the first American composer-pianist to make her name without having studied in Europe.

In recent years, thanks mainly to the efforts of feminist scholars such as Adrienne Fried Block and the advocacy of some perceptive pianists, Amy Beach's music has become much better known; a volume of her short piano pieces increasingly forms part of amateur piano collections. However, what Amy Beach was up against in terms of patriarchal attitudes is shown by Dvořák's remark to a Boston newspaper interviewer on the occasion of his first American visit in 1892. Asked what he thought about women writing music, Dvořák said, 'Here all the ladies play. It is well; it is nice. But I am afraid the ladies cannot help us much. They have not the creative power.'[98]

This patronising attitude was to survive well beyond the nineteenth century. On the 150th anniversary of Amy Beach's birth, in 2017, the *New York Times* reported that no American orchestras had programmed any of her works that season, and in fact 2017 marked *a century* since the Boston Symphony, based in the city where she lived, had performed any of her orchestral works in full.[99] Her large-scale music is only now becoming known. Nevertheless, Amy Beach's piano music is gaining in popularity, and with luck the rest of her music will follow suit.

Amy was an exceptionally gifted child, memorising songs and singing them perfectly in tune when hardly more than a baby. When little Amy was two, her mother was startled to hear her making up descant parts to melodies sung to her at bedtime. At four, Amy was writing her first little piano pieces. Her mother, also a talented pianist, started teaching her when she was six. Unfortunately her musical education was marked by an unusual degree of parental control. She had three piano lessons per week and was set strict practice times. Her mother, a member of a Calvinist church, used music as a way of rewarding or punishing her daughter. If Amy was naughty, she was not allowed to go near the piano. Even more disturbingly, her mother, knowing how sensitive Amy was to sad music, would sometimes punish her by playing a sentimental tearjerker like Gottschalk's *The Last Hope*, to make her cry. One hardly needs to be a trained psychologist to see that this approach would complicate one's feelings about music.

When Amy was seven, the family moved to Boston and she began to give concerts, playing her own compositions as well as standard repertoire. Several well-known Boston musicians tried to persuade the Cheneys to send her to study in Europe, this being the path successfully taken by previous American musicians (such as Amy Fay). But the Cheneys would not hear of it. On the contrary, they restricted Amy's public appearances and turned down the notion of her studying in Europe on health grounds; Amy was too delicate. Sending her to Europe would be a dangerous step on the path to becoming a performer. Moreover, her mother believed that flaunting oneself publicly for money was the opposite of the demure behaviour which the Bible advised for women.

At sixteen, Amy performed several virtuoso piano concertos – by Moscheles, Mendelssohn and Chopin – earning wholehearted praise from the Boston press. These concerts seemed to indicate that her parents were coming round to the idea of her being a performer, but perhaps they were merely keen to advertise her 'accomplishments' to an eligible husband. For at eighteen, Amy married a much older man, Dr Henry Harris Aubrey Beach, a respectable Boston surgeon. Dr Beach was an enthusiastic amateur musician himself and quite amenable to Amy writing music, but he drew the line at her performing in public for money. He asked that she restrict her solo recitals to one a year; any income was to be given to charity. She was not to teach piano, because that would have involved the sordid task of negotiating fees. For a similar reason she was not to receive composition lessons, but he thought it was fine for her to study on her own.

Amy embarked on solitary study of orchestral masterpieces, acquiring treatises on orchestration and translating them if necessary. She went to concerts and attempted to write down from memory the works she had heard without ever having seen the scores. She wrote out Bach's preludes and fugues from memory. In short, she devised a training probably at least as thorough as she would have had at a European conservatoire, but had none of the camaraderie of studying with like-minded musicians. She was ruefully aware of this. 'Music is the superlative expression of life experience,' she once said, 'and woman by the very nature of her position is denied many of the experiences that color the life of man.'[100]

Beach was fortunate in having financial security and time for herself, two things denied to many women (the couple had no children). During her marriage she composed extensively, but, as she said wistfully, 'I thought I was a pianist first and foremost'.[101] Her piano pieces, which she went on writing throughout her career, demonstrate a wide range of styles, from sweeping Romantic ballads to experimental pieces like *Hermit Thrush at Eve, at Morn* (opus 92), in which she attempts to capture realistic birdsong, and from the sentimental *Scottish Legend* to the sparkling filigree of 'Honeysuckle' (from *Grandmother's Garden*, opus 97). One of her most touching pieces is *Dreaming* (opus 15, no. 3), a beautifully controlled series of musical waves that carry deep emotion. Her most impressive large-scale composition was her *Gaelic Symphony* incorporating Irish folk melodies; a success in its own day, it has been praised even more warmly by modern critics, including Jonathan Blumhofer, who wrote in 2016, 'To my ears, it is by far the finest symphony by an American composer before Ives ... somehow Beach's Symphony is never daunted by the long shadows Brahms and Beethoven cast across the Atlantic.'[102]

It was not until after the deaths of her husband (in 1910) and her mother (in 1911) that Amy felt free to return to the concert platform as a pianist. She appeared no longer as Mrs H.H.A. Beach, but just as Amy Beach. At last she was free to go to Europe, and she performed there extensively, playing her own piano concerto in C sharp minor (opus 45), her piano quintet and her sonata for violin and piano. Her piano concerto has caught the imagination of musicians because it seems to represent the tale of Amy's own battle to be allowed to perform. It was written during the solitary study years of her marriage and casts the soloist in a long struggle with the orchestra, 'vying with each other', as Beach put it.[103] The concerto (nearly forty minutes long) is cast in four substantial movements, perhaps in tribute to Brahms's second piano concerto. Three of the movements are based on Amy's own songs, with lyrics written by her husband. Gradually the soloist asserts herself, and by the final movement is triumphantly able to break free of the orchestra and be heard above it.

Beach dedicated the concerto to the Venezuelan pianist Teresa Carreño (see p. 96), obviously hoping that this doyenne of pianists would perform it, but Carreño's attempts to interest promoters came to nothing, perhaps because a female composer's name was not a box-office draw. It was Beach herself who was the soloist at the Boston premiere in 1900, and later performed it to warm acclaim in major German cities. After her European travels, she returned to the US and relished the freedom to perform as often as she liked. As she told *Musical America* in 1917, 'The joy of giving of your highest powers is beyond description. When I play, there is only limitless enthusiasm and enjoyment.'[104]

MARGUERITE LONG

Marguerite Long (1874–1966) was an eminent French pianist who became a *grande dame* of French music. Her special claim to fame was the working relationship she developed with three important French composers: Fauré, Debussy and Ravel. She studied each man's music in depth with him and wrote three books about her experiences – *At the Piano with Fauré*, *At the Piano with Debussy* and *At the Piano with Ravel* – which offer invaluable insights into their music and their characters.

Marguerite Long was born in Nîmes and was first taught piano by her older sister Claire. As a teenager, Marguerite moved to Paris to study at the Conservatoire and won the Premier Prix when she was only seventeen. Soon she was giving her debut at the Salle Pleyel in Paris. In 1902 she met her future husband, the officer Joseph de

Marliave, a great fan of Fauré's music which was not widely known at the time. At de Marliave's persuasion, Marguerite started looking at Fauré's piano music and was sufficiently intrigued to arrange to meet the composer. This opened a decisive chapter in her career. She studied with Fauré over a period of about a decade and became a tireless advocate for his music. She came to believe that hers was the gold standard of Fauré interpretation: 'During those years the validity of the interpretation of so many of his works firmly established itself with us,'[105] she wrote – a claim that has troubled other fine interpreters, for, as we know, it is not essential to have been physically present at a composer's side to have a deep understanding of their work. Marguerite Long's identification with the music of her favourite contemporary composers may have led her to be overly possessive of it. She felt she had a hotline to their innermost thoughts, but this conviction was not necessarily shared.

The fact that Fauré liked Long's playing did not mean that it was the only way he could imagine his piano music being played, and indeed it seems he felt ambivalent about her. Long was teaching a preparatory piano class at the Conservatoire where Fauré was the director. When a vacancy came up to take over a *classe supérieure* in 1907, Long applied for it, probably assuming that her friendship with Fauré would oil the wheels of her appointment. However, the post was offered to Alfred Cortot, and Fauré wrote to his wife that 'there will be much, much opposition when it [the appointment] ought to go through of its own accord, since Cortot is infinitely superior to other possible candidates, whom I know only too well, alas!'[106] This, we may take it, was a reference to Marguerite Long.

Knowing that Long would be hurt, Fauré wrote to explain that he was keen to help her in her career but preferred things to happen 'in due time'.[107] Her feelings towards Fauré were clouded by this rejection. Nevertheless, she continued to champion his music. In 1909 she was the first pianist to devote an entire recital programme to Fauré's works, and his 'Ballade' (opus 19) for piano and orchestra was one of her most frequent concerto pieces. It is worth remembering that around this same time, the young Nadia Boulanger was trying to win the Prix de Rome and encountering what we would call institutional sexism, so perhaps Marguerite Long was a victim of it too. At any rate she was passed over for promotion again in 1913 and did not get a 'superior class' at the Paris Conservatoire until 1920, when she had been a successful pianist for many years.

Long's husband Joseph de Marliave was killed in action near the start of the First World War in 1914 and she never remarried; she threw herself into her work and once said, 'What is important is not to spoil your life but to be able to say to yourself: I did all I could. It is the only thing that can bring a little happiness.'[108] Ravel dedicated the toccata from his *Le Tombeau de Couperin* to the memory of Joseph de Marliave in 1917, and Long gave the premiere of the whole *Tombeau* in 1919.

Long had never felt convinced by her own or anyone else's interpretation of Debussy's piano music, and after meeting Debussy a number of times when he came to adjudicate at the Paris Conservatoire, they had a talk about it. As a result, Debussy invited Long to come and study his latest piano music with him in the summer of 1917. Long was still getting over the loss of her husband and Debussy was suffering from cancer, so it was a difficult summer, but Long relished their collaboration. Later that year, she gave the premiere of Debussy's technically challenging *Douze Études*, dryly described by the composer as 'a useful warning to pianists not to take up music as a profession unless they have remarkable hands'.[109] For many years thereafter, Long played a memorial concert on the anniversary of Debussy's death.

Her friendship with Ravel deepened in the 1930s and she was the soloist at the premiere of Ravel's piano concerto in G major, originally conceived as a vehicle for the composer himself to perform. But by 1932 Ravel was suffering from the first symptoms of the neurological condition from which he died in 1937, and Marguerite Long was invited to be the soloist at the 1932 premiere, which Ravel conducted. Together they introduced the concerto in about twenty cities. Long was the soloist at the first recording, three months after the premiere, with Ravel (then physically fragile) supervising proceedings from the control room. When a critic complained that Long's interpretation of the concerto lacked poetry, Ravel published a riposte, insisting that Long's interpretation fulfilled his expectations and should be considered a model for future performers. Long herself quoted Ravel as saying, 'I do not ask for my music to be interpreted, but only for it to be played.'[110] He clearly appreciated the clarity and energy of Long's playing. But he did not always respond in that way to the same qualities in other people's playing – Long cited the example of a pianist who played Ravel the Prélude of the *Tombeau* and was advised to play 'not so quick as Marguerite Long'. Long later asked Ravel why he said so, and Ravel answered that 'so far as you are concerned, one is sure to hear all the notes'.[111] So we know that he valued the precision of her touch, which she could maintain even at a fast tempo. Her recordings demonstrate the élan with which she played – a style found a bit heartless by some, but clear and energetic by others. The success of the G major piano concerto led Darius Milhaud, an old friend of Long's husband, to write his own piano concerto for her, and she gave the premiere in 1934.

Long became known as a representative of the French school of piano-playing, a vital link to the music of the three great French composers she worked with. Finally getting her own advanced piano class at the Conservatoire in 1920, she taught there with distinction until 1940. After that, she and her violinist colleague Jacques Thibaud opened a music school with the aim of providing parallel classes in piano and violin so that violinists could learn the important repertoire of sonatas for violin and piano with good pianists (and vice versa). In 1943, they went further and founded the Concours Marguerite Long-Jacques Thibaud for pianists and violinists. Long's final public performance was at a concert sponsored by the French government in February 1956 in honour of her contribution to French musical life. At the age of eighty-one she performed the Fauré 'Ballade' for piano and orchestra, and eight French composers contributed a variation each to a composite orchestral work entitled *Variations sur le nom de Marguerite Long*. Long told her students, 'If my career has been what it is, it is because I never gave up, I always worked. My joy in life is work, because it will never betray you.'[112]

WANDA LANDOWSKA

Wanda Landowska (1879–1959) was a Polish pianist who had an epiphany on encountering a harpsichord of Bach's era and devoted herself to reviving eighteenth-century harpsichord music.

She was born in Warsaw to Jewish parents and studied the piano with leading teachers who emphasised the study of Chopin. She composed, too, and at the age of seventeen was confident enough to write to Edvard Grieg to ask for his approval of her piano music. She seemed set for a career as a pianist until, while studying in Berlin, she visited a collection of historic keyboard instruments and was captivated by the sound of a Bach-era harpsichord. She determined to switch course and become an advocate for early keyboard instruments. This was an unusual decision for the time. In 1903 she first brought a harpsichord on stage alongside a piano and played them both during her recital, explaining to the audience how different the sound and playing style of the harpsichord was.

It is interesting to remember that at this point, the piano had dominated the keyboard scene for over a hundred years. At the beginning of the twentieth century only a few pioneers were interested in 'early music' and there was little public appetite for performance on historical instruments. Landowska was not the only artist who saw the potential for a harpsichord revival, but she was the one with the strongest personality and the greatest flair for self-publicity.

Touring Russia in 1907, she arranged to take a harpsichord out to the country estate at Yasnaya Polyana of the great Russian writer Leo Tolstoy; a photo taken by Tolstoy's long-suffering wife Sonia shows the author in his peasant smock, standing unsmilingly behind Landowska as she turns from the keyboard to look at the camera. The meeting was extensively reported in the press.

Landowska married a Polish ethnologist, Henri Lew, who devoted himself to helping her establish her career as a historical-keyboard specialist. It seems that theirs was a *mariage blanc*. Landowska taught piano at the Schola Cantorum in Paris from 1900 to 1912, and then (except when interned during the First World War) she taught harpsichord at the Berlin Hochschule from 1912 to 1919. Her husband died in a car accident after the war. In 1923 she toured the United States with no fewer than four harpsichords – several instruments perhaps being necessary because harpsichords were never meant to stand up to the rigours of touring and constant changes of temperature.

In 1927 she established her own École de Musique Ancienne at her home at Saint-Leu-la-Forêt outside Paris and taught her acolytes there until the outbreak of the Second World War. Landowska was a frequent visitor to and performer at the celebrated Paris salons of Natalie Clifford Barney and of the Polignacs (see p. 113). At her home she built up an impressive library of historical scores and books and a collection of instruments. Composers of new music had become intrigued by her and her harpsichords; she had concertos written for her by Manuel de Falla and Poulenc. Falla's *El retablo de maese Pedro* gave the harpsichord its first role in a modern orchestral piece.

In her prime, Landowska famously played a huge Pleyel harpsichord specially built for her, designed to have enough power for the modern concert hall, rather than merely copying the old instruments. It had two manuals (keyboards) and a sixteen-foot stop which added an extra bass octave. The pedals enabled various types of tone colour and timbre, for example by moving the leather plectrum closer to the string, or by controlling little shutters that opened and closed, allowing the player to produce the effect of a crescendo or diminuendo, which was not available on old harpsichords. Landowska was said to have concert gowns specially made so that her full skirt concealed the pedals and made it impossible for rivals to see how she was pedalling.

She provoked controversy because she claimed to be revealing how things actually sounded in Bach's day, meanwhile allowing herself to invent repeats not written in the score, or introducing 'looming up and fading away' dynamic effects not indicated by the composer. And, of course, her high-profile public career was unlike anything that would have been available to a harpsichordist of the Baroque era, let alone a female one. Not everyone was a fan of Landowska's sound; many thought it admirably clear and dry, but others found it brittle and mechanical. Some were cynical about her claim to be 'reviving the Bach sound' on a huge custom-built Pleyel harpsichord the like of which Bach would never have heard. However, everyone recognised the force of her personality and its value for her self-appointed mission.

In 1940, when the Nazis entered Paris, Landowska was forced to flee. Hours before her departure she made a famous recording of Scarlatti which happened to capture the noise of Nazi bombardment in the background. The sound engineers fled on hearing the noise and realising what it meant, but Landowska continued playing imperturbably to the end of the sonata. Together with her long-time assistant and partner Denise Restout, she managed to escape via the south of France and Lisbon to the United States, arriving at Ellis Island with only a small amount of luggage on the very day that the Japanese attacked Pearl Harbor. Her home in Paris was ransacked by the Nazis, her instruments and library of scores and books confiscated and dispersed to various outposts. Landowska spent the rest of her life trying in vain to obtain restitution. Meanwhile, she pressed on with her career in the US. In 1942 she gave the first modern performance of Bach's *Goldberg Variations* in New York's Town Hall. Composer Virgil Thomson reviewed it for the *New York Herald Tribune*. It was, he said, 'as stimulating as a needle shower. Indeed, the sound of that princely instrument, when it is played with art and fury, makes one think of golden rain and of how Danaë's flesh must have tingled when she found herself caught out in just such a downpour.'[113]

Landowska refuted the idea that music 'progressed' through history – she was at pains to point out to audiences that the music of Bach, Rameau, Couperin and Scarlatti could be as satisfying as anything that came later. This was an important insight that fed the early-music revival of the later twentieth century. On a 1959 archive clip, she can be heard introducing the Bach two-part inventions. In her charming Polish accent, she tells us that the inventions were written for Bach's son Friedemann, but that, unlike us, Friedemann would not have needed to study scholarly books to know the right way to play the pieces because he was always in his father's company, hearing him play harpsichord, violin and organ and being present at rehearsals and performances. Steeped in live music, the right style would have come naturally. 'What today is for us *erudition*, was for him daily bread and the life experience,' she says.[114]

OLGA SAMAROFF

Olga Samaroff (1882–1948), born Lucy Ann Olga Agnes Hickenlooper in San Antonio, Texas, was a leading American pianist who racked up a long list of 'first woman to …' achievements. She was influential in her belief that studying in Europe or making one's name through European concerts should not be considered the one and only gold standard for American pianists.

Lucy Ann Hickenlooper grew up in Texas and was taught piano by her mother and grandmother. She progressed so quickly that when she was only fourteen she was sent abroad to study in Paris. Arriving in Paris with her grandmother, she became the first American woman to be admitted to the piano class of the Paris Conservatoire. However, she felt she was looked down upon because she was American, and she was disappointed by teaching methods at the Conservatoire, where interest in the student ended with the last note of the lesson (sadly, this attitude is not confined to turn-of-the-century Paris). Conservatoire professors took no interest in how students were getting on with their life more generally, even if they had just crossed the Atlantic and were struggling with a foreign language. In 1898 she moved to Berlin for further study and lived there for six years, during which she was briefly married to a Russian diplomat who made the mistake of asking her to give up her musical ambitions.

Back in the United States in 1904, Lucy Ann decided to flout tradition and give her debut in Carnegie Hall. As she was unknown, she had to borrow money to hire the hall, and was in fact the first woman to self-produce her Carnegie Hall debut. In January 1905 she hired the New York Symphony Orchestra and conductor Walter Damrosch to join her in a performance of Tchaikovsky's first piano concerto, which was a huge success. As Europe was still considered the home of great pianism, a concert promoter advised her to adopt a European-sounding name. She already possessed the name Olga as a middle name, and someone in the family suggested the surname Samaroff, a distant part of family history. Ironically, she already *had* a surname of European origin, Hickenlooper being an old Dutch name meaning something like 'hedge-runner'. But Dutch names were not synonymous with pianism and Hickenlooper sounded rather angular, whereas Samaroff rolled off the tongue and carried a romantic suggestion of being from Russia, a country associated with great pianists.

As 'Olga Samaroff' she was the first American female pianist to give her debut in Carnegie Hall, and in 1908 she was one of the first American pianists to make a recording. Soon she was playing up to ninety concerts a year with leading orchestras in America and Europe. To her intense annoyance, however, she discovered that she was offered lower fees than men performing the same concertos. This was a problem that irked her throughout her career. Thirty years later, on the eve of the Second World War, she was still pointing out that male and female pianists were treated quite differently by managers and promoters, and that women pianists were paid less than men no matter how distinguished their reputation. No doubt she would be exasperated to learn that even today, we have not succeeded in eradicating this inequality.

In 1911 she married the promising conductor Leopold Stokowski and did all she could to promote him while continuing with her own career. In 1920, Samaroff was the first American pianist to perform all thirty-two Beethoven piano sonatas in a series of concerts. Hans von Bülow (in the 1870s) was the first pianist to perform the complete

Beethoven sonata cycle; Samaroff was the second, and Artur Schnabel (in 1927) the third – but although von Bülow and Schnabel are often mentioned in connection with these pioneering feats, Samaroff's feat is rarely mentioned. Blockbuster achievements were associated with men and continued to be so even after women had shown that they too were capable of them. In 1937 Samaroff commented wryly, 'During all the years of my career as a woman pianist, at least eighty percent of my press reviews either stated that I played like a man, or alluded to my playing like a woman. When the critic said I played like a woman, it meant that he did not like me at all.'[115]

As Stokowski's star rose, Samaroff's became somewhat overshadowed. They divorced in 1923 and Samaroff turned her mind to music education in the broad sense. She became a music journalist, reviewing concerts but also writing articles about piano-playing and teaching. In 1924 she became the first American-born professor on the staff of the newly founded Juilliard School in New York; a few years later she took up a parallel position at the Philadelphia Conservatory, and for twenty-five years she was a beneficial influence on a whole generation of young American pianists. Making good the omissions of the teaching methods she experienced as a teenager, she made sure that her students were introduced to relevant books and sent to museums, galleries and opera houses where they could see for themselves the artistic counterparts of the music they were learning. She trained her students to study scores away from the piano, so that their understanding of the music was not dominated by the physical problems of playing it.

She invited them to meals in her New York apartment, where they might find themselves sitting next to Bruno Walter, Myra Hess or Fritz Kreisler. She held fortnightly soirées (always ending with scrambled eggs and champagne) where her students had to dress formally and perform not only in front of one another but for an invited audience that might include conductors, promoters and the social elite of New York. This was inspired networking on behalf of her students. But she was also alert to her students' difficulties, helping them out with living expenses or the cost of putting on concerts. Even more unusually for an elite teacher, she was not set on turning them all into concert performers. She recognised that some of them were better suited to going back to their hometowns and helping to raise the local standard of piano-playing, and she encouraged them to value this pathway.

'The world is full of slick pianists,' Samaroff said.

> By that I mean the pianist who can play a great many notes at once, achieve great speed, read well at sight and memorise a great many pieces. This is all praiseworthy and requires a great deal of hard work, but unfortunately one can do all these things without being an artist. It is the right combination of being and doing which produces the real artist.[116]

She explained that 'the only thing that can come out of your fingers is who you are inside'. Her breadth of approach is illustrated by her remark that 'one cannot be musically mature while one is humanly immature'.[117]

NADIA BOULANGER

Nadia Boulanger (1887–1979) was one of the twentieth century's most important and influential teachers of composition. She was also the first woman to conduct some of the top orchestras in the US and Europe. She was a concert pianist for a while in her early adult years, she held professorships in *accompagnement au piano*, and she used the piano as her main teaching tool throughout her long career.

Nadia Boulanger's father, Ernest, was sixty-two when he married the nineteen-year-old Russian student Raïssa Mychetskaya, and he was seventy-two when Nadia was born. Ernest Boulanger was a composer, conductor, singing teacher, a chevalier of the Légion d'Honneur and winner of a prestigious French composition prize, the Prix de Rome. Nadia was intensely sensitive to music and often found it upsetting to listen to, but at the age of five her response changed to fascination, and she began to pay close attention to the lessons her father was giving to his students.

When Nadia was six, her younger sister Lili was born. Her father – now aged seventy-eight – made Nadia give a solemn promise to look after her sister. Lili turned out to be wonderfully gifted at music and Nadia was devoted to her.

At nine, Nadia became a student at the Paris Conservatoire, where she studied composition with Gabriel Fauré. Her father died in 1900 and, discovering that her mother was not practical with money, Nadia assumed responsibility for earning the family income. She performed in concerts as a pianist and organist and undertook international tours playing piano-duet programmes with the Mozart specialist Raoul Pugno. As a composer, her aim was to win the Prix de Rome as her father had done. Women had not even been allowed to enter the competition until 1903, so Nadia was one of the first women eligible to compete. The awarding of the Prix de Rome was keenly followed by the French press. The first round involved the writing of a vocal fugue on a theme composed by a member of the jury. In 1908, having failed to win the competition twice already, Nadia entered for the third time.

After studying the given fugue theme, she decided that it was not suitable for voices and wrote a fugue for string quartet instead. The stages of the Prix de Rome were closely followed by the music-loving public and this was seen as a defiant gesture towards the jury. Her boldness was reported on the front pages of Paris newspapers (hard to imagine now) and became known as *l'affaire fugue*. People were scandalised that a young woman, one of the cohort of females so recently admitted to the competition, would dare to criticise a theme issued by the distinguished jury, whose chairman (and in fact the composer of the aforementioned fugue theme) was the great Saint-Saëns. After heated dispute, the jury decided to accept Nadia's instrumental fugue, and gave her the second prize. Traditionally, this would have put her in a promising position to win the first prize the following year, but when 1909 came, she entered the Prix de Rome again and won nothing. *L'affaire fugue* was still rankling in certain quarters. When she applied for a teaching position at the Paris Conservatoire in 1910 she was not successful, and in fact she was not engaged by the Conservatoire until after the Second World War. In the meantime her teaching positions had to be with new or less prestigious institutions, where as a woman she stood a better chance of getting a job.

A few years after *l'affaire fugue* her younger sister Lili became the first woman to win the Prix de Rome. Although Nadia was deeply proud of Lili's achievement, it must have been a bitter blow to be sandwiched between her prize-winning father and prize-winning younger sister. From then on, Nadia threw herself into teaching rather than writing her own music – a characteristically stern decision and too hard on herself, for her music is well crafted and appealing.

When the First World War began, Lili Boulanger, who had gone to Rome to take up the residency offered by her prize, came back to Paris and started a charity to supply food, clothes, money and (if wanted) harmony and counterpoint lessons by post for French soldiers who had been musicians in civilian life. The work exhausted her, her health collapsed and she died in 1918. In memory of her sister, Nadia vowed to make maximum use of the time available to her. She gave lecture-recitals, taught piano masterclasses and accepted invitations to conduct symphony orchestras. She did all she could to promote Lili's music and to keep her memory alive.

During her years as a composition teacher, many of the leading young composers passed through her studio in the rue Ballu, which she eventually persuaded the French government to rename as the place Lili Boulanger. The French School for Americans opened in Fontainebleau in 1921, and Boulanger joined the staff as a teacher of harmony. (This was the start of her long association with young American composers, which gained momentum when Boulanger was living and teaching in the United States during the Second World War.) Aaron Copland and Virgil Thomson were in her class in the 1920s, Elliott Carter and George Gershwin in the 1930s, Philip Glass in the 1950s. (Gershwin was only briefly her student, for when she looked at his music she told him, 'I had nothing to offer him. I suggested that he was doing all right and should continue. I told him what I could teach him wouldn't help him much ... and he agreed.'[118] Gershwin retold this story many times, taking it as a compliment – as perhaps it was.

Not only 'art music' composers were keen to learn from her: she also taught the jazz musicians Quincy Jones and Donald Byrd, Brazilian guitarist Egberto Gismonti and, famously, the Argentinian tango specialist Astor Piazzolla. Piazzolla later recalled that she was bored with his attempts at composing until she heard him play his own tangos, which she immediately recognised as his unique gift. She had an encyclopaedic knowledge of music and insisted on students learning the techniques of Renaissance and Baroque masters as well as engaging with the new. Familiar with the works of Schoenberg and Stravinsky, she preferred Stravinsky, whom she considered a truer inheritor of what she called *la grande ligne*.

In 1937, Nadia Boulanger, together with a hand-picked ensemble of singers, made a landmark recording of Monteverdi's madrigals, little known at the time. She herself played the piano for several of them. The ensemble also recorded Brahms's *Liebeslieder Waltzes*, written for voices and piano duet, and here Boulanger was partnered by the brilliant young Romanian pianist Dinu Lipatti, who was taking composition lessons with her four times a week. 'These lessons give me so much pleasure that I don't miss a word she says,' Lipatti wrote to a friend.[119]

As a teacher, Boulanger had a complex mixture of qualities. Although she herself had had to battle against gender prejudices, she was not always supportive of female students in her class; many of them felt she was kinder to the men. She was not in favour of women having the vote, believing that women 'lacked political sophistication'.[120] She was conservative, nationalistic, religious, a monarchist and a great admirer of the aristocracy – people said she was always nicer to students from upper-class families – yet she would allow anyone to enter her class, as long as they wanted to learn. Many of her students were Jewish, but in private she was said to hold anti-Semitic views. Despite her prejudices, she was notably open-minded about musical talent. She had an astonishing ability to see where each student's strength lay, and encouraged them to pursue 'their path' even if it was not to her personal taste.

Her manner when teaching or conducting was far from the prevailing ideal of femininity. She adopted a severe form of dress, a stern, intellectual approach and an authoritative, almost priestly manner. Perhaps she had found such a style useful in averting any suspicion that she might not have the power to control a class of ambitious young men or an orchestra of male musicians. As it was, she reigned supreme over them. Philip Glass recalled her as 'a tough, aristocratic Frenchwoman elegantly dressed in fashions 50 years out of date'. At their first meeting, he sat waiting while she leafed through his scores in silence. Finally she pointed to one bar and said, 'There. *This* was written by a *real* composer.' This was a discouraging start, but Glass admitted that her forensic inspection methods trained him to *hear*.[121]

My favourite Boulanger observation was quoted by the pianist Daniel Barenboim in a TV documentary about his life. He passed through Boulanger's class too, to hear her advice on his interpretation of Beethoven sonatas. She told him, 'You know how to feel the emotions of music, and you also know how to analyse music. Now your task is to bring the two together. You must learn how to *feel* the structure of the music, and you must know how to analyse the emotions.' Barenboim commented, 'I have thought about that remark every day of my life since then.'[122]

MYRA HESS

Myra Hess (1890–1965) was one of the leading British pianists of the twentieth century, renowned for her poetical performances of Bach, Mozart, Beethoven and Schumann. Today her name is most associated with the series of lunchtime concerts she founded at the National Gallery in London during the Second World War, but long before the war she was a hugely popular figure in Britain, Europe and the United States.

Myra was born to Jewish parents in north London and started lessons at the age of five. She later became one of the star students of piano professor Tobias Matthay, who also taught Clifford Curzon, Harriet Cohen, Moura Lympany and other successful pianists. At the age of seventeen, Myra's family funded her concerto debut, in which she played a group of solos plus Beethoven's concerto no. 4 in G major with the New Symphony Orchestra and a young Sir Thomas Beecham conducting. Shortly after this she played a solo recital at Aeolian Hall in London, and was soon being invited to play all over Europe. In 1922 she made her debut in New York. As she was unknown there was a very small audience, but the *Tribune* reported that:

> She is every inch an artist; every fibre in her comely and well poised body is musical. Her knowledge, instincts, technical skill are of the highest order. She possesses not only fancy but the higher gift which is imagination. Her expositions are not merely intellectual, they are poetical also. The book of music is open to her.[123]

(Note that although the review is respectful, her 'comely and well poised body' is mentioned.) Hess acquired a top American agent and quickly became a favourite of US audiences, broadcasting on the popular *Ford Sunday Evening Hour* and earning very high fees (for example, in 1937 she was allegedly paid $4,000 for a radio appearance).

When the Second World War was declared, Myra Hess chose to remain in London. Shortly after the conflict began, she started to organise the famous series of lunchtime concerts in the National Gallery that made her name with a wider public.[124] London theatres, concert halls and entertainment venues were closed in the evenings because of the blackout. The paintings held by the National Gallery were whisked away to secure hiding places in Welsh slate mines and the like. For concert-goers, London seemed bleak. Hess suggested to Kenneth Clark, director of the National Gallery, that the empty rooms could be enlivened by lunchtime concerts at cheap prices. Clark was enthusiastic and a small army of volunteers was enlisted to make it happen. The first concert was scheduled for 10 October 1939.

Hess volunteered to play a solo programme in case only a few people turned up. But shortly before the doors were due to open, the staff peeped out and saw a huge queue of people stretching round Trafalgar Square; in the end, Hess played to almost 1,000 people. Her programme began with Scarlatti, continued with Bach preludes and fugues and Beethoven's 'Appassionata' sonata, and ended with a short piece that became closely associated with her: her arrangement of Bach's chorale 'Wohl mir, dass ich Jesum habe', or 'Jesu, Joy of Man's Desiring' as it was known in Britain.

The public's appetite for the National Gallery concerts continued right through the war, with lunchtime concerts five days a week and occasional repeat performances at teatime. Famous artists took part; young artists were given opportunities to play, and musicians from the RAF orchestra performed, many of whom were well known, such as horn player Dennis Brain, flautist Gareth Morris and the Griller Quartet. Some artists appeared only once, while others played regularly. All were paid five guineas regardless of their status. The royal family often attended.

The audience was told they could bring their lunch, and could wander in and out between the pieces or movements. Quickly, however, the noise of rustling paper bags became an unwelcome counterpoint to the music, and this led to the setting up of canteens. The comedian Joyce Grenfell was one of the canteen volunteers and recalled the fare: raisin and honey sandwiches, cream cheese and date sandwiches, 'good damp station cake' (a fruit cake) and strong coffee. Audience members had counters where they could stand and eat their own food while listening to the music. During the Blitz, concerts moved downstairs to the basement, but the audience still queued up. Occasionally bomb-disposal units could be heard working nearby.

It quickly became clear that Hess could not be expected to organise these concerts on her own. She asked her friend, the composer Howard Ferguson, to help, and he took over the artistic programming, with a team of helpers looking after the practicalities. Hess's long-time assistant Anita Gunn kept daily notes on what was played, along with brief notes on the war ('News bad', 'News worse').[125] Altogether they presented 1,698 concerts through the war, with Hess performing in about 150 of them and playing a large repertoire including all Mozart's piano concertos, and piano quintets with the Griller Quartet. There were many touching moments, such as the appearance of the German singer Elena Gerhardt in 1940, the day after Germany had invaded the Netherlands. Gerhardt phoned Hess to cancel her performance, explaining that nobody would want to hear the German language at such a moment. Myra disagreed and offered to play the piano for the concert. Gerhardt was nervous as they walked on stage, but the audience gave them such a warm ovation that all her nerves disappeared.

After the war, now created a dame for her contribution to wartime morale, Hess resumed touring in Europe and America and continued doing so with great success until 1961. Touring life was facilitated by the presence of Gunn, her long-time secretary and companion, who for thirty years saw to travel arrangements, dealt with phone calls and agents, did the shopping and ironing, and played double solitaire with Hess backstage. Hess was persuaded to make recordings but hated the process and felt that she was never at her best in the recording studio; luckily, there were also recordings of live concerts, which capture her performing style more naturally. She recorded concertos, solo pieces, chamber music and piano duets with her friend and fellow Matthay pupil Irene Scharrer.

Myra Hess's playing and indeed her platform persona are often described as dignified, spacious, limpid, poetical, mature and thoughtful. Yet in private life she was a jolly person, full of jokes and fun, a keen card player, a wicked impressionist who could mimic people's accents. Her niece recalled how, when she was a child, Aunt Myra would thrill her by making 'teeth' out of a piece of orange peel and inserting them behind her lips for fun. If the doorbell rang, Aunt

Myra would open it and innocently greet the visitor with a smile, startling them with her orange-peel teeth. Yet by a strange alchemy this same woman could hold audiences spellbound with the spiritual atmosphere of her performances of late Beethoven piano sonatas.

GUIOMAR NOVAES

Guiomar Novaes (1895–1979) was a Brazilian pianist whose debut concerts in Europe and the United States had critics reaching for ecstatic phrases to describe the beauty of her playing. Her recordings are so persuasive that it seems astonishing she is not mentioned in the same breath as Paderewski, Rubinstein and co.

Guiomar Novaes was the seventeenth of nineteen children born to her parents in São Paulo. Her gift for piano-playing became evident at the age of three. Her parents were not wealthy, but neighbours helped them to gather enough money for piano lessons, and when she was just fourteen she won a Brazilian government scholarship to study for four years at the Paris Conservatoire. First, however, she had to win one of the two places open to foreigners. After crossing the Atlantic to reach France she learned that there were 388 applicants for those two places. Guiomar played for a jury that included Fauré and Debussy. 'The most artistic of all the candidates was a young Brazilian girl of 13,' Debussy told a friend in a letter of 25 November 1909. 'She's not beautiful, but her eyes are drunk with music and she has that ability to cut herself off from her surroundings which is the rare but characteristic mark of the artist.'[126] Considering Guiomar's youth, the long-distance travel, the foreign language and the circumstances of the audition, this is remarkable proof of her self-possession.

Guiomar won first place in the entrance auditions and began to study with the renowned piano teacher Isidor Philipp, who soon realised that although she was quiet, she knew her own mind. After only two years, she won the coveted Premier Prix du Conservatoire and began to play public concerts in France and England. When the First World War broke out she returned to Brazil but at the age of twenty was invited to give her US debut in Carnegie Hall. The critics were rapturous: 'More inspired playing has never been heard in Aeolian Hall, and Aeolian Hall audiences have heard all the foremost pianists of the time, including Paderewski,' the *Evening Post* said.[127] 'She is the greatest woman pianist now before the public, and even some of the men must look to their laurels.' The *New York Times* called her 'a musician by the grace of God'. *The Boston Globe* said she was 'a young genius of the piano'. 'Miss Novaes seems to get her inspiration direct from heaven ... [She is] one of the seven wonders of the musical world,' said the *Evening Post* on hearing her again.[128] Because of her lovely Chopin-playing she was dubbed by critic James Huneker 'the Paderewska of the Pampas'[129] – Paderewski was particularly renowned for his playing of Chopin.

In 1925 Guiomar married Dr Octavio Pinto, an architect and composer, and returned to Brazil, where she enjoyed family life with their two children. Each year she returned to play in New York, where she was a great favourite. The critic Harold C. Schonberg once said she had 'velvet paws'. This allusion to the feline species may seem patronising, but Schonberg was probably referring to her much-admired controlled relaxation:

> With the most graceful movements of arm she forms and molds the tone to such quality she desires. She plays with controlled weight, but it is weight that is alive, vital, not lumbering and 'dead'. With this condition of poise in arm, wrist and hand, every tone she produces, from feathery pianissimo to the utmost fortissimo, has a searching, vibrant quality, a quality that makes an instant appeal to the listener. Even a single tone has the poignant quality that makes a thrilling effect. She produces these tones without apparent effort; yet they carry a message quite apart from the studied tones of other pianists.

So wrote Harriette Brower in her book of interviews with early-twentieth-century pianists.[130]

Novaes became known especially for her interpretations of Chopin and Schumann, though she once admitted that her own personal preference was for the music of Bach and Mozart. She was not a fan of modern music. 'Will this music last forever? Sometimes it sounds artificial,' she said.[131] Nor was she overawed by her contemporaries. 'Modern pianists are so well trained they sound alike,' she told the *New York Times* in 1972. 'They are not allowed an opportunity to show their own personalities, for the most part. It was different before. We could easily recognize the tone, the interpretations of each great one.'[132]

Novaes's tone was unforced yet full and singing, with what critics described as a thrilling quality (in that sense, she was like Teresa Carreño, another Latin American pianist). She liked pianos and they liked her back. 'The piano is something that seems to have soul to transmit our feelings,' she said. 'I don't like to see pianos left abandoned, carelessly. My mother used to say, "Keep yourself faithful to your piano; he is your best friend." I have done my best for this.'[133]

Audiences noted that she never played a piece the same way twice; she was relaxed enough to be spontaneous. Yet she did not play to the gallery – on the contrary, she seemed absorbed in the enjoyment of playing and admitted that in concerts she often forgot that the audience was there. She delighted in illuminating details in the music, as though her mind were always open to passing thoughts and observations even under the pressure of live performance. She did genuinely seem to find things easy. Asked how she memorised so much music, she replied, 'I really do not know ... it all comes to me very quickly. I find it very amusing to learn by heart. You do not think I should say amusing? Well then, I shall say I find it interesting.'[134] Audiences loved her because she made everything sound natural, even if the music was of enormous technical difficulty; she had the ability to drop technique into the background. She once said, 'All my life everything has come to me without struggle. Art for some is drudgery. For me it is the greatest joy. Well, I shall play better next year. I wish to give back all that life gives to me.'[135]

CLARA HASKIL

Clara Haskil (1895–1960) was a Romanian pianist whose much-admired purity of tone and musicianship were achieved against a background of physical suffering. The Clara Haskil Piano Competition was set up in her memory in 1963 in Vevey, Switzerland.

Clara Haskil was born in Bucharest into a talented family of Sephardic Jewish origin. She was named after her maternal aunt Clara, an outstanding pianist, who died of tuberculosis at the age of twenty. Clara had two sisters, Lili and Jeanne; all three became musicians although Jeanne once said, 'We have talent, but Clara has genius.'[136] As a child, Clara could play by ear anything she had heard, and could transpose it into any key. Her father died of pneumonia when she was just four. When she was seven, her uncle Avram decided that her musical talent had to be developed and took her to live in his home in Vienna, where she studied with the well-regarded piano teacher Richard Robert. In Vienna she took up the violin after going to a concert in which the violinist Joseph Joachim played Brahms; she made predictably rapid progress, which probably influenced her approach to tone production and the art of achieving *cantabile* on the piano.

A few years later, when Clara was ten, Richard Robert recommended her to Gabriel Fauré, director of the Paris Conservatoire, in the hope that she could study with Alfred Cortot. As she was so young, she first spent two years working with Cortot's assistants, but finally passed into his class and graduated at fifteen with a Premier Prix du Conservatoire. Concert invitations followed and in 1911 Clara was playing all over Europe, including a concert in Zürich where composer-pianist Ferruccio Busoni was so struck by her talent that he invited her to study with him. But Clara was only sixteen, and to her lasting disappointment her family did not approve this plan. By now she was showing signs of scoliosis, a curvature of the spine. She had to spend four years in a nursing home in a plaster cast to correct the condition, but its after-effects were long-lasting.

From 1927 to 1934 she lived with her uncle in his Paris apartment. It was at this period that she frequented the famous artistic salon hosted by Winnaretta Singer, Princesse de Polignac (see p. 113). Through her appearances there she was heard by a number of wealthy arts-loving patrons who, admiring her talent but perhaps also realising that she was not well suited to self-promotion, supported her financially. At the Polignacs' she met and struck up a warm friendship with her fellow Romanian pianist Dinu Lipatti; the playing styles of these two gifted pianists are in some ways comparable, being characterised by lucidity and sensitivity.

At the approach of the Nazis in 1940, Haskil fled Paris and took refuge in the south of France, where her health problems continued. She developed a tumour on her optic nerve which brought vision problems and headaches. A Jewish surgeon travelled from Paris to operate on her, but the procedure did not cure her of headaches. In 1942, she and her sister Lili managed to move to Switzerland, where she became a Swiss citizen in 1949.

The same year, a Dutch concert manager pursued a successful campaign to get her the concert invitations she deserved. This led to a halcyon period in the 1950s when Haskil gave solo recitals and appeared with leading orchestras in Europe and America. Her repertoire was focused on Mozart, Beethoven, Schubert and Schumann, but she was a very fine player of Scarlatti and Debussy. She also proved a superb chamber musician, playing duets with Lipatti and partnering many fine string players such as the cellist Pablo Casals, the violinists George Enescu and Eugène Ysaÿe, Joseph Szigeti, Isaac Stern, Henryk Szeryng, Yehudi Menuhin and, in her most celebrated artistic partnership, the Belgian violinist Arthur Grumiaux, with whom she made an exquisite recording of six Mozart duo sonatas. Grumiaux was also a talented pianist and it is said that sometimes he and Haskil would swap roles for fun, she playing the violin – although she had not practised it for years – and Grumiaux playing the piano. (It need hardly be said that few piano–violin duos have possessed this double ability.) Haskil also made a series of fine recordings such as her eleven Scarlatti sonatas of 1950 and her Schumann piano concerto of 1951, but she never enjoyed playing for the microphone. This decade brought Haskil a remarkable career high in her fifties, though she was never free of pain caused by her headaches and her spinal condition.

In 1960 she and Grumiaux gave a violin–piano duo concert in Paris, to be followed by a tour of Grumiaux's native Belgium. But when Haskil arrived by train in Brussels, she tripped and fell down the stairs at the railway station. She was unconscious when taken to hospital and died the following morning. As conductor Ferenc Fricsay said, 'With the death of Clara Haskil we have become the poorer, but our existence has been enriched by her life.'[137]

Haskil's reputation is unusual because she was the opposite of the larger-than-life extroverts who bound colourfully through the piano world. She was serious and shy, inclined to dress austerely for concerts, uncomfortable about smiling for photographs.[138] (Today, these qualities would make it hard to build a career in the public eye.) Her appearance of serenity on stage was hard-won. Her musicianship is characterised by a beautifully even tone in which every note seems clear and unforced yet also soulful and sensitive. Her pedalling is very light, and notes are not blurred. Like other great pianists she gives the impression of having mastered technical difficulties to the point where she has all the time in the world to listen to herself play and to shape the sound as the music requires. Her appeal to piano fans has not faded over the years.

MARIA YUDINA

Maria Veniaminovna Yudina (1899–1970) was an extraordinary Russian pianist who never performed in the West. Her strongly held religious convictions led to her being *persona non grata* with the Soviet authorities. Although she was much admired as a pianist, she never possessed her own piano.

Yudina is known in the West mainly because of Armando Iannucci's blackly comic 2017 film *The Death of Stalin*, based on the French graphic novels *La Mort de Staline*. The film tells how, in 1944, Stalin heard a live radio performance of Maria Yudina performing Mozart's piano concerto in A major (K488) and asked for a copy of the recording. As no recording had been made and the radio producers were too frightened to admit as much, they knocked on Maria

Yudina's door in the middle of the night and dragged her back into the studio to record a fresh performance with a hastily assembled orchestra and audience. In Iannucci's film this episode is followed by a dramatic coda in which Yudina daringly writes Stalin a letter reproaching him for his great sins against the people, which causes Stalin to have a heart attack. There is no firm evidence for this letter, and the midnight recording session is unproven, but Yudina did record Mozart's A major concerto in 1948.

These stories fit with the drama of the real-life Yudina's personality. She was born to a Jewish family, but converted to the Russian Orthodox church at the age of twenty, becoming deeply involved in theological studies. She started living a life of service to others and renounced worldly goods. She joined the Josephite movement, a branch of the Orthodox church formed by members who resisted church leaders' call for loyalty to the Soviet government. Her beliefs brought her into constant conflict with the Soviet authorities. She saw herself as a champion of the persecuted and used to barge into government offices to protest on behalf of people she thought had been unjustly treated. She used her concerts to publicise the plight of the unfortunate. Ironically, it may have been because she was a woman that the authorities let this kind of thing go on as long as they did.

Yudina studied at the Petrograd (later St Petersburg) Conservatory, and after graduation was invited to teach there. As a young woman she was friendly with Shostakovich and the poets Boris Pasternak and Osip Mandelstam. She was very keen on modern music and learned works of Béla Bartók, Paul Hindemith, Ernst Krenek and Igor Stravinsky at a time when these composers' music was either little known or banned in Soviet Russia (perhaps her support of 'dissonant' music was a metaphor for rebellion). She corresponded with the philosopher Theodor Adorno and championed the music of Pierre Boulez and Karlheinz Stockhausen.

However, she also adored the music of Mozart and was one of the few Russian pianists who performed Bach's *Forty-Eight Preludes and*

Fugues in recitals at a time when, as Sviatoslav Richter recalled, 'the Forty-Eight were considered good enough only for examination pieces'. Richter remembered that:

> during the War, she had given *The Well-Tempered Clavier* at a splendid concert, even if she polished off the contemplative Prelude in B flat minor from Book Two at a constant *fortissimo*. At the end of the concert, Neuhaus, whom I was accompanying, went to congratulate her in her dressing-room. 'But, Maria Veniaminovna,' he asked her, 'why did you play the B flat minor prelude in such a dramatic way?' 'Because we're at war!!' It was typical of Yudina.[139]

Her ceaseless attempts to uphold her religious convictions resulted in her being dismissed 'for perverting Soviet youth' (by talking to them about religion) from three institutions where she taught – from the Petrograd Conservatory in 1929, the Moscow Conservatory in 1951 and the Gnessin Institute in 1960. Recording her recitals was forbidden. Undeterred, Yudina took to reading Boris Pasternak's poems from the stage and incurred a five-year ban on performing altogether. However, large numbers of ordinary Russians admired her spirit and flocked to her concerts when the ban was lifted. She often appeared on the platform dressed in nun-like black robes, walking slowly, carrying a crucifix and crossing herself before she played. Her friend Shostakovich said, 'She always played as if she were giving a sermon.'[140] 'For my own part,' said Sviatoslav Richter, 'I found her behaviour exaggeratedly theatrical and her religious beliefs somewhat false and ostentatious.'[141] Yudina had a fearsome piano technique and could impart a great sense of drama to her performances, but often played things much more loudly or fiercely than the composer indicated. 'By the end of her concerts I used to have a headache,' Richter recalled.[142] In her later years Yudina became increasingly eccentric and isolated, devoting her time to caring for the poor and living 'like a tramp' in Moscow.[143] Richter summed her up in his memoirs as a 'sacred monster'.[144]

A friend and colleague of Yudina's was Maria Grinberg (1908–78), the first Russian pianist to record all Beethoven's piano sonatas. Grinberg's promising career never recovered from the traumatic experience of having both her father and her husband arrested and executed by the Soviet government in 1937. Grinberg herself was viewed with disfavour and not invited to tour abroad until after Stalin had died. Even then her concerts were not recorded, and critics omitted to review them. In her fifties and sixties she enjoyed a kind of rehabilitation and in 1970 was invited to record a thirteen-disc box set of Beethoven sonatas for the Melodiya label. Grinberg and Yudina had a prickly relationship, but when Yudina was considering which musicians she would like to play at her funeral, Grinberg's was the only name she gave.

LILI KRAUS

Lili Kraus (1903–86) was a Hungarian pianist whose musical training brought her into contact with several of the greatest musicians of the twentieth century – Bartók, Zoltán Kodály and Schnabel. Her renown as a pianist helped to save her when she was imprisoned by the Japanese while on tour in Asia during the Second World War.

Lili Kraus was born to a poor Jewish family in Budapest. Her father was a charming but impoverished Czech who made a meagre living by sharpening knives in his cutlery shop. Her Hungarian mother had a beautiful singing voice and wanted to be a singer, but her parents forbade it on the grounds of respectability. Lili's mother was prey to depressive episodes and the atmosphere at home was often unhappy.

Kraus herself would have liked to become a dancer, but strangely, in the light of her own experience, her mother forbade it because she said it was not much better than becoming a prostitute. Music was

Lili's second choice, and she wanted to play the violin, but her mother refused this too, allowing her however to learn the piano 'because it belongs to decent households'.[145] Somehow the family acquired a jangling old piano with stiff keys. Lili enjoyed learning to play it, in the process acquiring the muscular finger technique that characterised her playing in later years.

At the age of only eight, she auditioned for the famous Franz Liszt Academy in Budapest, which normally required applicants to be at least fourteen years old. The Academy had set pieces for pianists to prepare, but Lili turned up for her audition with pieces of her own choice. When asked why she had not presented the set pieces, she replied that she did not like them. Her bravado impressed the audition panel and they admitted her to the Academy. Over the years she studied music theory with Kodály, piano with Arnold Székely (a student of Ferruccio Busoni) and chamber music with Leo Weiner, to whose lessons she went without having prepared properly because her mother regarded chamber music as a waste of time for Lili when she could be training to be a soloist. Her mother frequently dragged her to the piano by her hair and hit her if she made mistakes. It is a mark of the misery she felt at home that from the age of seven to seventeen, Lili visited the local zoo every day, usually by herself, and cultivated imaginary bonds with some of the wilder animals, on one occasion even bribing a zookeeper's son to let her into the lion cubs' cage when the mother lion was nearby (luckily she was seen and rescued).[146]

In Kraus's final year at the Academy her teacher died. With her plans disrupted, she took a one-year job teaching piano in the small town of Losonc. Here one of her students was Eugene Fodor, founder of Fodor's travel guides. He recalled that 'she was a very very stunning young woman. The whole town, whether young or old or man or woman, simply fell madly in love with her.'[147] At the end of the year Lili went back to Budapest to study piano with Béla Bartók. This was a formative period for her. Bartók was the opposite of coercive; he would listen to her play something and then sit in silence waiting for her to feel like playing it better. This was surprisingly effective. Sometimes he would say something like, 'Have you considered what it *could* be?' or 'But don't you find ...?' And Kraus would consider ... and find. Bartók's own playing was very different from hers, but she loved it: 'He had very thin fingers, and he was not a sensuous man. Sometimes you had the feeling that bone hit against bone, so it was not a luxurious sound, but boy, every note had its meaning.'[148]

After graduating from the Liszt Academy, Kraus moved to Vienna to study with Severin Eisenberger, a Leschetizky student whose own solo career had foundered after he developed shell shock in the First World War. Aged only twenty, Kraus was soon offered a teaching post at the Vienna Konservatorium, a rare honour for such a young pianist. Concert invitations started pouring in and Lili's beauty was often mentioned in reviews. The tempo of her life increased when she met and fell in love with Otto Mandl, a wealthy Jewish mining engineer. He was married, with a wife and three children living in London, but when Kraus became pregnant he set about obtaining a divorce. In 1930 Kraus gave birth to her daughter Ruth just before Mandl's divorce came through; Lili and Otto were married shortly after. Somehow, Mandl's first wife Mary came to terms with the situation, and so did the children of Mandl's first marriage. His son William remembered:

> She [Lili] was ravishingly beautiful, dressed completely different than people were in London at that time ... Her movements were majestic and when she walked on the street, there was a queen walking. She tossed her head and people turned around because she was so beautiful, just marvellously beautiful.[149]

In the 1930s, when the shadow of Nazism started to fall on Europe, Lili and Otto converted to Catholicism. Vienna was notably anti-Semitic and the couple moved to Berlin, where Kraus took masterclasses with Schnabel. He too had an excellent influence and persuaded her to study the *Urtext* (the original text) of scores, to acquire an intellectual grasp of the structure of the work, to practise with the metronome to curb volatility, to understand that within a steady pulse there can be infinite flexibility around the beat, and so on. She learned from Schnabel that the composer's expression marks are not to be mechanically applied but are outward signs of what lives inside the music: 'You must have endless grades of emphasis depending on what the music says.'[150]

During the 1930s, Kraus formed the most important chamber-music partnership of her life with the Polish violinist Szymon Goldberg, one of Carl Flesch's star students. Together they recorded Beethoven and Mozart piano and violin sonatas for Parlophone in the mid-thirties. It's interesting that Kraus, who was forbidden from playing the violin and from studying chamber music when she was young, found happiness in this collaboration with a sensitive violinist. Many of her fans would probably refer to her recordings and performances with Goldberg as the artistic high point of her career.

When the Second World War broke out, Kraus and her family tried to move out of the way of the advancing wave of anti-Semitism, eventually moving to Indonesia where it was thought that Goldberg and she could safely tour with their piano–violin duo. In 1942, however, they were arrested by the Japanese along with their families and interned in different prisoner-of-war camps on the island of Java. Here Kraus had to stay for three years, separated from her children, who were taken to a different camp. It transpired that some of her Japanese captors were aware of her musical renown, and this probably helped her to survive. She was eventually even allowed to play the piano and was invited to play for her Japanese guards and for fellow prisoners.

After the camp was liberated by British forces in 1945, it naturally took Kraus some time to work her pianistic skills up to concert standard. She never returned to live in her native Hungary. She went to settle first in New Zealand, and then in South Africa. She resumed performing and touring in Europe and the United States, but critics noticed a certain eccentricity in her playing: her forthright style could tip over into brusqueness. Even her admirers felt that her wartime experiences had exhausted her. A *Gramophone* reviewer (male), seeing a 1960 photo of her on a reissue, felt entitled to describe her as 'a heavy-boned mittel-European hausfrau in a lace-trimmed gown that would have been old-fashioned in the 1930s', a style of comment he would not have made about a male artist.[151] Kraus was still ambitious, however, and in the 1966–7 season she played twenty-five of Mozart's piano concertos in New York, following that feat with all of his piano sonatas a year later. This led to her being offered a teaching position at Texas Christian University in Fort Worth, where she taught until retirement and was the only constant member of the Van Cliburn competition jury.

Her teaching style, lively and dramatic, could turn cold in a flash and her devastating remarks became the stuff of legend on campus. For example, her student and biographer Steven Roberson remembered that when one of her pupils was performing a Beethoven piano concerto with the university orchestra, Kraus suddenly stood up and shouted, 'Stop! I won't have the audience think it's supposed to sound that way.' On another occasion she told a student, on the night before his final recital, that she couldn't understand why he was supposed to be a musician. Hungarian music teachers are often noted for a robust and even biting style of criticism, but in my experience all the professors who exhibit those traits have been men, so it is interesting to hear of a woman who used the same style. It is no doubt intended to challenge the student in a creative way. If the student has fire in them, such a challenge may have good results, but it can be a shock to those brought up in a system where educators are trained always to say something positive.

EILEEN JOYCE

Eileen Joyce (1912–91) was a glamorous Australian pianist best known for her playing of Rachmaninoff's second piano concerto on the soundtrack of David Lean's film *Brief Encounter*. She was popular with audiences for her habit of changing her concert frocks and hairstyles to suit the music she was playing.

She was born into an Irish-Australian mining family in Tasmania; much later, when interviewed in London by John Amis, she told him that 'one doesn't realise, over here, how very primitive it is'.[152] She moved in early childhood to Boulder City in the goldfields of Western Australia, where her uncle had 'a tough pub' with an old piano which Eileen liked to play. Her father eventually bought it from the pub and wheeled it home for her. When her musical ability became evident she was sent to study at Loreto Convent in Perth, where Mother John Moore was a renowned piano teacher. The composer Percy Grainger came to play to the nuns in 1926, heard Eileen play and wrote a letter to the local newspaper, calling her 'the most transcendentally gifted young piano student I have heard in twenty-five years' and recommending that the people of Perth should sponsor her to study abroad.[153] Six weeks later, the German concert pianist Wilhelm Backhaus also came to give a concert at the convent, heard Eileen play and advised that she be sent to study in Leipzig. Financed by local subscription, at the age of only fifteen she travelled to Leipzig – 'the nuns packed for me' – and spent several years studying with Max Pauer and Robert Teichmüller.[154]

Eventually she moved to London to complete her studies with Tobias Matthay and to make her debut. Teichmüller gave her a letter of introduction to the conductor Albert Coates, who in turn introduced her to Sir Henry Wood. He invited her to play at the Proms, playing Prokofiev's third piano concerto, which was still fairly new to the British public. Soon she was sought after by other orchestras and conductors and learned an enormous repertoire of concertos. She gave the British premieres of Shostakovich's first and second piano concertos, and also made a point of performing British piano concertos by Bliss, Ireland, Howells and Rawsthorne.

During the Second World War she travelled extensively within Britain to perform in cities that had been bombed, sometimes playing in several venues per day or performing concerts twice in an evening. She became very popular with the public, who especially enjoyed hearing her play the big concertos by Grieg, Tchaikovsky (no. 1) and Rachmaninoff (no. 2). She also performed regularly at Myra Hess's National Gallery concerts (see p. 137). Until the 1940s she designed her own concert dresses and would change them between items to match colour to composer: green for Chopin, lilac for Liszt, red for Tchaikovsky, blue for Beethoven and so on. This 'gimmick' was frowned upon by critics but was popular with audiences.

In 1945 she recorded the piano music for two successful films, *Brief Encounter* and *The Seventh Veil*. Having been warned that 'serious people' would look askance at her involvement with commercial film, she remained anonymous for *The Seventh Veil*, but when it came to *Brief Encounter* her name appeared in the opening credits in letters even bigger than Rachmaninoff's, a mark of her popularity. She toured extensively, visiting South Africa, India, Australia, New Zealand, South America and Russia as well as Europe.

In 1946 Joyce was the subject of a Pathé newsreel in which we see her arranging flowers in a splendid living room – 'She's a success, and lives in a lovely Mayfair flat,' intones a narrator.[155] We see her cycling to 'her Chelsea practice studio' where she works for five hours a day. As Joyce practises in her studio, working men pause thoughtfully in their labours to listen; the milkman steps close to the window to marvel at her Chopin. In the film we also see her then six-year-old son John, whom she later said she regretted neglecting for the sake of her music and her intensive concert schedule.

Joyce must have had tremendous stamina, for she made a speciality of playing several concertos in a single concert. For example, at a

1951 concert she performed Chopin's first concerto, Rachmaninoff's second, the John Ireland concerto and Beethoven's 'Emperor' in one programme – a feat few pianists would attempt.

In the 1950s she became fascinated by the harpsichord, and recorded on that instrument, but critics found her playing of 'early music' rather stiff compared with her dashing performances of Liszt, Chopin and Brahms. In her later years she collected many honours, including an honorary doctorate from the University of Cambridge.

Eileen was brave as well as hard-working. She suffered from rheumatism, which flared up during the war when she was working as a volunteer firefighter. For a while she had to wear a plaster cast that covered her shoulders and back. This would have caused many a pianist to take a break from the concert platform, but Eileen persevered with her hectic wartime concert schedule, commissioning the royal dress designer Norman Hartnell to make her some flattering gowns that concealed the plaster cast. Even when her rheumatism was under control, she continued to wear concert frocks designed by Hartnell.

MARGARET BONDS

Margaret Bonds (1913–72) was the first Black person to perform as a concerto soloist with the Chicago Symphony Orchestra. She was a pioneer in composing politically inspired works that paid tribute to African American spirituals, and she founded a society dedicated to performing the classical music of Black composers.

Margaret was born in Chicago. Her father, Monroe Alpheus Majors, was a civil rights activist and the first Black physician in the American Midwest. When Margaret was four, her parents divorced and Margaret took her mother's surname, Bonds. At the age of five, Margaret wrote her first piece, *Marquette Street Blues*. Her mother, a piano teacher, was friendly with many Black artists, writers and musicians, who used to visit their home. One of them was Florence Price, who became a leading classical composer. While the young Margaret was still at school, she studied composition with Price and at the age of sixteen she gained a place to study at Northwestern University, which she later described as 'this prejudiced university, this terribly prejudiced place'.[156]

Attending university was her first sustained experience of racism. Although she was technically permitted to study for a music degree, she was not allowed to live on campus or use the university facilities, and many restaurants refused to serve her – bitter pills for someone who was struggling to fund her tuition. Margaret sought consolation in Evanston Public Library, where in the poetry section she was struck by a poem by Langston Hughes. In 'The Negro Speaks of Rivers', Hughes refers to the ancient rivers of the Euphrates, the Nile, the Congo and the Mississippi, alluding to Black people's long experience of migration and proclaiming, 'My soul has grown deep like the rivers'. 'I'm sure it helped my feelings of security,' Margaret recalled. 'Because in that poem he tells how great the black man is.'[157] She did not know it then, but Langston Hughes was to become a lifelong friend and inspiration.

During her student years at Northwestern, Bonds won a composition award for her song 'Sea Ghost', which unfortunately is now lost.[158] In 1934, when she was just twenty-one, she was the first Black person ever to perform as concerto soloist with the Chicago Symphony Orchestra (a piano concertino by the American composer John Alden Carpenter). Her success led to an invitation, the following year, to perform Florence Price's piano concerto in D minor with the Women's Symphony Orchestra of Chicago. In 1936 she met Langston Hughes, whose poetry she so admired. In 1939 she moved to New York, where she studied composition with Roy Harris, performed in a piano duo, taught piano and got involved in the musical theatre scene. She married a friend of

Hughes and had a daughter, Djane. Djane later recalled Hughes as a frequent visitor who stayed with them every Thanksgiving and Christmas.

Bonds gradually forged a New York career as a piano soloist and in duos with singers, often performing her own music. Her *Spiritual Suite*, weaving spirituals and folk dances into the music, was a success, and its third movement, 'Troubled Water', an intriguing blend of hard-hitting jazz style and rippling Rachmaninoff-style figuration, remains her most popular piano piece. She also founded the Margaret Bonds Chamber Society, a group of Black musicians dedicated to performing the classical music of Black composers. This was a pioneering initiative.

In 1954 she and Hughes collaborated on *The Ballad of the Brown King*, a Christmas cantata that tells the story of Balthazar, believed to be 'the African king' from the three kings who visited Jesus after his birth. Bonds and Hughes dedicated the work to Martin Luther King. The original choral version was expanded and Margaret provided an orchestral accompaniment for a CBS Christmas broadcast of *The Ballad of the Brown King* in 1960. The cantata comprises nine movements which incorporate blues, gospel, hymns, calypso, jazz, spirituals and recitative. It is Bonds's most frequently performed work, a testament to her belief that American identity must reflect the rich history of African Americans.

When Hughes died in 1967, Bonds became deeply depressed. She made the drastic decision to leave her husband and daughter and move by herself to Los Angeles, where her depression deepened. Her last work, *Credo* for chorus and orchestra, was premiered by the Los Angeles Philharmonic under Zubin Mehta in 1972, just months before she died. One of Bonds's last acts was to throw many of her music manuscripts and letters into a waste container in the street. Some of them were rescued, but it is unknown how much of her music and history was lost.

ANNIE FISCHER

Annie Fischer (1914–95) was a Hungarian Jewish pianist admired by fellow pianists such as Sviatoslav Richter and Maurizio Pollini and cited as an influence by Martha Argerich, András Schiff, Peter Donohoe and many others.

She was a child prodigy who performed Beethoven's piano concerto no. 1 at the age of ten. She studied at the Franz Liszt Academy in Budapest with Ernst von Dohnányi and Arnold Székely. In 1933 she won first prize in the inaugural Franz Liszt piano competition and this led to many European concerts. In 1937 she married the critic and later opera director Aladár Tóth, with whom she was very happy. Shortly afterwards, life became very difficult for them because of anti-Semitic feeling in Budapest. In 1941 the Fischers fled to Sweden, where they waited out the Second World War, Annie passing the time by teaching more than she did at any other period of her life. When the war ended, they returned to Hungary and Annie renewed her European concert career with appetite.

I remember hearing Annie Fischer when she came to Edinburgh. I missed her much-praised 1961 Edinburgh Festival recital, but I did hear her play with the Scottish National Orchestra in the Usher Hall. My (female) piano teacher admired her to the extent of forgiving her for playing in a sleeveless dress, a style my teacher considered unattractive. Annie Fischer at the piano, serious and strong, in a plain green dress with her hair in a no-nonsense bun, made a great impression on me. Here was no feminine posturing or smiling at the audience; she was there to represent Beethoven and she threw herself into the task with conviction, enunciating every note with her strong fingers as though she really wanted us to 'get it'.

Her approach is often compared with Schnabel's because of its intellectual grasp and emotional intensity, combined with a surprising impulsiveness. As with Schnabel, impulsiveness – in the form of rushing forwards – sometimes led to a loss of control over note accuracy, but one can tell by watching film of Fischer's performances that the odd wrong note didn't bother her – she was aiming for accuracy at a higher level, that of poetic truth. Her style was often described as 'masculine' because of her muscular strength and decisiveness. She was a chain-smoker, sometimes even photographed with cigarette in hand, and in London some of the orchestras disrespectfully nicknamed her 'Ashtray Annie'.

She was never keen on recording, feeling uncomfortable with the idea that it pins down an interpretation in an artificial way, but she did allow live performances to be recorded, and it is these – particularly the filmed concerts – which give the best impression of her serious, eloquent style. In her sixties she was persuaded to embark on a project of recording all thirty-two Beethoven piano sonatas for the Hungaroton label. Naturally, her dislike of recording made this a challenge. She recorded the works in small sections, playing her own Bösendorfer piano whose tone had become slightly harsh after being subjected to years of energetic practice. Fischer was a perfectionist, and it took her fifteen years of intermittent work to complete the set. Even then, she was dissatisfied and forbade the recordings to be released until after her death. Once released they were widely acclaimed and placed on a level with the best 'complete Beethoven sonatas' of Kempff, Arrau and Schnabel.

Fischer is perhaps not as well known as she should be because she was not much interested in career planning. She only visited the United States a couple of times, years apart, and did not play in New York until her late sixties. When she did finally play in Carnegie Hall in 1982 (Beethoven sonata in C major opus 53, 'Waldstein', Schubert impromptus opus 142, Schumann *Fantasie* opus 17), the *New York Times* did her the favour of offering her a pre-concert interview with the legendary critic Harold C. Schonberg but Annie turned it down, saying that she had never given interviews and wasn't going to start now.[159] Ticket sales were slow, but at the last minute, word spread and her Carnegie Hall debut was sold out. A decade later, she gave her last triumphant London recital at the age of seventy-eight. As an encore, she played the fugue from Beethoven's 'Hammerklavier' sonata. Beethoven's torrential fugue is a feat for any pianist, and it was doubly so on this occasion.

NANCY WEIR

Nancy Weir (1915–2008) was an Australian pianist. As a young child, she used to entertain customers at her parents' pub in Lockhart, New South Wales, by playing the piano for them. At the age of ten she started studying with Amy Freeman Corder, a renowned Australian piano teacher. Nancy's first concerts attracted an exceptional degree of adulation, and by her teenage years she had got used to people in the street trying to touch the hem of her dress as a token of respect. At thirteen, she played Beethoven's third piano concerto with the Melbourne Symphony Orchestra. Such a crowd turned up to hear her that allegedly 3,000 people were turned away, but still so many people crammed into the hall that the organisers were prosecuted for overcrowding. After the performance, the car in which Nancy was being driven home was mobbed by cheering well-wishers, who ran after the car all the way up Collins Street. These scenes would seem to suggest that as well as being a fine pianist, Nancy Weir had remarkable charisma. Reviewers predicted that she would become one of the world's greatest women pianists.

When Weir was fourteen, the mayor of Melbourne organised a fundraising effort to gather money to send her to Berlin to study with Artur Schnabel. In 1930 she travelled to Berlin and, at not quite fifteen, became Schnabel's youngest pupil. She lived by herself in a *Pension* or boarding house, learning to speak German, with no supporters around her and no concerts to play. Despite her youth she was not overawed by Schnabel's deeply serious attitude to his art, which struck her as exaggerated. He once said that 'music is a great art, a high altar, and you will never be able to appreciate it unless you are ready to take a rope and hang yourself'. 'It was a silly way to talk to a child,' said Nancy later.[160]

She was the last person to have a lesson with Schnabel before he left Germany in 1933 to escape the rise of the Nazis.

Nancy then went to study in London with Harold Craxton and Tobias Matthay at the Royal Academy of Music, where her extraordinary aural skills were noted and compared with those of Mozart; evidently she had no difficulty in following five simultaneous lines of music and noting them down accurately. After graduating with excellent results, she played two solo recitals at London's Wigmore Hall in 1937. But then, as her biographer Belinda McKay astutely observed, 'She began to make career choices which deviated from the linear structure to which most concert pianists slavishly adhere.'[161] She joined the Bangor Trio, whose mission was to give concerts in Welsh schools. She decided not to enter the 1938 Ysaÿe competition in Brussels, opting instead to go on a paid concert tour playing for the singer Paul Robeson. Her classmate Moura Lympany from the Royal Academy of Music went in for the Ysaÿe competition, met Arthur Rubinstein there and came away with a promise to be represented by his concert management. Making use of similar strategies, several of Weir's classmates quickly climbed the career ladder, but she sidestepped it.

When the war came in 1939, she joined the Women's Auxiliary Air Force, apparently never thinking that as a skilled pianist she could have sought a musical role through which to contribute to the war effort. On the contrary – 'I kept it a deadly secret that I was a pianist because it was so marvellous not having to practise.'[162] Her knowledge of idiomatic German came to the attention of the authorities, and she was sent to work in intelligence. This took her to Cairo, Algiers and Italy, where at one point a bombed airfield in Rome led to an unusual way of arriving in the city: 'I think I am the only classical pianist in history who ever parachuted into Rome,' she said.[163]

After the war, Weir found it difficult to get well-paid concerts in London. When her father fell ill in Australia in 1954, she took it as a sign that she should go back. At first, her return was warmly greeted. But the stellar career predicted for her was not forthcoming in her homeland, and she was not the first pianist to find that the charm of being a child prodigy doesn't always translate into adult success. Moreover, at that time there was – rightly or wrongly – a widespread view that returning to Australia after overseas success was an admission of defeat. As her father's sole carer, Weir could not travel far from her home or for any length of time. When a male pianist left the Ormond Trio, Weir took his place, only to find that she was being paid one-tenth as much as her predecessor because 'women only needed pin-money'.[164]

She took up a piano lectureship at the Queensland Conservatorium, where her stimulating lessons had a huge influence on a new generation of Australian pianists. She started her 'Symphonic Safaris', taking students with orchestral instruments around Queensland in a big bus and performing informal concerts to remote communities. 'Surprise concerts in outback areas have often given untold joy,' she said, and many of the students involved in playing those concerts were profoundly influenced by the experience.[165]

In later years, when deafness limited her performing activities, Weir took to running community theatres, converting old churches and railway sidings into performance spaces, running a fish and chip shop and a grocery store, and raising money to send Australian music students overseas for performing experience. She was gifted enough to fulfil the hopes of the fans who touched the hem of her dress when she was a child, but her outlook on life – including a healthy dose of scepticism about the music profession – made it unlikely that she would ever choose the narrow path of the traditional concert pianist. With her commitment to making music accessible, her interest in collaborative music-making and her awareness of the deprivation in remote communities, she probably did more than her illustrious contemporaries to bring the joy of music into the lives of ordinary people.

ALICIA DE LARROCHA

Alicia de Larrocha (1923–2009) was a Catalan pianist widely recognised as one of the greatest of the twentieth century. Although her repertoire ranged from Scarlatti and Mozart to contemporary works, it was her advocacy of Spanish piano music by Granados, Albéniz, De Falla and Mompou that gave her career a special distinction.

De Larrocha was a small person, only four feet nine inches in height, but vigorous and strong. Much has been said about her having small hands, but this has to be seen in context. First of all, her hands were proportional to her size; she herself wouldn't have experienced her hands as 'small'. Secondly, she had an unusually long fifth finger, almost as long as the ring finger, which extended her reach. She also had an unusually wide stretch between the thumb and the index finger; when she stretched her hand fully, her thumb and her fifth finger formed virtually a straight line. So she had a big lateral stretch and worked to maintain it with exercises.

The bare facts about how wide an interval a pianist can stretch doesn't tell you as much as you might think. Firstly, there are many passages in piano music where rapid notes lie close together on the keyboard, requiring players to operate their fingers within a small space, and for those kinds of passages a smaller hand may even be an advantage. Secondly, it's not always the case that the notes of an interval, or chord if there are more than two notes, need to be sounded exactly together. In former times it was often the fashion to 'spread' the notes of a chord, or to allow a slight discontinuity between the timing of the two hands, which was considered to enhance the expressive effect. If a player can use lateral stretch (as De Larrocha could) to spread or roll a chord from one side to the other, or bring in a finger from the other hand to play one of the notes in a wide interval, then the size of the hand is less of an issue. This is in no way to belittle De Larrocha's fabulous technique, just to say that the smallness of her hand was probably less of a handicap than it has been made out to be.

Alicia de Larrocha came from a musical family. Both parents were pianists, as was her aunt, and her mother and aunt had been students of Enrique Granados at his piano academy in Barcelona. In due course, Granados handed over the academy to his pupil Frank Marshall (Spanish-born of English parents), who changed the name to Academia Marshall. When Alicia was only two, her aunt realised she was musical on hearing her picking out melodies and chords she had heard piano students play. She was said to have banged her head on the floor until her parents agreed to let her begin piano lessons. At the age of three, she began studying with Frank Marshall and gradually acquired a classical repertoire and an impressive technique. Her family was not pushy and concert invitations came her way without undue striving on anyone's part. She gave her first recital aged five and was heard by Arthur Rubinstein, who remained a friend and supporter. At the age of twelve she played Mozart's 'Coronation' concerto (in D major, K537) with the Madrid Symphony Orchestra. She did not encounter the Spanish repertoire that made her famous until she was an older teenager – asked about this later, she simply said that her teacher had not suggested it until then and it hadn't occurred to her to be interested. Once she encountered it, she understood its qualities – and its musical bone

ALICIA DE LARROCHA

structure – better than anyone. She once said, 'If you can't play Bach and Mozart correctly, you can't play Spanish music. The Spanish style is like Chopin mazurkas – free of melody, but solid at the bottom.'[166]

By the time she was twenty, her concerts in Spain were selling out. She did not, however, appear more widely in Europe until 1947, when she played in Lausanne, Switzerland, and started to be noticed internationally. In 1950 she performed Poulenc's concerto for two pianos in Barcelona, with the composer playing the second piano part. In 1953 she visited England, and the following year she played in the United States for the first time. In 1958 she married her fellow pianist Juan Torra, who gave up his own career in order to support her and took over many of the administrative tasks that underpin a concert pianist's schedule. He encouraged Alicia to tour abroad and volunteered to be a stay-at-home father when their two children were small. They jointly took over the directorship of the Academia Marshall after Frank Marshall died in 1959.

Once De Larrocha had acquired a top American agent in 1965, her career became intensely busy. She toured the US three times each year and made many recordings, particularly of Spanish piano music, which won all manner of awards – four Grammys, fourteen Grammy nominations, three Edison awards, two Grand Prix du Disque and so on. She became a great favourite in Japan and South Africa. Critics were bowled over by her alluring combination of warmth, energy, clarity and rhythmic vitality. She was very grounded, formidably equipped with technique yet also appealingly matter of fact and straightforward. Harold C. Schonberg, reviewing a concert at Hunter College for the *New York Times* in 1965, wrote that 'She has a technique that can honestly be classified as stupendous. This tiny Spanish woman is pianistically flawless with infallible fingers, brilliant sonorities, steady rhythm, everything. She plays with the strength of any of her male colleagues.'[167]

Unlike many pianists who use the pedal to cloak everything in a forgiving haze, she used the pedal very sparingly. In Spanish music, which often emulates the sounds of guitar, clapping, foot stamping, castanets and so on, she made every detail speak clearly. Listeners were entranced by the layers of texture they could hear in the music. Her way of playing was very natural and flexible, yet she somehow also imparted a feeling of classical restraint and elegance which took Spanish piano music beyond 'local colour' and upheld its essential seriousness. As her pupil Alberto Ráfols wrote, 'She never allowed the romanticism to slide into melodrama.'[168]

As well as being a champion of Spanish music, De Larrocha cultivated a large repertoire of concertos and recital pieces from Bach, Handel and Purcell through her beloved Mozart and Schumann to Brahms and Bartók, Debussy and Ravel. She was also a keen chamber musician, enjoying a partnership with the cellist Gaspar Cassadó, collaborations with string quartets and duo partnerships with the singers Victoria de los Ángeles, Montserrat Caballé and Pilar Lorengar.

When her husband died in 1982 she lost her principal supporter, but threw herself into her work and even increased her touring schedule, playing a hundred concerts a year in the 1980s and 1990s. At the age of eighty she decided to retire after an extraordinary career of seventy-five years.

Interviewed by Bob Sherman for WXQR radio in 1978, Alicia de Larrocha gave a very calm account of how her illustrious career had been built up. She declared she had 'never in my life asked for a concert'. How did her career happen then, the interviewer asked. She answered tranquilly that, well, someone had heard her somewhere . . . and invited her to play somewhere else . . . and then it kept happening! Sherman asked if she was pleased to be so busy now. She answered no, but a period of quiet time didn't seem to be on the horizon. 'Why not turn down some concert invitations, then?' She smiled and said she supposed she didn't have the strength to say no.[169]

It was clear that, although she was not ambitious in the usual sense, she simply loved playing the piano and would rather be doing that than anything else, even if it meant being far from home and family. Asked on one occasion when she realised she had become famous, she replied that she didn't know because she was too busy practising to notice what was happening in the outside world. In that respect she seems to have been rather like the Brazilian pianist Guiomar Novaes (p. 141), who similarly fell in love with the piano and let the wind take her where it would (which was all over the world). These days, when so many pianists compete for concert work with tireless efforts to promote their 'brand', it seems most unlikely that anyone could immerse themselves in practising, 'take no thought for the morrow' and end up with a spectacular world-class career, but it is nice to know that it can happen.

TATIANA NIKOLAYEVA

Tatiana Nikolayeva (1924–93) was a powerful Russian pianist closely associated with Shostakovich, who wrote his *Twenty-Four Preludes and Fugues* for her, and with the music of Bach, which she recorded with great success.

Nikolayeva was born in the year that Stalin came to power in the Soviet Union. Her mother was a professional pianist who had studied in Moscow with Alexander Goldenweiser, himself a friend of Scriabin, Rachmaninoff and Medtner. Tatiana in her turn became a pupil of Goldenweiser at the Moscow Conservatory, an institution with which she was associated for many years and where her name appears on the marble plaques of honour both as pianist and as composer. In 1950 she entered the Bach competition that was organised in Leipzig to mark the 200th anniversary of Bach's death. Shostakovich was on the jury and was impressed by the playing of this young woman from Moscow.

At this period, Shostakovich was still reeling from the official denunciation of his music under the so-called Zhdanov doctrine of 1948. Not only had his music been criticised as 'anti-democratic' and 'formalistic' (or abstract), but some of it had also been banned, and he had temporarily been removed from his position at the Moscow Conservatory. When he went to Leipzig he was still musing on the path that would bring him back into the artistic fold. Hearing Tatiana Nikolayeva play Bach preludes and fugues, he was inspired to write a collection of his own. Perhaps this gentle, thoughtful sort of music, inspired by the Baroque master, seemed a safe route for the moment.

Back in Moscow, Shostakovich took to writing a prelude or fugue every few days and summoning Nikolayeva to his apartment to try them out and discuss them. She too was composing at this period. Her own *Twenty-Four Concert Studies* date from 1951–3 and were probably composed in parallel with Shostakovich's preludes and fugues. Nikolayeva gave the premiere of Shostakovich's set in 1952 in Leningrad.

Stalin died in 1953, but his regime continued in other hands. Perhaps because of her early association with Shostakovich, Nikolayeva was never one of the top Soviet artists sent to perform abroad and it was not until late in her life that she was allowed to perform in the West. She started to teach at the Moscow Conservatory in 1959 and became a professor there in 1965. Her compositions grew to include a piano quintet, a piano sonata, a transcription for piano of Prokofiev's *Peter and the Wolf* and a piano concerto in the very unusual key of B major. Interestingly, the Russian composer Alexander Glazunov was one of the few who wrote a piano concerto in this key, and perhaps his was a model. Recognised for her devotion to the piano music of Shostakovich, she also became well known for her Bach playing, which was of a robust and full-toned character, using all the resources of the modern concert grand.

In her sixties, Tatiana Nikolayeva came to London and was a big hit with Proms audiences and beyond. By this time, some of the leading Russian (male) pianists were no longer dominating the scene: Emil Gilels had died, and Sviatoslav Richter only visited London occasionally. When Nikolayeva appeared on the platform looking like everyone's idea of their favourite Russian grandmother, stout and smiling, the British public took her to their hearts. She was received with equal warmth in the United States, where she died after suffering a brain haemorrhage on stage during a performance in San Francisco of one of Shostakovich's fugues. As the *Independent* said in its obituary, 'Everything radiated humility, generosity of spirit and, above all, happiness.'[170]

Her former student Nikolai Lugansky said of her, 'She was not a technician, although her technique was beyond question; she believed that technique was a response to a musical demand and that the important thing is how we think about music, how we listen to music.'[171]

YVONNE LORIOD

Yvonne Loriod (1924–2010) had an extraordinarily close musical and personal partnership with Olivier Messiaen, whose music she inspired, performed and recorded with great distinction for fifty years.

She was born in Houilles, near Paris, and began to learn the piano at the age of six. By fourteen, she had learned all the Bach preludes and fugues, all Beethoven's piano sonatas and all Mozart's piano concertos. She studied at the Paris Conservatoire, where her first piano and harmony teachers, both Jewish, were deported by the Nazis. In 1941, when he was released from a prisoner-of-war camp, composer Olivier Messiaen came to take over the harmony class. 'All the students waited eagerly for this new teacher to arrive,' Yvonne Loriod said.

> And finally he appeared with music case and badly swollen fingers, a result of his stay in the prisoner of war camp. He proceeded to the piano and produced the full score of Debussy's *Prélude à l'après-midi d'un faune* and began to play all the parts. The whole class was captivated and stunned and everyone immediately fell in love with him.[172]

Messiaen was an organist first and foremost and had already composed substantial organ works, but he quickly realised that he had an exceptional pianist in his class and began to write piano music with Loriod's technique in mind. At this point, Messiaen was married to the violinist Claire Delbos, who was suffering from a long illness and spent her last years in a sanatorium. Messiaen was not free to marry, but clearly felt close to his brilliant student. In 1943 he wrote his two-piano work *Visions de l'amen* for himself and Yvonne Loriod, allocating 'everything which is velocity, charm and sound quality' to her part while he took charge of 'everything which demands emotion and power'.[173] They gave the premiere in Paris while it was still occupied by the Germans. Two years later he wrote her the sparkling piano part in *Trois Petites Liturgies de la présence divine*. Any suggestion that he saw Loriod primarily as a purveyor of lightness and charm was, however, scotched by the colossal *Vingt Regards sur l'Enfant-Jésus*, which he wrote for her in 1945.

Loriod was still studying composition with Darius Milhaud, but she now decided to focus on being a pianist. Although she performed more than one 'complete Mozart concertos' cycle, she made her reputation primarily through contemporary music. Much of the new work by Boulez, Barraqué and Messiaen was of daunting technical complexity. Few pianists had summoned up the energy to learn it to performance standard, but Loriod tackled it all with huge commitment, giving the premieres of Boulez's second piano sonata (1950), *Structures II* (1961, in duo with Boulez), Barraqué's piano sonata (1957) and André Jolivet's second piano sonata (1959). She premiered all Messiaen's new piano music, including the many orchestral works that included a piano part for her; 'I always imagine her in the middle of the orchestra,' Messiaen said.[174]

Messiaen's first composition teacher, Paul Dukas, had told his students, 'Listen to the birds! They are great teachers.'[175] Messiaen took the instruction to heart, especially as he was already interested in birdsong, for him a kind of ideal, ego-less music. His interest in ornithology developed and he undertook constant trips around the world to record and transcribe the songs of exotic birds. In the 1950s his piano music was largely inspired by birds: *Réveil des oiseaux* (*Awakening of the Birds*), *Oiseaux exotiques* (*Exotic Birds*) and the *Catalogue d'oiseaux* (*Catalogue of Birds*) were all written for and premiered by Loriod. To the composer it seemed a delightful coincidence that Loriod sounds the same as *loriot*, the French name for the golden oriole.

In 1959 Messiaen's wife died, and he married Loriod in 1961. They gradually enlarged her apartment by buying up neighbouring flats and installing thick soundproofing so that they could play music at any hour. Messiaen lived in a rarefied world of imagination; Loriod had to be not only his muse but also his travel agent, manager and proofreader. She went along on his birdsong-collecting trips, wielding the tape recorder and getting up at first light to catch the dawn chorus. She became his editor, too, and spent two years on making a vocal score of his opera *St François d'Assise*. After Messiaen died, she even edited his 4,000-page *Traité de rhythme, de couleur, et d'ornithologie* (*Treatise on Rhythm, Colour and Ornithology*), and was probably the only person who could have done so with such deep authority.

From their earliest days together Messiaen was deeply appreciative of Loriod's pianistic skills. 'I have an extraordinary, marvellous, inspired interpreter whose brilliant technique and playing – in turn powerful, light, moving and coloured – suit my works exactly,' he said of her.[176] Those who knew the couple well said that Loriod's huge range of touch and command of tone colours – not to mention her appetite for work – inspired Messiaen to energise his style of writing for the piano. It is certain that without Loriod as an ideal and devoted interpreter, Messiaen would not have written so much or such fine piano music.

PHILIPPA SCHUYLER

Philippa Schuyler (1931–67) was an extraordinary child whose parents designed her for success even before she was conceived. Her story is intriguing and tragic.

Schuyler's father George was a Black American journalist, her mother Josephine a white, blonde Texan heiress who had been a 'bathing beauty' and was descended from a slave-owning family. George and Josephine believed that the white American race had become spiritually depleted and could best be strengthened if mixed-race couples had children. To prepare for this, Josephine spent several years purifying her body with special diets and spiritual exercises – to the dismay of her family, who broke off contact with her when they learned of her intentions. When Philippa was born in 1931, her mother put her on the same raw-food diet that she had followed. Even as a child, Philippa was eating not only raw vegetables but raw liver, raw steak and raw animal brains; her mother even had the cooker removed from their New York apartment so that nobody would be tempted to fry or bake anything. When they went to restaurants, Josephine made the startled waiters bring raw meat for her little girl to eat. Instead of sweets, Philippa was given slices of lemon.

She was intensively educated from early childhood and the results seemed to bear out Josephine's theories: Philippa could read and write by the age of two, had a huge vocabulary by three, and at the age of five was winning piano competitions with performances of her own compositions. Newspapers came to interview Josephine about how she had achieved it. Josephine did not indulge Philippa, hug or kiss her, but used to punish her with beatings if she did not follow her gruelling practice schedule. Philippa won so many prizes and became such a role model in the Black community that thousands of Black children were inspired to take up piano lessons. When she was only nine, she played two recitals at the New York World's Fair and Mayor LaGuardia declared that 19 June 1940 was to be called 'Philippa Duke Schuyler Day'. She was educated at home by private tutors and when she did attend school, she found she was far ahead of her contemporaries, who resented both her blackness and her superior educational level. She had a succession of piano teachers, who tended to distance themselves from the family when they became aware of the coercive nature of Josephine's project.

In her teenage years it became clear that Philippa's blackness was going to hold her back from total acceptance in the American arts world. For a while she switched to composing, and by the age of fifteen her works had been performed by the New York Philharmonic and the symphony orchestras of Chicago, San Francisco and Detroit. Composer Virgil Thomson heard her *Fairy Tale Symphony* in 1947 and said it was as interesting as the symphonies Mozart wrote at the same age. But around her thirteenth birthday, Philippa was shown the scrapbooks of newspaper cuttings her parents had compiled about her life. In article after article she read of how she had been in effect engineered as a prodigy, an experiment in genetics, nutrition and education. The realisation filled her with confusion and bitterness. She continued to practise and play concerts, but her devotion to piano-playing and fulfilling her parents' dreams was undermined. She began to wrestle with complicated thoughts about her identity and what she wanted from life.

In the 1950s she spent time in Central and South America, where she felt her mixed-race appearance was less of an issue, and she developed the idea of passing for white in certain contexts. She travelled to Africa and was shocked to see how African women were treated by their societies, yet she was also fascinated by African men, and this led her into some unhappy love affairs. In 1958 she undertook a huge world concert tour which ended with her 1959 Carnegie Hall debut, a glittering event attended by Leonard Bernstein. In the 1960s she renamed herself Felipa Monterro y Schuyler, at least for the purpose of playing in countries where she thought an 'Iberian' identity would help her. In her European tour of 1963 she performed as 'white' Felipa Monterro in France and Italy, but as 'Black' Philippa Schuyler in Germany.

Bizarrely, her father George came to espouse extreme right-wing views and, even more bizarrely, Philippa came to agree with him; father and daughter joined the John Birch Society, a right-wing group opposed to civil rights. She followed her father into the profession of journalism, gaining press accreditation. In 1966, she was invited to travel to South Vietnam to play the piano for American troops. The following year, aged thirty-five, she returned to Vietnam as a war correspondent for an American conservative newspaper. She joined a US Army mission to rescue Vietnamese orphans by helicopter, and was killed when the pilot lost control and crashed the helicopter into Da Nang Bay.

Today in Brooklyn, New York, the Philippa Schuyler School for the Gifted and Talented offers an arts-based education. For some years there has been talk of a film about Philippa's life, starring Alicia Keys, herself a talented and classically trained pianist, but it has not yet materialised.

So was Philippa a good pianist, or was her appeal based largely on her good looks and the audience's curiosity about her bizarre upbringing? Her tormented feelings about her life and purpose clearly tied her in emotional knots and made it impossible for music to flow through her in a simple way. Reviewers tended to think she was impressive in fast and dramatic pieces, less so in sensitive and lyrical ones. Archive recordings show that although she could play with great facility and finesse, there was a brittle, almost mechanical quality to her playing, a kind of emotional constriction – hardly surprising when one considers the love–hate relationship she had with the piano. It is a great pity that this intelligent girl was compelled to put her life at the service of her parents' eccentric theories.

ZHU XIAO-MEI

Zhu Xiao-Mei (born 1949) is a Chinese pianist whose studies were interrupted by Chairman Mao's Cultural Revolution, during which she was forced to spend five years as an agricultural worker in a remote province.

Today, China is the world's largest source of piano manufacturers, astonishing Western observers with the number of pianos being ordered by and produced for Chinese music conservatoires. The Chinese performer Lang Lang is one of the world's most successful classical pianists, inspiring millions of children to want to learn the instrument. Yuja Wang has an enormous performing career, and a huge social media following, and appears on the cover of fashion magazines. Young Chinese pianists are winning international competitions. Western music may have been banned during the Cultural Revolution, but new generations have worked up a huge appetite – and aptitude – for this music. Being able to play the piano is a high-status accomplishment in today's China, and some Chinese pianists are media stars and fashion ambassadors. Therefore it is poignant to learn about the experience of Zhu Xiao-Mei, who came of age in China at a time – not so long ago – when the piano and its Western repertoire were anathema to the communist regime.

Zhu Xiao-Mei was born in Shanghai in 1949 and was already playing the piano on Beijing radio and television at the age of eight. In 1966, on the verge of her full-time studies, Chairman Mao launched his Cultural Revolution, closing schools and universities and outlawing Western music alongside much else. Staff and students of the Shanghai Conservatory were targeted for their treacherous allegiance to Western music, and during the ensuing decade, twenty musicians from the Conservatory lost their lives. The director of the Conservatory was physically abused on public television for defending the 'dirty' music of Claude Debussy. Hundreds of pianos at the Conservatory were aggressively smashed up. The members of Zhu Xiao-Mei's family were separated and sent to different work camps for 're-education'; she herself was sent to Hebei province and spent five years doing manual labour. Her experience was typical of young Chinese people of her age.

Zhu had already formed a deep attachment to the keyboard music of Bach and she managed to take a copy of the *Goldberg Variations* to the re-education camp with her, copying it out by hand to share with other secret music lovers. At times, she had access to a broken-down old piano in an outbuilding, on which she could occasionally practise when it was not too cold. After her years in the countryside she returned to Beijing but found it difficult to catch up on her missing years of piano tuition. Mao died in 1976 and there was soon some relaxation of his regime. Three years later, the American violinist Isaac Stern visited China, and with his assistance, Zhu obtained a visa to study for a master's degree at the New England Conservatory in Boston, financing her study by taking on cleaning jobs.

Just before her United States visa was due to run out, she got the chance to move to France to take up a teaching job. In Paris she had no instrument of her own but used to practise in various locations where she could borrow a piano. Slowly various friends and patrons became aware of her artistic skill and tried to find performing opportunities for her. Her first Paris concert was in 1994 at the Théâtre de la Ville; its success led to other concert offers. Her repertoire included Scarlatti, Haydn, Mozart, Beethoven, Schubert and Schumann, but Bach remained her first love and gradually his music asserted itself as the focus of her performances. In recent years, she has recorded a large number of Bach's keyboard works but has become particularly known for her interpretation of the *Goldberg Variations*. This cornerstone work has inspired some iconic recordings, but Zhu Xiao-Mei's has been praised as among the best. She still lives a frugal life in Paris and dislikes using her background story to garner publicity. In 2014 she went back, with some misgivings, to visit China, where she was given the title of professor emerita at the Beijing Conservatory. Unable to forget her own years of suffering, she now tries to help young musicians. As she says, 'The worst of all privations is the closure of schools and universities and the actual denial of an education.'[177] She may be considered a kind of bridge between the generation of Chinese pianists forbidden to play Western music and today's young Chinese pianists who move with such ease and success between East and West.

Zhu has said that in Bach's *Goldberg Variations* she has found 'all that is needed to live'. For her it is meaningful that Bach's name, the German word for 'stream' or 'brook', is synonymous with water. She values the way that Bach gives each musical line its own integrity, allowing it to combine with or come into contact with other lines without losing its individual power or energy. When the Aria, or opening theme, comes back at the very end of the thirty variations, she likens this to the principle of 'return' which the ancient Chinese Taoist philosopher Laotzi (formerly known as Lao Tzu) described as fundamental to 'the movement of the Way'; the return of the beginning is a sign of hope and renewal.[178] She likes to play Bach on a modern Steinway, using a full and mellow tone, her hands in deep contact with the keys. Her personal history adds an extra layer of meaning to Bach's music, one that gives her performances an intensely inward quality.

JAZZ AND LIGHT-MUSIC PIANISTS

LOVIE AUSTIN

Lovie Austin, née Cora Taylor (1887–1972), is the first of several examples in this book of a type of pianist new in the early twentieth century: the jazz pianist. Jazz arose in the late nineteenth and early twentieth centuries from Black communities in the United States, in the first instance from the plantations of the South, where enslaved people from Africa had been brought to work. It drew on African songs and rhythms as well as European harmonies, and became an increasingly rich cultural heritage as it spread further afield and gathered in other ingredients.

Austin was one of the first women pianists to make an impact on the US jazz scene in an era when it was the norm for women to sing and for men to play instruments (a tradition that has not entirely faded). The life of a blues or jazz pianist was, of course, very different from the life of the classical pianists we've been talking about, and it's striking to reflect on the difference between Lovie Austin's career and those of her classical-pianist contemporaries.

One of the main differences was that most jazz pianists were not playing notated music – at least, not specified note by note as classical compositions generally are. In jazz there was almost always an element of improvisation and flexibility. In this sense, jazz kept alive a tradition of improvising that was once commonplace in classical music but which faded as the works of the composer became the pinnacle of the art form during the nineteenth century. Jazz had many composers, but their compositions were often musical cells (such as songs) which they and fellow players would build up into colourful, large-scale mosaics. Jazz pianists, particularly in the early days, usually performed in bars, brothels, theatres and clubs with upright pianos rather than in concert halls with grand pianos. Listeners were more likely to wander in and out during a 'set', or to talk and drink during the playing. Music was provided for background entertainment and jazz musicians were usually not well paid, though many blues and jazz pianists – some classically trained, some self-taught – were so good that they became the main attraction, often making the venues famous.

Lovie Austin was from a large African American family in Chattanooga, Tennessee. Undaunted by racist and sexist prejudices, Lovie studied music theory at Roger Williams University in Nashville and at Knoxville College. She began professional life as a vaudeville musician, touring American cities under the auspices of TOBA, the Theatre Owners' Booking Association, whose venues were the only theatres to allow unsegregated audiences in the American South. Austin was unusual on the jazz scene because as well as being a fine pianist she was trained to analyse harmonies, could notate music, and was an excellent sight-reader at a time when many jazz musicians played by ear. There's nothing inferior about playing by ear, as many jazz musicians have proved, but Austin's formal training gave her a degree of power when it came to making a living.

When the increasingly disreputable Storyville entertainment district of New Orleans was closed down in 1917, many musicians drifted towards Chicago in search of work and Austin was swept along in that current. She formed and directed her own band, the

LOVIE AUSTIN

Blues Serenaders, and her musical training enabled her to compose and make musical arrangements for the group. The Serenaders accompanied many leading singers: Ma Rainey, Ethel Waters, Ida Cox and Austin's lifelong friend Alberta Hunter, with whom she wrote 'Downhearted Blues', a song made famous by Bessie Smith. With other songs like 'Chirping the Blues', 'Bama Bound Blues' and 'Bo-Weavil Blues', Austin earned enough to buy a Stutz Bearcat, a glamorous open sports car with leopard-print upholstery, in which she liked to be seen driving about Chicago.

She also worked as a session musician for Paramount Records, playing on many recordings in the 1920s and 1930s and earning royalties for music she had composed or arranged. However, when Paramount Records was sold in 1935, the cheques stopped coming and Austin found that the rights to her songs had been sold on without her knowledge. She became music director at the Monogram Theater in Chicago ('a rinky-dink dump', according to Ethel Waters: 'You had to dress way downstairs with the stoker and come up to the stage climbing slave-ship stairs. While working there I took sick from the migraine headaches I'd had on and off for years. The air was very bad down there where the stoker was').[1] For over twenty years she worked there, accompanying visiting musicians, acting as a talent scout for emerging artists and, on occasion, transcribing what they played so that it could be published as sheet music. The pianist Jelly Roll Morton was one who benefited from her transcription skills.

Jazz pianist Mary Lou Williams remembered the first time she heard Lovie Austin:

> Now that woman really inspired me. No-one had been able to imitate her incredible ability to make music. My brother-in-law took me to see her when I was very young, seven or eight years old ... We entered the theatre and there was this woman, sitting up there with her legs crossed, cigarette in her mouth, playing with her left hand and writing with her right for the next act. Now I

saw that myself! Nobody does that! ... You see, during that period we didn't have many readers [meaning people who could read music notation] and this woman was a master reader.[2]

'Wow! I never forgot this episode,' said Williams. 'My entire concept was based on the few times I was around Austin. She was a fabulous woman and a fabulous musician too. I don't believe there's a woman around now who could compete with her. She was a greater talent than many of the men of this period.'

As the swing era took over from the blues, Austin's main sources of work began to dry up. She spent the Second World War working as a security inspector for a naval munitions firm. After the war, she worked as a dance-school pianist, living in obscurity until a final recording with Alberta Hunter in 1961 revived interest in her back catalogue. It was Hunter who later exhorted us, 'Never forget Lovie Austin.'[3]

Austin's piano style can be heard on archive recordings. She was a vigorous, laconic yet highly rhythmic player who didn't use much pedal and whose style has been described as masculine. However, although she was usually the band leader, composer or arranger (all more often masculine roles), she didn't take the opportunity to give herself piano solos; she preferred to provide crisp piano commentary and support in the background. Maybe this was just her temperament, or perhaps she felt that reticence was appropriate for a woman.

How jazz pianists saw themselves and were seen at this period is an intriguing question. Jelly Roll Morton, recalling his days of playing blues in New Orleans's red-light district in the first few decades of the twentieth century, made this startling comment to folk music collector Alan Lomax in the 1930s: 'Of course, when a man played piano, the stamp was on him for life, the femininity stamp, and I didn't want that on, so of course when I started playing, the songs were kind of smutty a bit.'[4] By this he seems to mean that playing blues with raunchy lyrics was enough to fend off any suggestion of un-masculinity.

Morton's association of piano-playing with 'femininity' is mysterious. Was it to do with the fact that the piano had by then become a popular parlour instrument, with a repertoire of pretty and sentimental pieces written for and played mostly by women? Was it because blues pianists often stayed in the background, as women were supposed to do, allowing 'soloists' to shine? Whatever the reason, the link between the piano and any perceived 'femininity' was severed as jazz became internationally popular. The vast majority of famous jazz pianists have been men, their style far from 'feminine', unless one thinks of decorative and virtuosic piano runs as somehow un-masculine. Ironically, later in the century, many female jazz pianists 'got the masculinity stamp' simply by being assertive or rhythmical, as the style often demands. Clearly there is an androgynous quality to jazz piano-playing, which is probably part of its enduring fascination.

RAIE DA COSTA

Raie da Costa (1905–34) was a very gifted pianist who died at the age of only twenty-nine. The child of a white Portuguese family, she grew up in Cape Town, South Africa, where she was classically trained and by the age of eighteen was performing Beethoven's 'Emperor' concerto with the Cape Town Municipal Orchestra. At nineteen she travelled to London to study with Tobias Matthay (Myra Hess's teacher – see p. 137), who had his own piano school in Wimpole Street. Matthay had a glittering cast of students, but he recognised Raie da Costa as a major talent. She was soon impressing audiences with her scintillating performances of Chopin and Liszt. Raie loved classical music but was also drawn to 'syncopated' and 'novelty' piano music of the type that the English pianist Billy Mayerl was performing with great success at the Savoy Hotel.

Finding it hard to make headway as a classical artist, Da Costa started playing 'novelty' piano music and devising her own virtuoso elaborations of popular songs by Gershwin, Cole Porter and Jerome Kern. She had large hands, an advantage when playing 'stride' piano style and putting down widely spaced chunky chords in the bass. Her career in popular music took off like a rocket. Among the stars of the Tobias Matthay Piano School she may have been only one of many, but on the popular-music scene she stood out as extraordinary. Her classical technique, particularly her flashing scales and sparkling arpeggios, gave her arrangements a thrilling quality. She sometimes played duets with Billy Mayerl, who was famous for his nonchalantly rapid fingerwork; Raie da Costa's piano technique was probably even more highly developed.

Just as Billy Mayerl had got into trouble as a student at Trinity College of Music in London when he let slip that he liked to play ragtime and syncopated music, Da Costa found herself somewhat alienated from the serious-minded piano class at the Tobias Matthay School. Not only was she 'slumming it' in their eyes by playing novelty piano music, but she was a *woman* slumming it, which was even less respectable. No matter: soon she was recording for HMV Parlophone and the BBC and was even shown on Pathé newsreels in the cinema, billed as 'a famous artiste known to millions of listeners'. In her long satin gown and outsize sleeve decorations made of feathers, she played pieces like her own *Fairies' Gavotte*, frequently turning to smile at the camera, a technique not used in classical piano. Innumerable stage shows, clubs and hotels booked her to perform 'a spot', and soon she was far busier than she would ever have been as a classical artist (and probably earning more).

She did not stop loving the classical repertoire she grew up with, however, and sometimes smuggled a classical piece into her popular sets. Indeed, in 1929 she went into the studio to record Liszt's *Rigoletto Paraphrase*, a now rare recording that makes her artistry very clear. In 1930 she published her *Modernistic Pieces for the Piano*, incorporating waltz and foxtrot episodes. Her schedule became so busy that she complained, 'My life has been one ceaseless rush from engagement to engagement. I have played somewhere for somebody every single day, on the variety halls, recording, official entertaining – until I almost begin to eat, sleep and drink syncopation.'[5]

Her recording career only lasted six years, from the age of twenty-three to twenty-nine, but in that short period she made a hundred recordings. Archive clips (available on YouTube) show her striking appearance, tall, thin and intense-looking, almost like one of the literary Sitwell family. When she was only twenty-nine and on the verge of becoming the leading light-music pianist of the day, she died from complications after an appendix operation. This was a great loss to popular music. Raie da Costa is an unusual example of a pianist who performed at the highest level in both classical *and* popular styles.

MARY LOU WILLIAMS

Mary Lou Williams, née Mary Elfrieda Scruggs (1910–81), was an African American pianist whose versatility and resourcefulness enabled her to remain a major figure throughout several jazz eras. She was one of the first women to found her own record company and publishing company, and the first jazz musician to compose sacred choral music. She played an important role in promoting the understanding of jazz as an art form.

Mary Lou was an observant child who could easily work out how to do things by watching others. 'I think I could build a clock just from watching,' she once said.[6] She learned to play the piano by copying her mother, who played by ear. The family was friendly with several professional musicians and the young Mary liked to imitate the powerful 'stride' piano style of the Atlanta pianist Jack Howard. Mary's stepfather bought a player piano, and she learned its repertoire of pieces simply by pressing her fingers down on the keys that went down as the piano roll played, until she had memorised the patterns. Relatives gave her money to play them Irish tunes and classical numbers, and sometimes sneaked her into bars to hear live jazz. Her playing was cherished by neighbours, who commented that they were less likely to get bricks thrown through their windows if Mary was playing the piano. Soon she was spending all day at the piano if she had the chance. 'The piano was just a natural place for me to be,' she said.[7] 'Kids would come to call for me – my half-brother would come over, he was about two years younger, he'd come over to play with me – but I'd be busy at the piano. Sometimes I'd stop and go and play with him a little while, and then I'd come back in to the piano, getting my own sounds, and I've been doing that all my life.'[8]

In her teenage years, Mary married the saxophone player John Williams and moved with him to Kansas, where he joined Andy Kirk's band Clouds of Joy in 1928. As the band already had a pianist, Mary was employed to drive the van, but soon she was 'sitting in' as a pianist with the group. 'The house would go in an uproar because although I was so tiny, I was playing heavy like a man,' she recalled.[9] Watching Andy Kirk at work, she became interested in composing. Kirk showed her how to notate music and she learned quickly. The Kirk band was a leading exponent of the style known as Kansas City swing. By the 1930s, Mary was composing tunes and doing arrangements for all the major big bands – Louis Armstrong, Jack Dorsey, Benny Goodman, Jimmie Lunceford. Two of her songs from this period, 'Roll 'Em' and 'What's Your Story Morning Glory', were huge hits for Goodman and Lunceford.

Mary Lou Williams later claimed that she never felt disadvantaged by being a woman in a male-dominated profession, but it's clear that she had exceptional self-possession. Her male colleagues – particularly Art Tatum – always sought her out to play with them in after-hours sessions. In 1941, Williams moved to New York, where she had a long-running engagement to play at Café Society Downtown. Her apartment in Hamilton Terrace became the meeting place for many jazz musicians, including Dizzy Gillespie, Miles

Davis, Charlie Parker and her piano colleagues Bud Powell and Thelonious Monk, who would seek her advice on their compositions. Perhaps inspired by the experimentation going on in classical music – such as bitonality and other new kinds of dissonance – they were interested in finding new directions for jazz, to free it from being tied to endlessly repeating chord charts and simple harmonies. When her friends had finished playing their money-making gigs at various bars and clubs, they would often gather at Williams's place to try out new sounds. In these late-night jam sessions, with Mary demonstrating innovative chords to the others, the concept of bebop was formed. She was ready for these leaps into the new: 'I experiment to keep up with what's going on,' she once said. 'I even keep a little ahead of them, like a mirror that shows what is going to happen next.'[10] In 1945 she wrote her *Zodiac Suite*, twelve movements based on the personalities of jazz musician friends born under different signs of the zodiac. Some of the movements were improvised live on her radio show, the *Mary Lou Williams Piano Workshop*. Later, she scored the suite for piano and orchestra and performed it with the New York Philharmonic.

It was during the bebop (or bop) era that Williams felt a desire for a more solid piano technique, so she went to a Russian concert pianist for lessons. This experiment was short-lived. 'When I began to realise I might lose some of the things Tatum gave me – like controlling the keyboard with my hands – I ran.'[11] This remark hints at fascinating insights. What could she have meant? Surely all pianists 'control the keyboard with their hands'? Tatum played with his hands close to the keys – perhaps Williams felt that classical technique involved expressive movements that would lessen her sense of contact with the keys. She was scathing of pianists who played handfuls of unnecessary notes. 'The only time we'd do all that running up and down the keyboard was when we were lost and had stopped thinking,' she said.

In the 1950s Williams became disillusioned with the jazz scene. Famously, she walked off the stage when playing at Le Boeuf sur le

Toit, a café in Paris, in 1954, and retreated from the profession for several years. Fellow jazz pianist Hazel Scott, on a visit to Paris, found Williams at a low point and counselled her to turn to religion for consolation. After long reflection, Williams did so. One of the outcomes of this experience was that she started writing sacred music in jazz language; she composed three masses, and a hymn to St Martin de Porres which became widely known on her 1964 album *Black Christ of the Andes*. She became deeply involved in charity work, prioritising that over her musical career. But she did not disappear from the jazz world: Dizzy Gillespie invited her to play with his band at the Newport Jazz Festival in 1957, and in 1958 she was one of the few women included in the famous photograph of fifty-seven great jazz musicians, 'A Great Day in Harlem', taken by Art Kane for *Esquire* magazine.

In later life, Williams became an artist in residence and a revered teacher at Duke University in North Carolina as well as a broadcaster and mentor to young artists. She started a foundation to promote the public understanding of jazz as an art form and was given many honorary awards. Her intelligence shone in her answer to a question from an interviewer: 'Do you do much practising now?' 'Yes, with my mind,' Williams answered. 'My mind moves my fingers.'[12]

WINIFRED ATWELL

Winifred Atwell (1914–83) was a Trinidadian pianist, the first Black artist to sell a million records in the UK, the first to have a number one hit in the UK singles chart and, to date, the only female instrumentalist to do so. In the 1950s she was by far the biggest-selling pianist of her time, enjoying huge popularity in the UK and later even more so in Australia. Her boogie-woogie records and copies of the sheet music sold in their millions.

As a child growing up in Trinidad Atwell learned the piano and often played for American airmen on the Piarco air force base. There she encountered the boogie-woogie piano style, then popular in America, and quickly learned to play it, composing *Piarco Boogie* to entertain the servicemen.

Her ambition was to become a classical pianist. In her early thirties she went first to New York to study piano, and then to London, where in 1946 she gained a place at the Royal Academy of Music and excelled in her exams. Like Billy Mayerl and Raie da Costa a few years earlier, Winifred slipped away to play ragtime and boogie in clubs and hotels in the evenings to earn some money. It rapidly became evident that this offered a speedier route to success. She married a stage comedian, Lew Levisohn, who gave up his career to manage hers.

Soon they had developed the stage act that made Atwell famous. It involved a two-part performance with her first appearing in a dignified concert gown and playing classics on a highly polished grand piano, then announcing that she was going to play 'my other piano' and sitting down at a honky-tonk upright with its front panel removed, exposing the mechanism. Here she would delight the audience by bursting into boogie-woogie numbers such as *Black and White Rag* (a 1908 number by George Botsford), which started a honky-tonk craze in Britain and was used as the theme tune for the BBC's *Pot Black* snooker programme. The sight of Atwell in her concert gown, winking at the camera as she threw herself into her vigorous boogie-woogies, was warmly received by everyone, including the queen and Princess Margaret at the Royal Variety Show in 1952. Atwell bought herself a Cadillac, which became a familiar sight in Brixton. In the 1950s she even opened a beauty salon for Black women, catering to the women of the *Windrush* generation.

For the rest of the decade Winifred Atwell reigned over the popular-music scene, fronting her own television shows, acquiring 50,000 members of her fan club and touring with her 'other piano', which was said to have travelled half a million miles by air during her career, touching down in the Sydney Opera House and a Las Vegas hotel among others. Her hits included 1954's 'Let's Have Another Party!', which spent five weeks at number one in the UK charts, and 'The Poor People of Paris', which spent three weeks at number one in 1956. Her love of classical music led her to extract the eighteenth variation (the slow, romantic one) from Rachmaninoff's *Rhapsody on a Theme of Paganini* and record it as a single, 'The Story of Three Loves', which many fans assumed she had written herself. In 1955 she was the soloist in one of the first stereo classical recordings in the UK, playing Grieg's piano concerto with the London Philharmonic Orchestra – though her favourite drummer recalled that 'that took an awful lot of guts, and she had to practise like crazy to get up to it'.[13] At this point, her hands were insured for £40,000, a fortune in the 1950s. Rumour had it that one of the conditions of the policy was that she must never do the washing up.

Her tours of Australia were phenomenally successful and inspired her to settle there in the 1970s. For her television shows in Sydney she put together a huge wardrobe of glamorous concert gowns – thirty-nine dresses and twenty-six sets of jewellery. She spoke out against the racism meted out to Australian Aborigines but denied that she herself had experienced racism, and claimed that the public had always spoiled her. 'My money can buy me minks, diamonds and Cadillacs,' she once said. 'Maybe it buys me the tolerance and friendship of white people too? I prefer not to think so – but perhaps it does.'[14]

Winifred Atwell's use of two contrasting pianos, one 'serious' and one 'fun', raises interesting questions about how classical and popular music are presented. There is no doubt that the heart of her act, the one that everyone was waiting for, was when she crossed the floor from the grand piano to the old upright with her fans' initials scratched on the case. The honky-tonk was deliberately de-tuned so that it had the jangling sound of a pub piano. The implication was clear. Enough of being serious – let's have a party!

As she clattered cheerfully around on her 'other piano', dressed somewhat incongruously in a regal concert gown, Atwell would turn to the camera, smiling widely. As noted in the case of Raie da Costa (p. 185), it is quite tricky to play virtuosic piano music while turning your head through ninety degrees, because it prevents you from orienting yourself by looking at the keys, and risks disturbing your balance. Atwell had a wonderful smile, but now and then on archive clips one can see her smile freeze for a second as she has to concentrate on getting through a tricky passage of music. The contrast between her demeanour as a serious classical performer and her physical vocabulary as a fun-loving honky-tonk pianist illustrates the conventions that grew up with each style.

Winifred Atwell didn't improvise – she played 'novelty' pieces she had learned from notation.[15] Not being an improviser, she was never really a part of the jazz world, and she moved away from the classical one, creating a composite career which was hard to categorise. In terms of money, popularity and audience numbers she was far more successful than her classical contemporaries, yet when new kinds of popular music swept the world in the 1960s, her 'novelty' piano style passed out of fashion and has left only a faint trace on music history.

HAZEL SCOTT

Hazel Scott (1920–81) was the first Black performer to have her own nationally syndicated TV show in the United States and the first to have it written into her contracts that she would not perform for segregated audiences. Her glittering career was halted by clashes with the House Un-American Activities Committee during the McCarthy era of the 1950s. Of all the women I mentioned in my book *The Piano: A History in 100 Pieces*, the one whose archive clips provoked the most joyful surprise among my readers was the glorious Hazel Scott. 'Why had I never heard of her?' people asked.

Hazel Scott was born in Trinidad but immigrated with her mother to Harlem in New York when she was four. Her mother, Alma Long Scott, was a professional pianist, at one point a member of Lil Hardin Armstrong's band, and later a band leader herself. When she arrived in Harlem, however, Alma was forced to take a job as a maid to make ends meet. Young Hazel showed precocious talent for the piano, auditioning for the Juilliard School at the age of eight (when most applicants were twice that age). Although she was too young to be formally accepted, one of the piano professors, Paul Wagner, agreed to teach her privately. When she was a teenager, Hazel had her own radio show as a result of winning a local competition. She developed a classical repertoire and a fine technique which she put to splendid use when she switched to playing popular music. At the age of nineteen she got a job with Café Society, one of the first jazz venues to welcome a racially mixed audience. She entertained customers with boogie-woogie-flavoured versions of Chopin waltzes, Bach inventions and Liszt Hungarian rhapsodies, cheeky adaptations that showed her rebellious spirit.

Hazel was beautiful as well as brilliant, and before long she was being courted by Hollywood. Film producers wanted to cast her in roles where she would have a cameo opportunity to play a musical number, but these turned out to be roles of Black maids and washerwomen, and Hazel refused to play them. She did, however, appear in several successful films in the 1940s, listed in the credits as 'Hazel Scott as Herself'. By 1945, she was earning the equivalent of $1 million a year from records such as *Bach to Boogie*. In that year, too, she married the charismatic Adam Clayton Powell, the first Black congressman from New York. Both were stars in their respective fields, and their wedding (complete with wedding cake in the shape of the White House) attracted a scrum of press photographers and so many well-wishers that a police guard was required.

1950 was a dramatic year in Scott's life. She became the first Black performer to have her own nationally syndicated television show in America, with three fifteen-minute weekly shows in which she both played piano and sang vocals. Just as she was about to settle into national prominence, she was named in the notorious 'Red Channels' booklet, which purported to reveal the names of communist sympathisers in the entertainment industry. Scott was not a communist but her egalitarian views had been noted. Ignoring her husband's advice, she volunteered to appear in front of the House Un-American Activities Committee (HUAC) to answer the charge that she had performed for organisations with communist affiliations. She explained to them that when she was booked to perform somewhere, there was no way she could know the promoters' political affiliations, but the Committee was unconvinced. Weeks later, her TV show was cancelled and her concert bookings started to evaporate. Her husband had already requested her to stop playing in nightclubs because he felt it was incompatible with his image as a respectable congressman, so Hazel had few avenues left.

Before long her marriage had broken down, and for a while, so did her mental health. In 1957 she went to live in Paris, where several Black American artists were living. Her apartment on the Right Bank became a sort of salon where fellow musicians such as Lester Young, Dizzy Gillespie and Mary Lou Williams (see p. 187) would hang out. During her decade in Paris, Scott recuperated and continued her commitment to civil rights activism. In 1963 she joined the author James Baldwin on a march to the United States embassy in Paris in support of the March on Washington, the demonstration at which Dr Martin Luther King delivered his famous 'I Have a Dream' speech. In 1967 she returned to New York, but the public's taste in music had changed. Motown and British pop music such as the Beatles were all the rage. Scott continued to play occasionally in nightclubs and on daytime television, but never recovered the momentum of her Café Society years.

Hazel Scott's 1955 trio album *Relaxed Piano Sounds*, with bassist Charlie Mingus and drummer Max Roach for the Debut label, has come to be considered one of the best jazz albums of the twentieth century. Made in the fallow years after her bruising encounter with HUAC, it is a glimpse of Hazel in quieter mood. For sheer élan, her earlier performances – such as 'Black and White Are Beautiful' or the film reel she recorded for the troops during the Second World War, singing songs like 'It's Gonna Be a Great Day' – are irresistible.

NINA SIMONE

Nina Simone, originally Eunice Waymon (1933–2003), wanted to be a classical pianist, but events propelled her into popular music instead, and into a life of civil rights activism.

Eunice spent her childhood in the town of Tryon in North Carolina. Her mother was both a Methodist minister and a domestic worker employed by a white family. Eunice's musicality was evident to her family from her earliest years, when she began picking out hymn tunes on the piano. Soon she was playing piano in her mother's church services; to spare her precious hands, her family exempted her from washing dishes and other housework. Her talent was noticed by her mother's employer, who paid for Eunice to have piano lessons with a local white teacher, Muriel Mazzanovich.

Eunice developed a deep affection for the music of Bach, Beethoven, Schubert and Chopin. At the age of twelve, she gave a classical piano recital in her mother's church. This was a decisive experience. Her parents were seated happily in the front row when she came in to play. However, she spotted an usher asking her parents to move to the back of the church so that a white couple could sit in their seats at the front. Eunice refused to play until her parents were moved back to their original seats, and she got her way.

When she was old enough to audition for the prestigious Curtis Institute in Philadelphia, her community collected enough money for her to have preparatory lessons at the Juilliard School in New York. Her unsuccessful audition for the Curtis Institute was another turning point in her life. 'I was rejected because I was Black,' she told an interviewer in 1993, and this belief became a cornerstone of her activism.[16] In later years, music historians tried to establish the truth of the story. It appears that in the year Eunice auditioned, there were seventy-two pianists applying for only three places. So, although she was turned down, so were sixty-eight other young pianists, and who knows? Eunice may have been number four on the list. In any case, she felt she had been rejected by the classical world she had intended to join. She started to move towards the world of popular music.

In 1954 she got a job playing piano at Atlantic City's Midtown Bar and Grill, where she began with a potpourri of classical numbers and gospel tunes, but the proprietor told her she'd have to sing as well, if she wanted to keep the job. This was when she discovered how to use her remarkable singing voice, which brought her a whole new audience. Her voice was low and could be harsh and rasping but also sultry and expressive; as she said herself, 'What I was interested in was conveying an emotional message, which means using everything you've got inside you, sometimes to make a note; or if you have to strain to sing, you sing. So sometimes I sound like gravel, and sometimes I sound like coffee and cream.'[17] She also decided to change her name. Knowing how distressed her deeply religious mother would be to know she was playing 'the devil's music' in a bar, she disguised her activities by taking the name Nina Simone – Nina, apparently, after a nickname her then boyfriend had for her, and Simone after the French film actress Simone Signoret. Soon she was being invited to play in leading jazz clubs and nightclubs in major US cities. Despite her renown as a singer, she always sat at the piano and often incorporated classical references into her songs, using classical technique to deepen the textures. Her recording of Gershwin's 'I Loves You, Porgy' was a hit in 1959. 'Saying what sort of music I played gave the critics problems because there was something from everything in there, but it also meant I was appreciated across the board – by jazz, folk, pop and blues fans as well as admirers of classical music,' she recalled.[18]

In the 1960s she became friendly with a group of Black activists including James Baldwin, Langston Hughes and the playwright Lorraine Hansberry, who continually prompted her to ask herself what she could do for 'the cause'. She also married New York police detective Andrew Stroud, who became her manager and the father of her daughter Lisa, born in 1962. Many years later it was revealed that Andrew Stroud had been physically and psychologically violent towards her.

1963 was another decisive year. In that year, Simone played Carnegie Hall, but she played it as a jazz singer, rather than with the classical recital she had once imagined herself giving there. The poster contained a quirky little poem about her by Langston Hughes: 'The letters l-i-v-e that spell LIVE mean exactly the same as the letters N-i-n-a that spell NINA. As for that word SIMONE – be cool, Jack, be cool!'[19]

That was the year of the famous March on Washington, the huge demonstration calling for civil rights for Black people. The same year, civil rights activist Medgar Evers was murdered in Jackson, Mississippi, and several Black girls were killed in the bombing of a church in Birmingham, Alabama. 'In a rush of fury, rage and determination',[20] Simone wrote the song 'Mississippi Goddamn', expressing her anger at the treatment of Black people and calling for immediate change: 'My people just about due.' The song caused a furore, copies of the record being broken and posted back in pieces to the record company by angry radio-station executives. However, it marked Simone's transformation into a publicly recognised spokesperson for Black rights. From then on, her songs often included a political element, to which her hard-edged, passionate voice gave perfect expression.

Dr Martin Luther King was assassinated in 1968 and his death sparked a sense of disillusionment. Simone's album *'Nuff Said*, recorded shortly after Dr King's death, includes a lament for him and an impatient call for freedom, 'I Ain't Got No/I Got Life'. She lost faith in the United States and went to live first in Barbados, then Liberia, then Switzerland, the Netherlands and finally France. During these extended travels her mental health became increasingly fragile. She still had the commanding stage presence and improvisatory skill that drew so many fans to her concerts, but she took to turning up extremely late for performances or not turning up at all. On stage, she was given to outbursts of temper and swearing. All these were later thought to have been symptoms of bipolar disorder, not diagnosed until the late 1980s.

One legacy of Simone's classical training was that she wanted her audiences to be quiet when she was performing – not for her the traditional jazz musician's battle to prevail over background noises. Her love of Bach surfaced frequently in her song arrangements. The delicious 'My Baby Just Cares for Me', made famous in Europe when it was used in a perfume commercial in 1987, features a loping

Bach-flavoured piano solo, which she often extended in live performances. 'Love Me or Leave Me' has a candid homage to Bach's keyboard music in the middle, while 'For All We Know' of 1961 is a beautiful Bach-inspired aria, Simone for once not in defiant mood but floating her melody line above delicate Baroque piano tracery, her expression far away as if remembering her mother's church services.

FURTHER PERSPECTIVES

The fifty women pianists in this book are just a selection of all those I might have included. There have been many others who attempted public careers. Some were successful, some prospered for a time and then faded, some put their careers on hold when they married, others found the struggle against convention and prejudice too much. There were a number of interesting women pianists who lived in the shadow of their much more famous husbands, and probably deserved more of a share of the limelight themselves: Rosina Lhévinne (considered as talented as Josef Lhévinne but adamant about staying in his shadow), Marguerite de Pachmann (whose career was restricted by having to look after the eccentric Vladimir de Pachmann). These examples echo the experience of women in other fields who were eclipsed by their male relatives, assisting them without receiving their share of credit: Dorothy Wordsworth, who provided inspiration for her brother William; Mileva Marić, who helped her husband Albert Einstein with his ground-breaking calculations; Marie Curie, who had to share her husband's portion of the Nobel Prize money.

One way in which women pianists were often given meagre recognition compared with their male colleagues was as composers.

Many of the great (male) pianists of history were also composers: Mozart, Beethoven, Robert Schumann, Felix Mendelssohn, Liszt, Chopin, Brahms, Busoni, Rachmaninoff, Prokofiev. Each of these in turn was renowned for performing his own music, and their latest works were eagerly awaited. It was routine for male pianists to compose, right through from the eighteenth to the early twentieth centuries. Many of the women in this book also composed, though it's my impression that the number of female pianist-composers declined through the nineteenth century and beyond. Some women were acknowledged as composers more generously than others, but none were treated as being in the league of the great male 'composer-pianists', and many did not compose at all. Why was this?

One important reason is that women did not have regular access to the same level of music tuition as men, and sometimes they had no access to tuition at all. Women were assumed not to need training as composers, and it was only in the late nineteenth century that most music conservatoires began to open their theory and composition classes to women. Even women who had access to tuition did not always receive the same training offered to men. The courses women were offered were often more basic, shorter and less comprehensive than men's, because it was assumed that few women would be able to devote their lives to composition. As late as 1939 the composer Ernst Krenek, teaching at Vassar College in New York, was told not to teach twelve-note technique to women students because most women were amateurs and wouldn't need such sophisticated information.[1] Lack of training is a crucial handicap, because, as anyone who has tried to write down music will know, specific skills in notation are required, all the more so if one wants to write in orchestral or opera score, with many different instruments playing different parts at the same time.

Women pianists who might have wanted to compose were also hampered by lack of opportunities for networking. Women might meet potential supporters in salons, but other avenues were barred to them. Women did not hold professional posts with built-in opportunities to interact with other important figures in the musical world, people who could say the word and make doors open for their friends and protégés. Women were not directors of conservatoires, conductors of orchestras or managers of opera houses. There were limits on how much a woman could do to get herself or her works into the public domain. Behaviour that was tolerated as necessarily assertive in a man was out of the question for a woman, especially those of a certain social status. Women were most unlikely to have been present at the kind of informal conversations that resulted in an agreement to 'give something a go' in the concert hall. They were not at the Freemasons' lodge when projects were mooted. They did not enjoy the privileges of the gentleman's club where influential men might meet and exchange ideas over a brandy and cigar. For all these reasons, women were less likely than men to attract wealthy sponsors.

These social factors also go some way towards explaining why women were less likely to compose in large-scale orchestral or operatic formats. Quite apart from lacking the time and peaceful working surroundings necessary for thinking up and writing down a huge score, most women must have thought it vanishingly unlikely that they would ever have a pathway to a performance of anything 'grand' they had written, no matter how ambitious they were. Women did not play in orchestras until the late nineteenth century, when the first women's orchestra was founded in Berlin, and it was not until 1913 that the first few women were hired by a major orchestra, the Queen's Hall Orchestra in London. Therefore, women were not routinely in the swing of how orchestras worked. They did not have the chance to listen at close quarters to all those instruments ranged around them – strings, woodwind, brass, percussion – and get to know what worked well with what, or which registers of each instrument were most suited to which kind of music. They did not, as various male composers have done, emerge from the ranks of a symphony orchestra with a symphony of their own. Nor did women have the chance to gaze for hours on end at a conductor, analyse his stick technique and his rehearsal method and work their way up through conducting smaller orchestras to presiding over a major one. Women conductors were unknown until the twentieth century, and even then the few who made it onto the conductor's podium were met with significant prejudice. In this light it is hardly surprising that such a large percentage of women's music is in smaller-scale formats such as piano music or songs with piano, which could more easily be written down in quiet moments snatched from domestic duties, and which lent themselves to performance in domestic settings, over which women did have some sort of control. Throughout history, most composers have been pragmatic, writing music which had a chance of being performed.

These disadvantages for aspiring women composer-pianists are self-evident, and different versions of them extended from the eighteenth to the twentieth centuries. But this did not stop prominent figures declaring that the lack of female composers was mainly down to want of talent or aptitude. In 1885 the leading German critic Eduard Hanslick explained why women had 'achieved nothing as composers'. It was because the function of a composer was essentially constructive, like that of a sculptor. Women had plenty of feeling, but 'It is not the feeling, but a specifically musical and technically-trained aptitude that enables us to compose.'[2] Hanslick was saying that women lacked not just the training, which was true, but also the basic aptitude, for which he had no evidence. This was a common prejudice, and for that reason generations of women were brought up surrounded by the belief and assumption that composing was men's work. As recently as the late twentieth century, the composer Nicola LeFanu, daughter of the composer Elizabeth Maconchy, said she had learned early on that composing was considered 'a gentlemen's club, of which the chairman was Beethoven'.[3]

Women in literature and the visual arts have faced equivalent prejudice. Women writers have often published their works under male pseudonyms, or have used initials to disguise their gender. Women's compositions have also been published under the names of men – several of Fanny Mendelssohn's songs were included in her brother Felix's collection. But for the woman *pianist* before the age of recordings, there was no concealing her identity. Women who wanted to perform as concert pianists simply had to appear on stage as themselves. They knew they risked being seen as 'forward', but they had to believe their prowess would overcome the audience's preconceptions. And they had to believe they were bringing something distinctive to the concert platform, not just asking the audience to accept them as substitute men. Today we are always reading that we should 'believe in ourselves' and 'follow our dreams', but in previous eras such messages of female empowerment were not readily available to women, and their positivity is all the more impressive.

These women, denied the status of the male composer-pianist, were pianists first and foremost. And that raises another question of hierarchy. The history of Western music, unlike the history of most other cultures, has traditionally been focused on the history of composers. This has pros and cons. On the one hand, we have precious documents written by the hands of Bach, Mozart and Beethoven. On the other hand, the high status of such written works means that many other types of music-making have been undervalued.

Arguably there has been too great a distinction drawn between composer-pianists, and pianists who were 'only' interpreters. Hanslick talks about the function of the composer being like that of the sculptor, but this is true of any musician whose task is to bring a piece of composed music to life. A musician must know how to guide the audience's attention to this and that, how to impart energy to the piece, to build contours of high and low, to clarify characters; how to indicate foreground or background, how to suggest sunlight and shadow. They must try to sense the composer's motive for writing what they wrote and convey the message to the listener without getting in the way. They must, in a sense, feel that they are originating the music. Mediating between the work and the listener is a serious task and calls for qualities of mind and imagination as well as the purely executant skills that pianists practise every day. Not just composers but also the women pianists who were 'merely' players deserve recognition as creative artists too.

The sense of engaging an audience in this creative act would have been especially powerful in an age when women had few opportunities to command the attention of a room in which men were present. On a public stage, they were able to experience that sense of communication to an audience that the poet Kae Tempest expressed so vividly when describing live performance: 'I am granted access to a freedom so resolute it leaves me shining head to toe . . . Looking out at the crowd, I see reality at last. People really feeling things.'[4]

In the twentieth century the habit of playing at home dwindled. When the radio and the gramophone (and their successors) became available and affordable, many people were content to swap their old upright piano for a music-playing machine that didn't require effort and didn't leave the standard of playing to chance. Meanwhile, pressures of space and inadequate soundproofing have made the acoustic piano increasingly *persona non grata* in city apartments, to the point where some neighbours can't understand how anyone can be so selfish as to install a big musical instrument that lacks a 'silent mode'.

We are a long way from the days when domestic music-making was a widespread social scene in middle- and upper-class homes, in which women played a starring role. In her memoirs, the English composer Ethel Smyth gave us entrancing descriptions of the Röntgen family whom she got to know when studying in Leipzig in 1877: 'a family that could raise a piano quintet among themselves, and together with their Röntgen cousins a small orchestra'.[5] She described how Frau Röntgen, playing the piano in this or that chamber work, would dash off between movements to supervise some crisis in the kitchen, while her daughter took over the playing of the piano part until she came back. This scene of enthusiastic music-making woven into the fabric of family life seems adorably picturesque, but also archaic. How many of us know such families now?

There are, however, still thriving amateur music societies and lots of people who choose to make space for a piano (acoustic or digital) in their homes. Their leisure hours at the instrument make them part of a great network of music lovers who hold a collective understanding of our musical heritage. When I was a member of the National Youth Orchestra of Great Britain (playing my second instrument, violin), conductor-composer Pierre Boulez told us we might wonder what the point was in training so intensively when most of us were not going to take up music as a profession. We should understand, he said, that discipline and teamwork skills were transferable into any field, and even if we did not become musicians, understanding what goes into the making of a performance would make us ideal listeners in the future.

Nevertheless, once the training reaches a certain level, it seems natural that a pianist should want to try performing in concerts, despite the challenges and obstacles. Women concert pianists who make it to the concert platform have something in common with women mountaineers, who have often faced sustained opposition in their quest to climb mountains. Even though today there are celebrated female climbers, the situation has not wholly changed since the days of the first *alpinistes* in the early nineteenth century; climbing a mountain is considered a noble aspiration for a man, but a woman risks accusations of selfishness for undertaking an activity incompatible with motherhood. We even have the equivalent of 'rugged peaks' in music, such as late Beethoven sonatas. They were viewed as wild and forbidding when they first appeared, but later as sublime works of art which all aspiring pianists should tackle once they had built up their stamina and learned to breathe at artistic altitude. Both male and female pianists have wanted to tackle these peaks of musical achievement, but reading archive reviews one sometimes has the sense that onlookers were surprised to find ladies clambering among Beethoven's jagged rocks in their long skirts and pretty shoes. If those ladies gave a convincing performance they were praised for having 'masculine' strength, but such terminology just underlines that for most onlookers, the default pianist was male. Comparisons like this have not entirely gone away, and are seen at their clearest in the modern phenomenon of the piano competition.

WHERE ARE WE NOW?

THE RISE OF PIANO COMPETITIONS

When audiences went to hear the performances of the pianists described in this book, they usually went to hear one particular pianist, either on her own or (more often) appearing in a mixed programme with other artists. One might go to hear a famous male pianist, or a famous female pianist, but these would be on different occasions. Generally speaking, one did not have the opportunity to compare different pianists, let alone different men and women pianists, directly on the same stage. It was not really until the middle of the twentieth century that the idea arose of holding piano competitions in which men and women pianists would compete against one another.

After the Second World War, in which many women discovered their potential in terms of working outside the home, there was growing acknowledgement that women deserved more access to the professional world. The gradual approach of equality legislation (for example, the Civil Rights Act of 1964 in the United States, and the Sex Discrimination Act of 1975 in the UK) was also an important factor, motivating the movers and shakers of the music world to create events open to everyone. Women pianists welcomed the chance to compete on equal terms with their male counterparts.

Piano competitions, many launched in the mid-twentieth century, became crucial stepping stones for a career in music. The International Chopin Competition in Warsaw was founded in 1927 and has been held every five years since 1955. Over a decade or two in the mid-century, there was a rash of new competitions. The ARD International Competition in Munich was first held in 1952, the Maria Canals International Competition of Barcelona in 1954, the Moscow Tchaikovsky Competition in 1958, the Van Cliburn International Competition of Texas in 1962, the Leeds Piano Competition in 1963, the Clara Haskil Piano Competition of Vevey, Switzerland, in 1963, the Santander International Competition in 1974, the Gina Bachauer International Competition of Salt Lake City in 1976. Significantly, several of these were founded by strong, determined women pianists or teachers – the formidable British piano teacher Dame Fanny Waterman founded the Leeds Competition, Paloma O'Shea founded the Santander Competition, and Maria Canals founded the one in Barcelona. Two of the competitions – Clara Haskil and Gina Bachauer – are named after women pianists.

Competitions have proliferated hugely in the last few decades and they are now found all over the world. Each has its own stipulations, age restrictions, repertoire slants, prescribed works, prize money and 'added value' privileges, such as masterclasses with jury members, who might advocate in the real world for a candidate whose playing they admire. Candidates feel positive about major competitions because, even though they involve a lot of work and stress, they offer more than just an immediate prize. Competitions work in partnership with festivals and series which stand ready to offer engagements to the winners. In short, if you win a big competition you are launched on an efficient circuit that saves you from the vagaries of the word-of-mouth recommendations pianists once relied on. Word of mouth produces interesting results, but it's a much hazier process.

Today, many ambitious young pianists study the dates and requirements of competitions and work out how to enter as many as possible, using the same repertoire over and over again if they are allowed to, until they win something – which, given so many different juries, is quite likely if they stick at it long enough. I now expect to see a list of prizes – a second prize here, an audience prize there, a prize for the best performance of the commissioned piece somewhere else – on the CVs of accomplished young pianists. Few musicians *enjoy* competing, but it seems to be generally thought that to try to make a career any other way is simply too slow and unreliable.

Equal-rights legislation was supposed to guarantee equal treatment for women and men, but, as we well know, legislation and public opinion don't always march in step with one another. Despite the involvement of women in founding these competitions, the reality was that the first female competitors were often at a disadvantage, because society was doubtful about women aspiring to 'masculine' solo careers. I remember as a child watching the 1966 Leeds Piano Competition on television and admiring the playing of the Russian pianist Viktoria Postnikova. I was convinced she was going to win and was upset when she came second to Rafael Orozco. The adults in my life, including my (female) piano teacher, tried to explain that it was natural for the jury to want a man as the first-prize winner, because a man was likely to be freer of family responsibilities and therefore more able to take up the offers that would come his way. What was striking about these explanations was that they were nothing to do with Postnikova's talent or skill, which indeed we all admired. People were not saying, 'She's not good enough for an international career.' They were saying, 'A woman is more bound into her family and community.' The situation has changed since those conversations took place, but not utterly.

In its sixty-year history, the Leeds Piano Competition has only been won twice by female pianists. One wonders whether competitions can ever be a level playing field for men and women, because competitions by their very nature are trials of nerve and chutzpah. Throughout history, many public competitions have been demonstrations of strength and speed – running faster, jumping higher, pulling more strongly, punching harder, swimming further – proofs of physical prowess. Dragging music into the realm of competition has produced a strange kind of hybrid. Physical strength and speed *are* elements of elite music performance, but there are other important elements, more subjective and not so easily marked. Any musician will tell you that it is difficult to produce a performance of poetic intensity under competitive conditions – or that such conditions are likely to produce a kind of performative 'intensity' rather than the real thing, which tends to blossom in quieter surroundings. Since many of the mysterious elements of music elude marking systems, judges often focus on the things that can objectively be given a mark. This tends to prioritise the same sort of qualities that produce winners at contests of physical strength.

Piano competitions are more akin to end-of-year exams – which, as we know from educationists, play to the strengths of boys – than to continual assessment, which plays to the strength of girls. If the audience takes sides vociferously, as they sometimes do, the competition can take on the character of a gladiatorial contest. There is still an international preference for 'masterful' playing and a hunger for the performance which ends with sizzling double octaves and provokes a roar of acclamation. Believing (rightly or wrongly) that masterful playing is a prerequisite for a top career, female pianists sometimes try to conform to this style, even though it may not suit them. Now and then audiences develop a special affection for someone (usually a woman) who plays with poetic inwardness, but that person doesn't usually go on to win the first prize. In piano competitions there is also the question of whether hand size matters. Women tend to have smaller hands than men, famously Alicia de Larrocha, but there have also been some celebrated male pianists – Josef Hofmann, Vladimir Ashkenazy, Daniel Barenboim – with small hands. There have also been successful women pianists, such as Clara Schumann, who had large hands.

Candidates in piano competitions are all choosing from the same repertoire list. Most of the competition repertoire was composed by men, often with male pianists in mind. Typically, the pieces that make the biggest impression on an audience are the barnstorming nineteenth-century piano concertos, for which big hands and a strong physique are an advantage. But we all know that today there are some young women who play the most fearsome piano concertos with aplomb, so the question of whether hand size matters is not straightforward to answer. It may be that access to excellent training and even to excellent nutrition has dispelled some of the disadvantages under which women used to labour.

Additional elements come into play when the competition is not for solo piano but for piano chamber music. This involves repertoire ranging from duo sonatas (e.g. for piano and violin) and piano trios (piano, violin and cello) to piano quartets (piano, violin, viola and cello) or piano quintets (typically piano and two violins, viola, cello) – a repertoire in which the piano is central. Most of the big works – for example Beethoven's 'Archduke' trio or the Brahms piano quintet – were written by male composer-pianists who conceived of the pianist as 'first among equals' in chamber music. The piano part is the most complex and is to a great extent directorial in nature, shaping the musical narrative. When the pianist in such a group is a woman, observers sometimes have to fight back a mild sense of unease, especially if the rest of the players are men. Even members of the jury can be uncertain how to respond to a female pianist who is authoritative and commanding, even though the music requires it.

It is not just the competitors in any piano competition who can find themselves at a disadvantage. Just as women competitors can be subtly intimidated by a male-dominated atmosphere, the same can be true of women on the jury. In my experience of international juries, women have usually been in the minority. It is sometimes difficult for a woman to find her way into the social life of the jury if the men appear to have bonded immediately and are always sitting together at meals, discussing their careers with gusto, and going out together in the evenings. Some women are good at creating a niche for themselves in such settings, but others may feel left out. In turn, this can have an effect on the tone and even the outcome of jury discussions.

A pianist with international jury experience wrote to me about 'the remarkable degree of misogyny, unconscious or otherwise, that I've seen first-hand in the piano world'. Lest anyone think that this is a fiction, let them spend some time exploring the websites of major piano competitions, where they will find confirmation of what I have claimed in this chapter: lists of past winners make it all too clear that the great majority have been men.[1] Moscow, Chopin, Van Cliburn, Leeds – all appear to have the male soloist as the default winner. (There are occasional exceptions, such as Martha Argerich, but they remain exceptional.) Women do make fairly frequent appearances in the tables of second and third prizes or special prizes for the best performance of this or that, but a few minutes of studying such tables will demonstrate that female pianists have an uphill task on their hands.

As recently as September 2021, in the Leeds International Piano Competition, the five finalists were all male. In October 2021, in the International Chopin Competition in Warsaw, there were nine men and three women in the final. The top four prizes all went to men, and so did all the special prizes. In 2022, thirty pianists were chosen to appear in person before the Van Cliburn competition jury in Texas – of those thirty pianists, twenty-seven were men, and the gold medal was won by a man. In September 2022, all three prize-winners at the ARD International Competition in Munich were men. As these judgements are partly subjective, one will never be able to *prove* that the results were unjust, but they certainly raise some questions.

I have discussed some of the possible reasons why men keep winning. Perhaps men have simply played better. Maybe women have steered clear of competitions. Perhaps the repertoire is slanted towards the male pianist, partly because of hand size. Perhaps women have been disadvantaged or demoralised by the 'macho' competitive atmosphere. Or perhaps, despite equality legislation and the efforts of campaigning groups, juries in 'open' competitions have an unconscious bias against women. It's difficult to prove, but everyone has their stories.

TODAY'S PIANOS AND PIANO TEACHERS

Arthur Loesser concluded his 1954 book *Men, Women and Pianos* with a somewhat downbeat assessment of the piano's future, admitting that it was 'not obsolete, nor is it likely to become so in the appreciable future', but also pointing out that 'as a source of passive musical enjoyment it has been all but snuffed out by the phonograph, the radio and the television set'. He ended his book with the discouraging words, 'The low plateau has no slope than we can now see. Our tale is told.'[2] At that point, he believed not only that the traditional piano had passed the peak of its popularity, but also that the electronic piano had 'never caught on' and there was no sign that it would.[3] However, contrary to his expectations, the digital piano has now become as popular as the acoustic piano and is probably more prevalent in modern life. Happily today the piano – in whatever form – is still one of the world's most popular instruments, regularly topping polls of 'what instrument would you most like to be able to play?'

Perhaps there is still some association between the piano and the grandeur of the concert grand, but the upright piano diluted the link when it became a popular domestic instrument at the beginning of the twentieth century, and the digital piano seems to have broken the link entirely. A digital piano evokes no imagined link with people in frock coats or silken gowns. A gain for female performers is that nobody expects them to acquire an expensive, old-fashioned outfit to play a digital piano.

In concert halls where classical music is performed, the acoustic piano is still king. At the time of writing I have never come across a concert venue where the default piano is a digital one. It's interesting that pop musicians still choose to play an acoustic grand piano at certain prestigious appearances, such as when they have a guest spot on a nationally popular TV show.

But in most non-classical concerts, in private homes and in college accommodation, the digital piano seems to be gradually overtaking the acoustic piano, for practical reasons if not for musical ones. Along with this change comes a shift of musical focus, especially for young people who have grown up with contemporary repertoire less based on the classics and more linked to films, musicals, pop and ambient music.

On the other hand, opportunities to learn the skills needed to play and appreciate the classical repertoire are increasingly under threat. School education systems (certainly in the UK) treat music tuition as an optional extra, requiring parents to pay for piano or other instrumental lessons. This puts music lessons out of reach for many families, even though musical talent can appear in children of any background. Where music tuition is provided in school, time constraints and the competing claims of 'more important' academic subjects often mean that music is studied only at a basic level. This leaves large parts of the repertoire out of reach, possibly never to be encountered. Survey after survey has reported on the multiple benefits of being involved in live music, and yet music still has to fight for its place in the mainstream curriculum.

Women have been prominent in neighbourhood piano teaching since the nineteenth century, and at local level are still in the majority compared with male piano teachers. Anecdotally it still seems to be the case that women specialise in teaching 'early years', whereas advanced piano students often go on to study with a man. Early-years teaching is, of course, of great importance. However, while female piano teachers have been dominant at beginner's level, they have always been under-represented at conservatoire and university level. Since the late eighteenth century there *have* been renowned female teachers at the top level, but they have always been outnumbered by renowned male teachers, just as female concert pianists have always been outnumbered by male ones.

Although one-to-one lessons are common at all levels, advanced conservatoire or college teaching also usually includes masterclasses, taught in front of an audience. Masterclass teaching has developed as a kind of branch of theatre arts, in which mini-dramas are created for educational effect: 'masters' sometimes use a teaching style that incorporates an abrasive element, even of insult or humiliation for the student. Not all masters indulge themselves like this, of course, and some of them are models of consideration, but others use doses of criticism and praise to build up moments of catharsis in which the student makes some sort of breakthrough (though it is debatable whether such 'breakthroughs' last much longer than the time on stage). Occasionally, students in masterclasses are confronted with their own shortcomings with the aim of making them realise they don't have what it takes to be a high-level performer. Such moments of drama make for good television, as they say, but are very hard on the students.

This kind of forum is not ideal for female teachers, for a start because their voices tend not to be as loud as men's. If women don't use a microphone, they must try to project their voices, and this changes the tone of their comments. If they *do* use a microphone (while the student doesn't), there is an added flavour of artificiality. It's hard to disentangle the question of how women 'naturally' behave, as compared with the behaviour they're trained into because women are supposed to be 'nice and kind', but female teachers often prefer to work in an atmosphere of exchange and encouragement.

Unfortunately, collaborative exchange conducted in quiet voices is not conducive to audience entertainment. Masterclasses where 'hard-knock' methods are used with gusto are usually taught by men (though Lili Kraus was an exponent – see p. 150), and there is no doubt that some students – and audiences – enjoy seeing an authority figure merrily wielding power. All this creates something of an arena in which women feel they are expected to 'perform' like men do, but the gladiatorial arena is essentially a masculine construct.

Female students in masterclasses have their challenges, too. How should they respond to criticism from a 'master' in a public class? Is their situation exactly the same as that of a male student, or are there subtle differences that apply to women? Should a female student speak up and defend herself, or just keep quiet and listen? For a man to talk back to a masterclass tutor is perceived as legitimate self-defence, whereas a woman doing the same thing might be perceived as unattractively self-assertive. Both approaches are available to female students, but either way it costs them some effort. There are ingredients of the power relationship between a 'master' and a female student which are difficult to keep in balance. A masterclass conducted with respect can be a wonderful experience, but sometimes the inherent theatre of the situation brings specific problems for female students.

STILL STORMING THE CITADEL

Piano competitions these days are flooded with accomplished female pianists from all over the world, but one often loses sight of them in the years that follow their competition performances. The same is true in chamber music, which, because of its fabulous repertoire and opportunities for psychological exploration as well as meaningful artistic collaboration, attracts excellent female pianists but seems to have difficulty in retaining them. The factors that prevent women from thriving long-term in the music profession are similar to those that hamper women in many other fields, but they are significant. A hundred years ago, Fannie Bloomfield Zeisler observed that the female performer:

> assumes additional heavy burdens and is obliged to lead two entirely full lives – that is if she does her duty. In the case of the man who carries on a public career it makes little difference. He acquires in his wife someone who surrounds him with all of the comforts of domesticity and often stands between him and the unreasonableness of the outside world.[4]

Even in the modern age, many female concert pianists still find themselves leading 'two entirely full lives', in view of which their achievements are even more remarkable.

The music world today can boast many female pianists. Most of them are amateur, of course, since the majority of music-making is amateur. But there are also prominent female soloists who command great respect – and indeed many music lovers would say that the leading pianist of any gender in recent decades has been Martha Argerich. But despite having amply proved that their musicianship is as good as men's, few of today's leading women pianists are as well known to the general public as their male counterparts. Equal opportunity has in theory been established, but there is still some discrepancy between what women are entitled to do and how comfortable the public is with them doing it. Many women pianists would agree that there is still a sense of having to 'storm the citadel' in a profession where men are not only the celebrities but also the promoters, backers, critics and gatekeepers in general. It seems that it would take a revolution not only in career management but also in public perception to establish true equality of opportunity.

The same issues apply in jazz and popular music, where female instrumentalists still struggle to be taken seriously rather than to be seen as entertainers and ornaments. Despite high-profile female singers, the world of popular music is still dominated by men, both on stage and behind the scenes in the form of talent spotters and record executives. The piano is regarded as a prestigious instrument for performers to use on stage, even if they only play it a little – its very appearance seems a guarantor of musical worth. But most of the performers who attract enormous crowds specifically *as pianists* are men. The kind of adulation accorded to the Italian pianist Ludovico Einaudi, who straddles the classical/popular divide and whose grand piano functions as a pseudo-shrine, could scarcely be accorded to a female pianist because even today, only a man would be thought to have the necessary gravitas.

Sexism is still a barrier, and so is ageism, although it is technically outlawed, too. Famously, the piano is an instrument which people often continue to play into old age, partly because the technique of playing the piano does not subject the body to the twists and torques which can become hazards of other instruments' playing techniques. One often reads admiring comments about venerable male pianists who were still playing at major halls in their eighties and nineties (Arthur Rubinstein, Vladimir Horowitz, Mieczysław Horszowski, Leon Fleisher, Menahem Pressler), but few female pianists are actively pursuing a concert career at that age, even if they still have the appetite and the artistry.

By old age, the serial disadvantages that await women at various stages of life have made a cumulative impact. Those who have successfully made the transition to being senior performers have usually managed to cultivate a priestess- or sage-like image, as Nadia Boulanger did. Nobody actually *tells* women of venerable age to stay away from the concert platform, just as nobody tells them in so many words not to run for president, but most women are only too well aware of the importance that society places on youth, glamour and 'fitness' – priorities that can be seen in any concert-series brochure that carries photographs of its performing artists.

Women are aware that older women in public life are not always viewed with the same indulgence as older men. The difference in society's attitude towards older men and older women is neatly summed up by a quote in Ogden Nash's humorous poem about becoming a grandparent, 'Come On In, the Senility Is Fine': 'I don't mind being a grampa but I hate being married to a gramma.' This punchline works because we all recognise the situation. There are some strong-minded older women who insist that age is not going to stop them doing what they want to do, but more who look around them ruefully and feel unsure that they are still welcome. Because of ageist attitudes, the world of music is probably losing the input of many female musicians who have valuable things to contribute.

WOMEN CONCERT PIANISTS AND HOW THEY FEEL ABOUT THEIR STATUS TODAY

When I was writing biographies of women for this book, I stopped before we got to today's concert pianists because I felt it would be invidious to proceed. There are so many good female pianists today, and probably many up-and-coming ones that I don't know. How would I decide who to include and who to leave out? I did, however, think it would be interesting to ask some leading female pianists whether they had any observations on what it is like to tackle the music profession *as a woman*. Have they found that being female is an advantage, a disadvantage or a matter of no relevance? And so on.

After sending off a list of questions to various pianist colleagues, I began to wonder whether my plan was doomed to failure, like a project I tried to organise in the 1980s. At that time, at least in London, one could rely on important concerts being reviewed in several newspapers and music journals. I was performing quite frequently and collecting reviews of my concerts. I was also attending lots of concerts, mostly when friends were playing. I kept noticing that the way critics described the event was very different from the way I had experienced it myself. They often seemed to miss the point, get the wrong end of the stick or spend their few column inches expounding some theory about the composer's place in music history, leaving remarkably little space for evaluating a performance or an interpretation that had probably taken months to prepare. In concerts of collaborative music, say violin and piano duos with enormous piano parts, I constantly found that 'the soloist' (the violinist) was written about as though they alone were responsible for the artistic effect while 'the accompanist' was thrown a little compliment in the last sentence – a titbit that bore no relation to the work they had put into the occasion. It all seemed very different from how musicians themselves would describe their efforts.

It occurred to me one day that it would be interesting to get some top performers to review *their own* concerts, saying what they had hoped to do, and whether they had achieved it – if so, why; or if not, why not. (This later surfaced in educational settings as 'reflective practice'.) I approached a music journal with my idea and they jumped at it. I made a list of artists performing at major London concert halls in the next months and wrote to them with my idea. They were all very enthusiastic, agreed that it was very frustrating when reviews went off at a tangent, and said they'd love to join in. I asked them to send me a 'self-review' of the chosen concert once it was over, and sat back to await their replies.

One by one, the performers got back in touch to say that they had thought it over and decided it would be unwise to participate. To review their own performance honestly, they realised, would mean revealing things they didn't want to get into the public domain: for example, that they weren't at their best that night, that they were at odds with their musical partner(s), that they hadn't rehearsed enough, were disappointed with the piano, or were struggling with some medical condition (such as a hearing difficulty) that hadn't been made public. Even if they felt they had been superb, they were reluctant to say so, in case it seemed boastful. Better to leave it to a respected commentator to say they had played wonderfully, they felt,

WHERE ARE WE NOW?

and better for the public not to know that they were struggling in any way. In short, I ended up with not a single 'self-review' to use. I sympathised, of course, because I had my own share of things I would have felt shy of disclosing. The experience taught me what I should have known already, namely that most performers strive mightily to put forward a positive image and go to enormous lengths to conceal stresses and strains.

Remembering that experience, I started to wonder if female pianists, no matter how much they might have to say in private, would not wish to reveal any gender-specific problems they had faced in the music profession because it is too sensitive a topic and makes them look vulnerable. To some extent this turned out to be true. Some people never answered my request at all. Others promised to send comments but never did. And a valiant group of women responded very generously with tales of their experiences.

I found myself with some comments the pianists had agreed I could make public, using their real names, but with other comments they asked me not to quote, or not to attribute to them personally. ('I'm just telling you to let off steam.') It seemed a pity to leave out some of their most telling remarks. But now it was my turn to get cold feet. I began to feel I didn't want to cause problems for them further down the line because they had confided in me in a moment of solidarity. Gradually I realised that I couldn't provide a full picture of what they had said unless I kept them anonymous, as I finally decided to do. The reader will have to take my word for it that my interviewees are high-profile pianists of various nationalities.

Their responses all tallied in some respects. In answer to my question about whether being female was an advantage, a disadvantage or irrelevant, one international soloist made the splendid observation that she was lucky to have been born female, because had she been a boy, her traditionally minded father would have wished her to become a lawyer or doctor, whereas piano-playing was an approved occupation for girls in her country. Most women, however, began by saying that they had tried to ignore the whole issue of gender and simply focus on being the best musician they could be, trusting that talent would shine through and that fairness would work in their favour.

Just because *women* were trying to rise above gender prejudice, however, it did not mean that everyone else was rising above it too. One woman, looking for new management after winning an international competition, was told by a leading London agent that she 'was at a disadvantage being a woman'. When she challenged him to explain what he meant by that, he was embarrassed and didn't know what to say. Another competition laureate recalled how she had been belittled by a male conductor when rehearsing a Liszt piano concerto. After she had played the cadenza, the conductor stopped the proceedings and asked her in front of the orchestra, 'Miss X, do you *really* mean to play it like that?' Members of the orchestra told her afterwards that 'he does that to all the ladies to see how they'll react'. Another male conductor, after a disagreement about tempo when they were recording a piano concerto, refused to speak to her after she stood up for herself in front of the orchestra. For the rest of the recording session he refused to look at her and passed the necessary information to her via the (male) orchestral leader. 'Mr X, will you tell Ms Y that we're going from bar 120?'

One competition-winning pianist recalled having recorded a disc for a top international record label, only to be told that it was going to be difficult to market her unless she could get herself involved in some scandal which would 'give the publicity department something to get their teeth into'. The brilliance of male pianists was, it seemed, 'a given' which needed no ingenious marketing, but a brilliant woman needed something extra, something non-musical, to catch the attention of listeners. This 'something extra' not being forthcoming, the record company declined to offer her another album.

My question, 'Do you feel you have had to work harder than men in order to get the same opportunities?' produced some memorable answers. Two or three leading female soloists said there was no point in asking whether they had worked harder than *men* when the truth was that they had worked harder than *anybody*. Their commitment to work was, they said, not a reflection of their gender but simply a proof of their single-mindedness. They had left no stone unturned in their efforts to build a high-powered career; indeed, some of them were still pursuing arduous practice schedules at a stage when one might expect them to be resting on their laurels, if not wearying of the whole business and easing into retirement. Their commitment was admirable, but possibly also showed that they were still seeking a level of fulfilment and recognition that had been granted earlier and more straightforwardly to their male colleagues.

Given these pianists' status in the public eye, one would expect that they were all satisfied with what they had achieved, but in fact only one international soloist felt she had not suffered from being female and had no complaints about the trajectory of her career. Otherwise, all my interviewees had doubts about whether things had gone fairly. One or two gave the music profession a lukewarm endorsement by saying that on the whole they did not feel they had been *disadvantaged* by being female ('and anyway, how would one know?' as one of them said reasonably). Most women, however, said they had struggled with belittling attitudes.

In some cases this included battling their own families for recognition of their hard work and achievements. They felt that whereas the boys and men of the family were readily praised for their successes, it is strangely hard for some family members (women as well as men) to acknowledge a successful woman.

Several women mentioned that it caused them emotional pain if family members did not attend an important concert. Or if they did attend it, they could not bring themselves to say anything nice about it afterwards but merely chatted about other things, as though the concert were inconsequential. The search for validation of one's achievements is not confined to women, but it was clear that praise can still be withheld from high-achieving women, even by those close to them, in some sort of complicated power game. No doubt this has ancient roots that take different forms in different cultures.

Praise withheld by family members is, of course, felt most keenly, but one or two women also noted how difficult it is for some male colleagues to be generous when a woman is singled out for praise. In collaborative situations, such as a female pianist working with a male conductor or other male musicians, it can happen that the woman's artistry is praised more highly than the man's or men's. A woman may find herself being given the silent treatment by men who would find it perfectly natural if *they* were singled out for praise, but – consciously or unconsciously – resent the idea that the most striking contribution was made by a woman. 'Conductors don't like female soloists who show them up and get better reviews than they do. This has happened to me so often,' one of my top soloists said. In chamber music, powerful piano parts make it likely that whoever is playing the piano will be prominent. When the pianist is a man, this prominence may seem agreeably natural, or at any rate frictionless. But when the pianist is female, some men have difficulty in acknowledging that critics and commentators may perceive her to be the dominant figure in the group. Women are aware of this, which can lead to strained relationships all round.

Some of the most outwardly successful women said they had not always had the access they deserved to prestigious halls and series where they felt they should be regular guests, or at any rate should be re-invited as reliably as their male counterparts are. Even today, most of the gatekeepers of the music profession – agents, promoters, festival directors, hall managers, record-label executives – are still men, who seem more comfortable dealing with a male network. Several leading pianists said they had been told – by agents and promoters – that they would have reached the top of the career ladder ten years earlier if they had been a man.

One famous female soloist had accidentally been sent a list of solo pianists' current fees, from which she learned with surprise that her fee was much lower than those of men of similar renown. Another renowned soloist said she had stopped seeking information on comparative fees because 'I have learned I may not get the full truth, or if I do, I would rather not have heard it, since managers can be brutal to you when defending their own shortcomings'.

Even if you do succeed in learning what your rivals are paid, however, it is difficult to use the information as each fee is agreed on a case-by-case basis, promoters often starting the conversation with an explanation of why *in this particular case* there is a limited budget. There are no set fees for concert pianists, which probably means that those who negotiate with chutzpah (or whose agent negotiates with chutzpah) do better than those who quietly ask what is available. An artist is, naturally, always told that the offered fee is 'the very best that we can do', but there is no way of checking. Who gets to decide on an artist's fee level? It's likely that most of those setting the fees are men. What criteria are they using, and are these criteria open to scrutiny?

Several women pointed out the difference in attitude to a man devoted to his career and a woman devoted to hers. One said that if a woman soloist over thirty-five has no children, she is considered 'career-driven' and probably hard, self-centred and ambitious, whereas a man of the same age is simply seen as successful. All agreed that women are much more likely than men to be asked whether they have children.

A number of interviewees spontaneously mentioned that many of today's top women pianists are child-free. Of course this may be a positive choice, but the complexities of practising, touring and concert-giving could make anyone nervous about taking on parental duties as well. When I say 'anyone' I really mean 'any woman', because all my interviewees had noted that male pianists with children appeared to continue their careers with scarcely a hiccup, whereas women pianists with children were immediately plunged into the 'two entirely full lives' syndrome that Fannie Bloomfield Zeisler described a hundred years ago.

This was especially the case for single parents. None of the single mothers I spoke to had *known* they were going to be lone parents – rather, various turns of events had left them in that position. One of those women pointed out that the music profession is particularly bad at providing any help for women with caring responsibilities. No concert promoter asks if you need a babysitter backstage or an extra bed for a child in your hotel room. No concert hall provides a creche. Concert agents' faces fall if you turn down work because of school holidays or children's illnesses, and warn that if you make yourself unavailable, others will rush in to fill the gap. One woman, whose ex-partner is also a concert pianist, said bitterly that she had turned down numerous concerts because the dates fell in her children's school holidays, whereas her husband never considered the children's school holidays when accepting concert engagements; he just assumed that *she* would have the matter in hand.

As with female freelancers in other walks of life, there is (in the UK at any rate) no maternity leave, no childcare facilities, no sick pay, no security and no pension attached to the job. 'Women pianists would worry less about the amount of each concert fee if they knew they had a pension waiting for them at the end of their careers,' one woman told me. It's also worth pointing out that in the days when Clara Schumann left home to go on concert tours, she had servants and maids at home to take care of the laundry, cleaning, shopping, food preparation and the children. Today, nobody has servants, so women professionals are trying to cover all the bases themselves.

Concert pianists are not a unionised group with the power to put collective pressure on employers. On the contrary: they are accustomed to being in competition – competing not only with men, but also *with one another*. For any solo piano recital in a major hall, only one pianist is needed, and there is hot competition to be that person. The cut-throat nature of the profession has not made it natural for pianists, or women pianists, to look out for one another. Their mindset has never been that of a community. They don't play together as orchestral players do, forming 'sections' or 'teams' which have lobbying power with their institutions. Some pianists do form teams with singers or other instrumentalists, but the nature of these groups is often transient – and in any case, chamber groups are not unionised either.

All women freelancers share these problems to some degree, but in the music profession the problems are acute because performers have to travel continually. Most freelancers can go home at the end of the day, and in these post-pandemic days many people choose to work from home, but this has never been possible for performing musicians, who often find themselves in another city or even another country at the end of a concert, unable to respond to an emergency at home by getting there quickly in person. The schedule of any successful pianist with a family thus involves a jigsaw of domestic arrangements in constant upheaval. The unpredictable delays of international travel make these arrangements unlikely to work as planned, so expensive margins have to be left. If there is no 'wife' at home, who can be at home to hold the fort? The answer usually involves money. For most people, concert fees are not enough to be able to pay for domestic help, especially if it involves evening work and overnight stays, as it inevitably does. Caregivers charge extra for working those unsocial hours, making the situation even more difficult.

'All the women I know who have children are on edge all the time,' one woman told me. 'Women have to be so incredibly high-functioning and organised!' She recalled being interviewed before a concerto with the (male) orchestra conductor sitting beside her. For the umpteenth time she was asked how she balanced work with being a mum. So she told the interviewer she would only answer if he asked the conductor the same question. To his credit, the conductor said it was a good question and admitted that . . . yes, his wife was at home looking after their children.

This arrangement is still the default, even in a profession that aims to be welcoming to women. Almost every one of my interviewees said they had had difficulty in managing their home life alongside their musical commitments. As one of them put it, 'I am absolutely not passing judgment on the life partners of some of my male colleagues, but constant support, organisation, discreet efficiency, offloading small practical tasks can make a huge difference to head space and energies (how often have I reflected on this when putting out the dustbins late on a wet night before an early morning departure ...).' Everyone echoed this point in one way or another. Several top soloists had realised that they had to employ people to take over various chores for them in order to protect their practice time. Of course, such a solution can only be considered if fees are high, and that is less often the case than the public might imagine.

Several women said that they had often been complimented on their 'masculine' playing if they played assertively or with authority. One woman's agent, touring Russia with her, had been told delightedly that 'she plays just like a man!' However, being 'like a man' was clearly not something to admire in every context. Several women had found that if they stood up for their rights or refused to be charming and flexible, they were accused of being 'bossy', 'hard', 'cold', 'unfeminine' and so on. Playing like a man = good. Acting like a man = bad. Clearly this is a no-win situation for female musicians.

In any case, what does 'playing like a man' even mean? Does it mean playing assertively, strongly, confidently, single-mindedly? Does it mean taking risks, not seeming emotional, not caring how we come across? If it's any of these, we could just say so. Terms like 'masculine playing' seem lazy and old-fashioned in an era when masculinity itself is being interrogated – and they show that the male pianist is still the default. Who can imagine a man being enthusiastically told that 'you play just like a woman'? Who can imagine a man rejoicing to be told so? I have some very open-minded male colleagues, but nevertheless I can't help picturing their quizzical expressions if they were to be complimented on their 'feminine' playing.

Several women mentioned that they often have to brace themselves after concerts to hear that their performance was 'delightful' – a compliment no doubt well meant, but one that seems to be uttered to women in particular. It grates because it feels like a refusal to acknowledge the full achievement. As one soloist said, 'Being told after a gruelling and emotionally draining recital that it was "delightful" is on every front such an insult and misunderstanding! And yes, it is almost invariably men who say it.' What is wrong with telling someone her performance was delightful? Well, just imagine yourself going backstage and saying it to Sviatoslav Richter after an epic solo programme.

In answer to my question, 'Has your appearance often been mentioned in reviews?', some women said no, but others said they had often had comments about their outfits or shoes, and occasionally about their personal attractiveness (which never seems to happen to men). Everyone noted that women performers are still subject to different expectations than male performers. No one bats an eyelid if a man wears the same suit at every concert, but women are expected to keep varying their outfits, shoes and hairstyle. They had noticed that the comments, or lack of them, varied from country to country. While in some places it's poor taste to make comments about appearance, in others the audience (and the press) positively look forward to seeing what outfit a female pianist is going to wear and may even take an interest in the designer.

Because women know their appearance is likely to attract comment, they feel pressure to keep changing their concert outfits. Quite apart from the variation expected from one concert to another, several women noted that during their careers they had had to overhaul their wardrobes when the fashion changed from formal gowns to floral frocks or to unisex black trousers and smart jackets. Almost everyone noted that men do not feel pressure to keep varying their outfits and do not have to worry about disappointing the audience by appearing in the same concert clothes they wore in that hall on a previous occasion (some women even keep notes of what they wore where). Women know the audience's reaction to them is compounded of a response to their skill plus a judgement on their appearance, a gauntlet that male pianists do not have to run.

It would be foolish to pretend that physical beauty plays no part in establishing a successful career, for a female artist's physical appearance is often far too relevant to how her career progresses. I have heard people comment that it is not surprising that so-and-so is famous, because she is so beautiful. Conversely, I've often heard people praise such-and-such a female pianist for her musicianship and then casually remark that it's a pity she is not better-looking, because she could have a bigger career. Are men similarly helped/handicapped by their looks? I don't think we need a scientific survey to tell us that women are judged more on their appearance than men are. How a male pianist *looks* is way down the scale of things that audiences find important.

However, being beautiful can be a mixed blessing. There are no doubt gorgeous female pianists, constantly complimented on their appearance, who sincerely wish people would talk about their perfect phrasing for once. The very first impression made by an attractive female artist who sashays onto the concert platform in sexually provocative clothing is likely to be that she is an artistic lightweight. Such a person may feel that she has to work especially hard to prove that she is serious about her music.

Although I don't in general wish to discuss today's artists by name, it would be remiss not to mention the Chinese pianist Yuja Wang, who has – as one musicologist put it to me – 'fundamentally changed the narrative when it comes to critical discourse on what a female artist chooses to wear to perform'. Yuja Wang's daring outfits and ultra-high-heeled shoes might prompt the suspicion that she hopes to detract from her pianistic shortcomings by dazzling the audience with her appearance, but in fact she is a rare example of a pianist who not only looks like a pop star but also plays with exceptional technical finesse and a command of piano repertoire previously judged 'best played by men'. Her youthful glamour has attracted many casual listeners to the classical piano repertoire, which is surely an important thing.

Expectations of female artists don't stop at clothes and hairstyle. The mood a pianist chooses to project on the platform is part of their appearance as well. There are male concert pianists who seem morose, even depressive on the platform, and this can even seem to be part of their allure. Yet I very much doubt that any woman pianist could get away with such body language in concert. In an older generation of pianists there were certainly women (such as Clara Haskil or Annie Fischer) who looked austere or unsmiling, but none of them looked morose. When I think of all the high-powered pianists whose concerts I've attended, I can recall several grumpy-looking and dishevelled male soloists but not, I think, a single grumpy-looking or dishevelled female one.

In answer to my question, 'Have you felt pushed into, or away from, certain repertoire because you are female?', several people mentioned that women's hands are smaller than men's. To some extent this had dictated the repertoire they were best equipped to master. Several women said that they had often been expected to play Chopin, whose music seems to be associated with women even though it often requires a large hand (Chopin himself had hands that were not large, but were exceptionally flexible). Others said they had made a point of learning 'tough' piano concertos or technically demanding contemporary music to prove that women today are in possession of the whole repertoire. One soloist, whose 'extremely flexible' hands have enabled her to master almost all of the classic repertoire ('with the exception of Bartók's second piano concerto'), struck a note of balance when she pointed out that it isn't always the case that women have small hands and men have large hands: Daniel Barenboim, for example, has a stretch of just an octave.

During my research for this book, I noticed on many occasions when looking through musical scores that the female pianists who composed piano music often seem to have had hands larger than the average – at least, they wrote music that requires a large hand, often a hand that can stretch more than an octave, and one may assume that they wrote things which they themselves could play. (Examples are Hélène de Montgeroult, Maria Szymanowska, Clara Schumann, Teresa Carreño and Amy Beach.) I found this interesting. Were these women consciously writing against type, or was it rather that female pianists who successfully broke through as performers were more likely to be those with large hands – hands that could more easily take on and conquer the 'male' repertoire?

One woman in my survey made the interesting point that men seem more drawn to 'totem pole' repertoire – meaning complete cycles of this or that, blockbuster achievements easy to market by labelling them 'the complete Beethoven sonatas', for example. But 'how can one be equally responsive to everything?' she asked, wondering whether 'certain women's instinctive empathy for such-and-such repertoire rather than the bulk buy is maybe not always as appreciated as it should be'. This is a good point – that a person who feels a deep affinity with a single Beethoven or Schubert sonata may be its greatest interpreter but is much less likely to make a splash than the person who has recorded the whole lot, regardless of how uneven that achievement may be. Widening out from that point, one might wonder whether our whole attitude to 'iconic' classical repertoire is influenced too greatly by the blockbuster achievements of male composers and the male historians and critics who revered them.

Ageism was raised by a few people as a troubling issue. It was noted that whereas some very senior male pianists are celebrated for continuing to perform, one rarely sees very senior female pianists on the concert platform. This phenomenon isn't unique to the music profession, as we all know, but it's certainly a situation of which female pianists are painfully aware. But getting older was viewed as having positive sides as well. Several women commented that most men seem to remain competitive in attitude and invested in jockeying for position right through their careers. This was less so for women, who seem to find it easier to become philosophical about such matters. One woman commented that 'there comes an age when you see all these things with hindsight and you really don't mind any more, it's not what matters. I am not sure that men have that attitude. I do not envy them.'

Several women brought up a point I hadn't even asked about: for them, their nationality or race had been as much of an issue as their femininity, and sometimes even more of an issue. The white European pianist (or 'pianist with a European-sounding name') is still, they felt, the classic image. My respondents expressed in various ways and with varying degrees of intensity that they felt they might have had an easier time in establishing themselves if they had not been Canadian, Japanese, Black and so on. They were conscious of not being European or having a European-sounding name that would have guaranteed entry to the club. Several had been told they 'would have reached the top of the ladder ten years earlier if they had had a German or German-sounding name'.

Not meeting the traditional image of a European concert pianist can, of course, be more of a problem for some than for others. We have seen in the biographies of Margaret Bonds and Nina Simone that it has been difficult for Black pianists to enter the classical music profession, and although the situation has noticeably improved in recent years, it is still not easy.

Some of my younger interviewees, themselves Black or mixed-race artists, have set out to perform and promote music that is under-represented, such as music by Black women and other neglected female composers. One of them curates a concert series of piano music by African composers, both from Africa (where male composers are in the majority) and from the African diaspora (from which music by female composers is more likely to be found). She told me she was raised by her father to 'rise above any societal or cultural prejudice' while her mother taught her that 'as long as you work hard and believe in yourself, your light will always shine through prejudice or injustice'. 'Today,' this young woman said, 'I still believe in this very strongly.'

In answer to my question, 'Have you found that being a woman in the classical music profession is an advantage, a disadvantage or irrelevant?', one of these young women gave a delightfully positive answer:

> My identity is tied into my work as a classical pianist. I see it as an advantage because, as a result, I have become aware of so much incredible repertoire that I would have never heard of or played before. Being a woman inspired my desire to learn more about the longer history of women in classical music. Through wanting to see more of myself reflected in classical music, I have become a champion of Black Renaissance women like Florence Price and Margaret Bonds, as well as neglected European female composers. [The 'Black Renaissance' was an era of rich artistry and cultural rebirth that unfolded in the United States through the first half of the twentieth century.] Their music brings me so much joy and fulfilment in a way I never experienced as a pianist playing the typical repertoire. What's more, I get to connect with wonderful audiences all around the world who are also keen to see more women of diverse backgrounds reflected in the concert hall.

For many of the historical women pianists in this book, of course, it would not have been possible to base a career on the neglected music of female composers, because in their day it was the paramount task for women pianists to show that they could master iconic repertoire by male composers. The strategies of these young Black women point to a new way for women to lead a satisfying life as concert pianists.

WHERE ARE WE NOW?

It was clear to me that all the women in my survey had approached their work with admirable resolve, open-mindedness and dedication. And the fact that there were so many women pianists to ask tells its own story. All the issues raised were very familiar and chimed with my own experience as a concert pianist. If there was a surprise for me, it was that other women were willing to speak about difficulties that are customarily kept quiet. Doing the interviews gave me a pleasant feeling of community with fellow pianists.

The difficulties they described are, however, variants of the difficulties that all the historical pianists in this book had to confront. Ultimately, for major change to occur, the gatekeepers will have to change. Many people outside the music profession don't realise that an artist doesn't just *decide* they want to play at Carnegie Hall, the Musikverein in Vienna, the Proms, Ronnie Scott's or wherever – they have to be invited. They can put themselves and their programme ideas forward for consideration – and indeed that task occupies a lot of pianists' administrative time – but ultimately someone (such as an artistic programmer or a concert-hall manager) has to decide to engage them. Artists sometimes hire halls and promote concerts at their own expense, as many of the earlier women in this book did, but such a gambit is undertaken only with the hope of kickstarting other invitations. Those other invitations are usually negotiated by a phalanx of agents and promoters who do 'deals' with one another and maintain a professional camaraderie. They have the power to open doors, or to keep them shut. Naturally, audiences only see whoever actually gets to appear on the platform – they never know who tried in vain to open the door. For more doors to open more easily for women, we will have to hope for a different breed of gatekeepers.

In the pop world, some young artists have managed to bypass gatekeepers and go straight from recording themselves in their bedrooms to having a worldwide audience of fans, without the involvement (initially at least) of a team of middlemen. This approach is rarer in the classical world, where it is traditional to hope that a string of successful live concerts may bring you to the attention of a recording company, and where a recording contract is considered the icing on the cake, not a first step towards a performing career. Some artists have created their own luck. Valentina Lisitsa led the way a decade ago with a straight-to-YouTube career that amassed a huge subscriber base and, as a result, opened doors to major concert halls.

Today, many artists have social media channels on which they post all sorts of content, from humorous to educational, but as well as establishing a presence and acquiring followers their goal still seems to be to build awareness of their live performances. On the whole, musicians who have been trained to work towards live concerts (which is most of us) remain focused on that format with its unique atmosphere and satisfactions. During the coronavirus pandemic, several well-known pianists recorded recitals in their own homes and uploaded them to the internet. These online recitals enjoyed a vogue when live concerts were forbidden. Listeners appreciated the close-up camera angles, which enabled them to see the pianist's hands better than they could in a traditional concert hall. However, it seemed that both artists and listeners eventually got tired of the artificial context and found themselves longing for a real-life trip to the concert hall. Performing at home to a microphone can be intense, but nothing can replace the experience of being immersed in live music along with other people, because each live audience generates its own magnetic field, which impacts creatively on the performer. So far, social media channels have not offered a satisfying alternative to live performance. But the world of technology is getting more and more ingenious, and it will be interesting to see what happens next. Should we, for example, start to worry that artificial intelligence will be able to mimic the performance style of any pianist whose recordings it has analysed, and make their 'avatar' play any piece of piano music in their signature style, dispensing with the need for the human pianist? Perhaps gender disparities will turn out to be the least of our worries.

CODA

When women have had for several centuries the same advantages of liberty, education, and social encouragement in the use of their brains that men have, it will be right to argue their mental inferiority if they have not produced their fair share of geniuses. But it is hardly reasonable to expect women during a few years of half liberty and half education to produce at once specimens of genius equal to the choicest men of all the ages.
Alice Stone Blackwell in *The Woman's Journal*, 29 August 1891

When I was learning the piano, I was aware of very few women pianists in history. Even when I was at university, women musicians were more or less absent from the curriculum, and I recall with embarrassment that their absence didn't forcibly strike me. We knew a few facts about Clara Schumann and Fanny Mendelssohn, but most of the women in this book were unknown to me and remained so for years. Like most musicians of my generation (and of generations before), I had been trained to look up to the male composers and pianists whose achievements run through the pages of history books and fill the catalogues of recordings. Men were the main theme. Women, if they were present at all, were just grace notes to that theme.

Thanks to the efforts of campaigning women and feminist scholars, however, I gradually became aware of more and more of my female predecessors. As I learned about them, I also realised that music historians (mostly male) had not considered them sufficiently important to preserve their stories and present them to us alongside the biographies of important men. If the study of historical music can be viewed as an institution, one would have to say that there has been institutional sexism. I believe this has left women with a lingering sense that they should still be on their guard against a long-brewed tendency for society to overlook female achievements, or to treat them with less *intent to remember* than men's.

Women of the past were obliged to try to be honorary men in terms of the repertoire they performed and the way they handled their careers. It has been shown that people who are asked to guess the gender of an artist, just by listening to their recordings, cannot reliably tell whether the player is male or female. In one sense, this proves that women have equalled men at their own game. Fine piano-playing is unisex: hooray! In another sense, it suggests that in order to get ahead in the music profession, women have had to assimilate to the male way of doing things. It therefore also raises the question of whether there is, or could be, a distinctively female interpretative space, free from expectation of how pieces 'should' be performed, which women have yet to carve out for themselves.

Women have more delicate physiques, less physical strength and generally smaller hands than men. That is only an issue if we are summoning history's concert pianists to the starting line as if they were a row of athletes in a contest to find the fastest or the strongest. In that imaginary line, women would be at a disadvantage. However, when it comes to music we are looking for more than merely strength and speed. We're hoping for the ability to touch the heart, an understanding of the world of beauty and expression contained in music, and an ability to share it with listeners.

Small hands and a slighter physique are no impediment to these goals. In terms of imagination, sensitivity and artistic insight, women have always had at least as much to contribute as men, and making it hard for women to participate has inevitably resulted in a somewhat one-sided expression of musical culture. In any case, 'power' is not a simple thing to measure. In a musical performance, the audience's estimation of power is dependent on the context. How a pianist balances the relationship between one part of a piece and another, between a melody and its accompaniment, and between the softest and loudest parts of their playing will create its own context. Within such a context, a small, fragile-looking woman can create as powerful and impressive an effect as someone whose sound is measurably louder or more forceful. There's an analogy here with the world of acting: the most powerful actors are not necessarily the ones with the loudest voices.

Admittedly many of the women in this book were 'outliers' in their own day. They were pioneers because they had to be. Yet if we could ask them whether they enjoyed being pioneers, they would quite possibly say that they would have preferred to be part of a community of women musicians. Today, we are making headway towards that possibility. We take it for granted that any little girl should be able to learn the piano and have access to training and opportunities that enable her to pursue her dreams as far as she wishes. Those aspiring to be concert pianists are unlikely these days to be steered away from repertoire considered unsuitable for a woman, as I was by some of my teachers (both male and female). When I was a young professional, I did not especially feel that I was part of a community of female musicians; rather, I saw it as my task to find a niche in the community of male musicians, because that was where power seemed to lie. Had I been more aware of my splendid female forebears, I would have drawn power from that sense of continuity.

Today's young women are not willing to be told that they should abandon their ambitions and stay at home. The public's perception of women musicians is gradually changing as more women enter the profession, and as they do, the need to fight for their rights should diminish. In her revealing book *Why So Slow? The Advancement of Women*, Virginia Valian recommends that 'women should try to work in fields and professions where women are well-represented. Some women fear a backlash against women as they make strides in areas formerly reserved to men ... but such a backlash can have only limited effects if there are enough women ... If a woman is one of many, she is less likely to be perceived in terms of her sex and her job is less likely to be perceived as a man's job.'[1] It would help, too, to have more feminist historians – or, more generally, scholars and historians alert to the danger of casual amnesia about women's aspirations and achievements.

The women pianists in this book were not able to be 'one of many' because of society's attitudes to women working, performing, earning independent money and having a high profile of their own outside the home. Nevertheless, they were driven on by their love of music and belief in their own powers. In a male-dominated world, their achievements were often set aside because they defied expectation, but thanks to recent discoveries we are now in a better position to appreciate them. The prohibitions they faced are being gradually chipped away. Surely those women would be glad to know that thanks to them and other campaigners, young female pianists are ready and able to open any door they wish in pursuit of a life in music.

> The history of all times, and of today, especially, teaches that women will be forgotten if they forget to think about themselves.
> Louise Otto-Peters, German feminist, 1849

ENDNOTES

Introduction

1. Simone de Beauvoir, *The Second Sex*, trans. H.M. Parshley (London: Jonathan Cape, 1953; repr. Penguin Books, 1974), p. 175.
2. Anne Tyler, *Redhead by the Side of the Road* (London: Vintage, 2021), p. 96.

From harpsichord to piano

1. Plato, *Laws* 7.802.
2. La Fontaine's poem (my translation) is quoted in the entry on Marie-Françoise Certain in the Sophie Drinker Institut lexicon of female instrumentalists: https://www.sophie-drinker-institut.de/certain-marie-francoise.
3. *Mercure galant*, July 1677.
4. Quoted in Edward F. Rimbault, *The Pianoforte* (London, 1860; repr. Frankfurt: Salzwasser Verlag, 2022).
5. Richard Maunder, 'Mozart's Keyboard Instruments', *Early Music*, vol. 20, no. 2 (May 1992), p. 214.

From the eighteenth to the nineteenth centuries: Women and the rise of the piano

1. Quoted in Christopher Page, 'Men, Women and Guitars in Romantic England, VI: The Guitar and "the Fair Sex"', Gresham College lecture, 23 April 2015.
2. Robert Southey, letter to Charlotte Brontë, 12 March 1837, Brontë Parsonage Museum, Yorkshire.
3. Friedrich Melchior Grimm, *La Correspondance littéraire, philosophique et critique* (Paris, 1763).
4. Wolfgang Amadeus Mozart, letter to his sister, 7 July 1770, quoted in *Mozart's Letters, Mozart's Life*, trans. Robert Spaethling (London: Faber and Faber, 2004), p. 17.
5. John Essex, *The Young Ladies Conduct: Or, Rules for Education, under Several Heads; with Instructions upon Dress, Both before and after Marriage, and Advice to Young Wives* (London: John Brotherton, 1721), pp. 84–5.
6. 'Democritus Junior' (pseudonym for Robert Burton), *The Anatomy of Melancholy* (Oxford: Henry Cripps, 1638), p. 532.

7. Candace Bailey, 'The Antebellum "Piano Girl" in the American South', *Performance Practice Review*, vol. 13, no. 1 (2008).
8. Jane Austen, *Sense and Sensibility*, chapter 7.
9. Elizabeth Grant of Rothiemurchus, *Memoirs of a Highland Lady* (Edinburgh: Canongate Classics, 1988), p. 221.
10. Hannah More, *Strictures on the Modern System of Female Education* (Salem, MA: Samuel West, 1809), p. 49.
11. J.H. Adeane (ed.), *The Girlhood of Maria Josepha Holroyd. Recorded in Letters of a Hundred Years Ago: From 1776 to 1796*, 2nd edition (London: Longmans, Green and Co., 1897), p. 14.
12. Jane Austen, *Emma*, chapter 9.
13. Howard Irving, '"The Necessity of Giving Continual and Fatiguing Lessons"': William Crotch on Music Teaching in London', *International Review of the Aesthetics and Sociology of Music*, vol. 35, no. 2 (2004), pp. 151–67.
14. James Kennaway, 'The Piano Plague: The Nineteenth-Century Medical Critique of Female Musical Education', *Gesnerus*, vol. 68, no. 1 (2011), pp. 26–40.
15. James Johnson, *The Economy of Health* (London: S. Highley, 1837), p. 48.
16. Lawson Tait, *Diseases of Women* (London: Williams and Norgate, 1877), p. 78.
17. Quoted in James Kennaway, *Bad Vibrations: The History of the Idea of Music as a Cause of Disease* (London and New York: Routledge, 2016), p. 75.

The dawn of the piano era

1. Rudolf Rasch, 'Description of the Sources', in Luigi Boccherini, *Sei sonate per tastiera e violino*, ed. Rudolf Rasch (Bologna: Ut Orpheus Edizioni, 2009), p. xciii. Translated in Rebecca Cypess, *Women and Musical Salons in the Enlightenment* (Chicago and London: University of Chicago Press, 2022), p. 134.
2. Bruce Gustafson, 'Brillon de Jouy, Anne Louise Boyvin d'Hardancourt, Biographie', https://www.mgg-online.com/mgg/stable/404316.
3. Freia Hoffmann, 'Brillon de Jouy', https://www.sophie-drinker-institut.de/brillon-de-jouy-anne-louise.
4. Benjamin Franklin, letter to William Carmichael, 17 June 1780, Library of Congress.
5. Anne-Louise Brillon de Jouy, letter to Benjamin Franklin, 30 November 1777, *The Papers of Benjamin Franklin*, https://franklinpapers.org.
6. *Mesmeric Therapy*, oil painting by a French (?) painter, 1778/1784, Wellcome Collection, 44754i.
7. Hermann Ullrich, 'Maria Theresia Paradis and Mozart', *Music & Letters*, vol. 27, no. 4 (October 1946).
8. Mozart, letter to his father, 28 March 1781, Internationale Stiftung Mozarteum online.
9. Mozart, letter to his father, 22 August 1781, *Mozart's Letters, Mozart's Life*, trans. Robert Spaethling (London: Faber and Faber, 2004), p. 280.
10. Mozart, letter to his father, 27 June, 1781, ibid., p. 270.
11. Mozart, letter to his father, 22 August 1781, ibid., p. 280.
12. Mozart, letter to his wife, 16 April 1789, ibid., p. 408.

13. Hermann Abert, *W.A. Mozart*, trans. Stewart Spencer (New Haven, CT: Yale University Press, 2007), p. 710, n. 106.
14. Michael Kelly, *Reminiscences* (London: Henry Colburn, 1826), p. 252.
15. Haydn, letter to Marianne von Genzinger, 20 December 1791, HC Robbins Landon, *Haydn, A Documentary Study* (London: Thames and Hudson, 1981), p. 131.
16. Haydn, letter to his publisher Artaria, 25 February 1780, 'Auenbrugger, Marianna', https://www.sophie-drinker-institut.de/auenbrugger-marianna.
17. Katelyn Clark, 'The London Pianist: Theresa Jansen and the English Works of Haydn, Dusseck, and Clementi', *Online Journal of the Haydn Society of North America*, vol. 2, no. 1 (2012), https://remix.berklee.edu/haydn-journal/vol2/iss1/2.
18. Haydn's remark in 1806 to his biographer Albert Christian Dies was included in Dies's *Biographische Nachrichten von Joseph Haydn* (Vienna, 1810), p. 131.
19. Quoted in Grand Piano Records sleeve note, https://grandpianorecords.com/Composer/ComposerDetails/286047.
20. Hélène de Montgeroult, *Cours complet pour l'enseignement du forte piano*, c. 1830, IMSLP Petrucci Music Library (my translation).
21. Jérôme Dorival, 'Hélène de Montgeroult, Pianist, Composer and Teacher', https://www.editionsmodulation.com/en/Hélène-de-montgeroult-pianist-composer-and-teacher.

Women in the age of the concert pianist

1. Quoted in Alan Walker, *Franz Liszt*, vol. 1, *The Virtuoso Years 1811–1847* (Ithaca, NY: Cornell University Press, 1987), p. 240.
2. K. Shalimov in *Moskovskiia vedomosti*, 6 May 1822, p. 1146.
3. *Allgemeine musikalische Zeitung*, 1835, column 640, my translation.
4. *Neue Zeitschrift für Musik* (1848) II, p. 70, my translation.
5. *Revue et gazette musicale*, 1830, p. 376, my translation.
6. Quoted in David Conway, *Jewry in Music: Entry to the Profession from the Enlightenment to Richard Wagner* (Cambridge: Cambridge University Press, 2012), p. 171.
7. Quoted in R. Larry Todd, *Fanny Hensel: The Other Mendelssohn* (Oxford: Oxford University Press, 2010), p. 146.
8. Sebastian Hensel, *The Mendelssohn Family (1729–1847) from Letters and Journals*, trans. Carl Klingemann (London: Sampson Low and Co., 1884), vol. 1, p. 82.
9. Paul Mendelssohn Bartholdy (ed.), *Letters of Felix Mendelssohn Bartholdy from 1833 to 1847*, trans. Lady Wallace (London: Longman, 1864), p. 116.
10. Charles Gounod, *Autobiographical Reminiscences with Family Letters and Notes on Music*, trans. W. Hely Hutchinson (London: William Heinemann, 1896), chapter 2.
11. Sebastian Hensel, *The Mendelssohn Family from Letters and Journals*, trans. Carl Klingemann (New York: Harper and Brothers, 1882), vol. 2, p. 116.
12. Fanny Mendelssohn, letter to Angelika von Woringen, 26 November 1846, quoted in Marcia Citron (ed.), *The Letters of Fanny Hensel to Felix Mendelssohn* (New York: Pendragon Press, 1987), p. 352, n. 9.
13. *The Times*, 9 July 1829.
14. *The Times*, 3 May 1836.

15. *The Times*, 4 April 1843.
16. *The Times*, 12 June 1844.
17. *Musical World*, 10 July 1845, p. 327f.
18. *The Times*, 18 January 1843.
19. https://en.wikisource.org/wiki/A_Dictionary_of_Music_and_Musicians/Dulcken,_Louise.
20. Silke Wenzel, 'Louise Dulcken', *Musik und Gender im Internet*, https://mugi.hfmt-hamburg.de/receive/mugi_person_00000202?lang=en.
21. *The Memoirs of Berlioz*, trans. David Cairns (London: Victor Gollancz, 1969; repr. Panther Books, 1970), p. 154.
22. David Cairns, *Berlioz*, vol. 1, *The Making of an Artist, 1803–1832* (Berkeley, CA: University of California Press, 1999), p. 388.
23. *Revue et gazette musicale*, vol. 12, no. 5 (2 February 1845), p. 38.
24. *Le Monde musical*, vol. 6, no. 14 (3 April 1845), p. 2.
25. Letters between Robert and Clara Schumann, June 1839–February 1840, quoted at https://www.schumann-portal.de/startseite.html.
26. Berthold Litzmann, *Clara Schumann*, trans. Grace E. Hadow (Cambridge: Cambridge University Press, 1913; repr. 2013), vol. 2, p. 263.
27. Katharine Ellis, 'Female Pianists and Their Male Critics in Nineteenth-Century Paris', *Journal of the American Musicological Society*, vol. 50, no. 2/3 (1997), pp. 353–85.
28. *Revue et gazette musicale*, vol. 12, no. 5 (2 February 1845), p. 38.
29. Bibliothèque Nationale de France, Département de Musique, Pleyel, Lettres Autographes, no. 21.
30. Hector Berlioz, *The Memoirs of Berlioz*, trans. David Cairns (London: Panther Books, 1970), p. 692.
31. Portraits on the Schumann portal, https://www.schumann-portal.de/around-1827.html.
32. Gerd Nauhaus (ed.), *The Marriage Diaries of Robert and Clara Schumann*, trans. Peter Ostwald (London: Robson Books, 1994), p. 185.
33. Quoted in Nancy B. Reich, *Clara Schumann: The Artist and the Woman* (Ithaca, NY, and London: Cornell University Press, 1985; rev. edn, 2001), p. 216.
34. Litzmann, *Clara Schumann*, vol. 2, p. 410.
35. Quoted in Joan Chissell, *Clara Schumann: A Dedicated Spirit* (London: Hamish Hamilton, 1983), p. 139.
36. *The Times*, 15 April 1856.
37. Eduard Hanslick, *Music Criticism 1846–99*, ed. Henry Pleasants (London: Penguin Books, 1950), p. 49.
38. Quoted on https://www.schumann-portal.de/wilhelmine-clauss-szarvady-1352.html.
39. *Signale* (1850), p. 381.
40. *Signale* (1850), p. 234.
41. *Signale* (1851), p. 107.
42. Quoted in *Signale* (1862), p. 71.
43. Quoted on https://www.schumann-portal.de/wilhelmine-clauss-szarvady-1352.html
44. *Süddeutsche Musik-Zeitung* (1852), p. 16, my translation.

45. *Signale* (1852), p. 58.
46. *Signale* (1853), p. 190.
47. Franz Liszt, *Briefwechsel mit seiner Mutter* (Eisenstadt: Land Burgenland, 2000), p. 473.
48. *Neue Zeitschrift für Musik* (1872), p. 341.
49. *Signale* (1863), p. 202.
50. *Musical World* (1853), p. 243.
51. *Musical World* (1853), p. 26f.
52. *Daily News*, 16 May 1853.
53. *Neue Zeitschrift für Musik* (1855), I, p. 38.
54. *Recent Music and Musicians: As Described in the Diaries and Correspondence of Ignaz Moscheles* (New York, 1873), p. 388.
55. Quoted in Harold C. Schonberg, *The Great Pianists* (New York: Simon and Schuster, 1987), pp. 251–2.
56. *Neue Zeitschrift für Musik* (1868), p. 180.
57. Quoted in Schonberg, *The Great Pianists*, p. 252.
58. Amy Fay, *Music-Study in Germany* (1880), https://www.gutenberg.org/files/37322/37322-h/37322-h.htm.
59. Amy Fay, *Music-Study in Germany* (repr. New York: Macmillan, 1922), chapter 19.
60. Franz Liszt, *Briefe aus ungarischen Sammlungen, 1835–1886*, ed. Margit Prahács, trans. Tilda Alpári (Budapest: Akadémiai Kiadó, 1966).
61. Ibid.
62. Quoted in *Monthly Musical Record*, 1 May 1881, p. 95.
63. *Signale* (1871), p. 566.
64. Edward Baxter Perry reviewing Sophie Menter in *Étude*, November 1899.
65. Quoted in Schonberg, *The Great Pianists*, p. 262.
66. Quoted in Joseph Horowitz, *Arrau on Music and Performance* (Mineola, NY: Dover Publications, 1982), p. 94.
67. Quoted on Marie Jaëll's page on the Sophie Drinker Institut website: https://www.sophie-drinker-institut.de/jaell-marie (my translation).
68. Article in *American Record Guide*, quoted at: https://en.wikipedia.org/wiki/Marie_Ja%C3%ABll.
69. Bethany Bell, *Classical Music's Unsung Heroines*, BBC Radio 3 (2015), https://wittgenstein-initiative.com/bbc-radio-3-leopoldine-wittgenstein.
70. Ibid.
71. From an interview in the *Montgomery Advertiser*, 12 February 1911, republished in Elise K. Kirk, *A History of the American Spirit* (Urbana, IL, and Chicago: University of Illinois Press, 1986), pp. 84–5.
72. Quoted in Steven H. Cornelius, *Music of the Civil War Era* (Westport, CT: Greenwood Press, 2004), p. 89.
73. *L'Art musical*, 17 May 1866, p. 190.
74. *Watson's Art Journal*, 24 August 1867.
75. *Novosti i birzhevaia gazeta*, 26 January 1891.
76. Quoted in Marie Agosin, *A Woman's Gaze: Latin American Women Artists* (Buffalo, NY: White Pine Press, 1998), p. 216.
77. Sir Henry Wood, *My Life of Music* (London: Victor Gollancz, 1938), pp. 147–8.
78. Marcia J. Citron, 'Gender, Professionalism and the Musical Canon', *Journal of Musicology*, vol. 8, no. 1 (1990), pp. 102–17.

79. Edward Baxter Perry reviewing Sophie Menter and Cécile Chaminade in *Étude*, November 1899.
80. Ward Stephens in *Étude*, June 1899.
81. Quoted by Charlotte Higgins, 'I Am Music's Nun', *Guardian*, 26 January 2002.
82. Richard Aldrich in the *New York Times*, 25 October 1908.
83. Higgins, 'I Am Music's Nun'.
84. Fay, *Music-Study in Germany*, chapter 13.
85. *New York Times*, 24 December 1886.
86. Tchaikovsky in his diary, 27 April [= 9 May] 1891, quoted in Modeste Tchaikovsky, *The Life and Letters of Peter Ilich Tchaikovsky*, ed. Rosa Newmarch (New York: Vienna House, 1973), vol. 2, p. 649.
87. Quoted in the *Chicago Daily Tribune*, 25 February 1894.
88. Harold Bauer, *Harold Bauer, His Book* (New York: W.W. Norton, 1948), p. 135.
89. Quoted in Beth Abelson Macleod, *Women Performing Music: The Emergence of American Women as Classical Instrumentalists and Conductors* (Jefferson, NC: McFarland, 2000), p. 80.
90. *Étude*, vol. 5, no. 4 (April 1887), p. 51.
91. Quoted in Schonberg, *The Great Pianists*, pp. 334–5.
92. Quoted in Abelson Macleod, *Women Performing Music*, pp. 85–6.
93. Steinway and Sons to Fannie Bloomfield Zeisler, 22 December 1903, from the unpublished Fannie Bloomfield Zeisler Papers, American Jewish Archives, Cincinnati, OH.
94. 'Fannie Bloomfield-Zeisler's Silver Anniversary', *Musical Courier*, 21 March 1900, pp. 19–20, quoted in Abelson Macleod, *Women Performing Music*, p. 86.
95. John C. Freund in *Musical America*, 18 February 1899, quoted in Sigmund Zeisler, American Jewish Archives, Cincinnati, OH.
96. Christina L. Reitz, 'Fannie Bloomfield-Zeisler: Concert Pianist Battling Gender Lines in the Early 20th Century', *International Journal of Arts and Commerce*, vol. 1, no. 1, https://ijac.org.uk/images/frontImages/Vol_1_No_1_/9_Zeisler_submission_humanities.pdf.
97. Quoted in Diana Hallmann, 'Fannie Bloomfield-Zeisler', *Shalvi/Hyman Encyclopedia of Jewish Women*, https://jwa.org/encyclopedia/article/zeisler-fannie-bloomfield#pid-13473.
98. Quoted in William Robin, 'Amy Beach, a Pioneering American Composer, Turns 150', *New York Times*, 1 September 2017, https://www.nytimes.com/2017/09/01/arts/music/amy-beach-women-american-composer.html.
99. Ibid.
100. Ibid.
101. Quoted in Denise von Glahn, *Music and the Skillful Listener* (Bloomington, IN: Indiana University Press, 2013), p. 33.
102. Jonathan Blumhofer, 'Rethinking the Repertoire #9 – Amy Beach's "Gaelic" Symphony', *The Arts Fuse*, https://artsfuse.org/141769/rethinking-the-repertoire-9-amy-beachs-gaelic-symphony.
103. Quoted in Hyperion Records sleeve note written by Nigel Simeone, 2017, for the Amy Beach piano concerto.
104. Ibid.
105. Marguerite Long, *At the Piano with Fauré* (Paris, 1963; English trans. London: Kahn and Averill, 1980), p. 67.

106. Fauré, letter to his wife, 31 July 1907 in J. Barrie Jones (ed.), *Gabriel Fauré: A Life in Letters* (London: Batsford, 1988), p. 127.
107. Cecilia Dunoyer, *Marguerite Long: A Life in French Music, 1874–1966* (Bloomington, IN: Indiana University Press, 1993), pp. 39–40.
108. Ibid., p. 67.
109. Debussy to his publisher Durand, quoted at http://www.bruzanemediabase.com/eng/Works/Piano-Etudes-Claude-Debussy.
110. Marguerite Long, *At the Piano with Ravel* (Paris, 1971; English trans. London: Dent, 1973), p. 16.
111. Ibid.
112. Dunoyer, *Marguerite Long*, p. 125.
113. Virgil Thomson, *New York Herald Tribune*, 22 October 1942.
114. Wanda Landowska, spoken introduction to recordings of J.S. Bach, *Two-Part and Three-Part Inventions* (RCA album, 1959), https://archive.org/details/J.S.BACHTwo-PartAndThree-PartInventions/01.+Spoken+Introduction+by+Madame+Landowska.mp3.
115. *Music Clubs Magazine*, September 1937.
116. Donna Pucciani, 'Olga Samaroff (1882–1948), American Musician and Educator' (unpublished doctoral thesis, New York University, 1979), p. 78.
117. Quoted at https://www.encyclopedia.com/women/encyclopedias-almanacs-transcripts-and-maps/samaroff-olga-1882-1948.
118. Quoted in *Pianist* magazine, 3 May 2021.
119. Quoted on Dinu Lipatti website: https://www.dinulipatti.org/about-composer-and-professor-nadia-boulanger-in-a-letter-to-mihail-jora-january-26-1936-en-a234.
120. Léonie Rosenstiel, *Nadia Boulanger: A Life in Music* (New York: W.W. Norton, 1998), p. 152.
121. Quoted at https://daily.redbullmusicacademy.com/2017/02/nadia-boulanger-feature.
122. Quoted from memory from a television documentary, *Daniel Barenboim in His Own Words*, Pegasus Productions, shown on BBC4 in the UK on 19 December 2021.
123. Quoted in Marian Cecilia McKenna, *Myra Hess: A Portrait* (London: Hamish Hamilton, 1976), p. 82.
124. Quoted on the website of the National Gallery, London, https://www.nationalgallery.org.uk/about-us/history/the-myra-hess-concerts/how-the-concerts-started.
125. Quoted on the website of the National Gallery, London, https://www.nationalgallery.org.uk/about-us/history/the-myra-hess-concerts/the-blitz.
126. Debussy, letter to André Caplet, 25 November 1909, *Debussy Letters*, trans. Roger Nichols (London: Faber and Faber, 1987), p. 216.
127. 'Guiomar Novaes, Leading Brazilian Concert Pianist, Dies', *New York Times*, 9 March 1979, https://www.nytimes.com/1979/03/09/archives/guiomar-novaes-leading-brazilian-concert-pianist-dies-played-for.html.
128. Quoted in Harriette Brower, *Piano Mastery: The Harriette Brower Interviews 1915–26* (Mineola, NY: Dover, 2003), p. 130.
129. Quoted at: https://www.encyclopedia.com/women/encyclopedias-almanacs-transcripts-and-maps/novaes-guiomar-1895-1979.

130. Quoted in Brower, *Piano Mastery*, p. 132.
131. 'Guiomar Novaes Declines to Call It a Piano Finale', *New York Times*, 2 December 1972.
132. Ibid.
133. Ibid.
134. Quoted in Brower, *Piano Mastery*, p. 132.
135. 'Guiomar Novaes, Leading Brazilian Concert Pianist, Dies'.
136. Ruth Rosenfelder, 'Clara Haskil', *Shalvi/Hyman Encyclopedia of Jewish Women*, https://jwa.org/encyclopedia/article/haskil-clara.
137. Ibid.
138. Ibid.
139. Quoted in Bruno Monsaingeon, *Sviatoslav Richter: Notebooks and Conversations*, trans. Stewart Spencer (Princeton, NJ: Princeton University Press, 2001), p. 51.
140. Classic FM, 'One Amazing Pianist Dared to Criticise Joseph Stalin – and Remarkably Lived to Tell the Tale', 23 August 2016, https://www.classicfm.com/discover-music/latest/maria-yudina-stalin/#:~:text=Maria%20Yudina%2C%20who%20dared%20to,17%20years%2C%20dying%20in%201970.
141. Monsaingeon, *Sviatoslav Richter: Notebooks and Conversations*, p. 51.
142. Ibid.
143. Ibid.
144. Ibid.
145. Steve Roberson, *Lili Kraus: Hungarian Pianist, Texas Teacher, Personality Extraordinaire* (Fort Worth, TX: TCU Press, 2000), p. 4.
146. For this and other tales about Kraus I have drawn on Roberson, *Lili Kraus*.
147. Ibid., p. 11.
148. Ibid., p. 13.
149. Ibid., p. 28.
150. Ibid., p. 39.
151. *Gramophone*, August 2006.
152. Eileen Joyce interviewed by John Amis, https://www.youtube.com/watch?v=swgikN-b3OQ.
153. Percy Grainger, letter printed in *Daily News* (Perth, Australia), 5 August 1926, p. 4.
154. Eileen Joyce interviewed by John Amis, https://www.youtube.com/watch?v=swgikN-b3OQ.
155. Eileen Joyce (1946), https://www.youtube.com/watch?v=iQW9DXZc5eI.
156. Quoted in Helen Walker-Hill, *From Spirituals to Symphonies: African-American Women Composers and Their Music* (Urbana, IL: University of Illinois Press, 2007), p. 156.
157. Ibid.
158. Ibid.
159. Slipped Disc, 'How to Fill Carnegie Hall? Shun the *NY Times*', 12 April 2015, https://slippedisc.com/2015/04/how-to-fill-carnegie-hall-shun-the-ny-times.
160. Belinda McKay, 'Engendering Nancy Weir and Musical Biography', *Coastscripts*, 1994, https://www.academia.edu/26292919/Engendering_Music_Nancy_Weir_and_Musical_Biography.
161. Ibid.
162. Ibid.

163. https://en.wikipedia.org/wiki/Nancy_Weir.
164. McKay, 'Engendering Nancy Weir'.
165. Ibid.
166. Quoted in ABC radio programme *Pianist Alicia de Larrocha*, broadcast 6 September 2022.
167. Alberto Ráfols, 'Remembering Alicia de Larrocha: Thoughts on Her Artistry, Teaching and Musical Legacy', *American Music Teacher*, August/September 2015, p. 25.
168. Ibid.
169. Bob Sherman in conversation with Alicia de Larrocha for New York's WQXR radio programme, broadcast in 1978, https://www.youtube.com/watch?v=lFwpirv0NeU.
170. Obituary by James Methuen-Campbell, *Independent*, 27 November 1993.
171. Quoted in the CD booklet for *Legendary Russian Pianists*, no. 8 (Brilliant Classics, 2014).
172. 'Yvonne Loriod: Pianist Who Became the Muse and Foremost Interpreter of the Works of Her Husband Olivier Messiaen', *Independent*, 20 May 2010.
173. Quoted in Yvonne Loriod's obituary, *Guardian*, 18 May 2010.
174. Quoted at https://www.oliviermessiaen.org/yvonne-loriod.
175. Quoted in Roderick Chadwick and Peter Hill, *Olivier Messiaen's Catalogue d'oiseaux: From Conception to Performance* (Cambridge: Cambridge University Press, 2018), p. 2.
176. Quoted in 'Yvonne Loriod, Pianist and Messiaen Muse, Dies at 86', *New York Times*, 18 May 2010.
177. Quoted at https://en.wikipedia.org/wiki/Zhu_Xiao-Mei.
178. Quoted in *The Return Is the Movement of Tao: Zhu Xiao-Mei and the Goldberg Variations*, film by Michael Mollard for Medici TV, 2014.

Jazz and light-music pianists

1. Ethel Waters, *His Eye Is on the Sparrow: An Autobiography* (Boston, MA: Da Capo Press, 1992), pp. 77, 173.
2. D. Antoinette Handy and Mary Lou Williams, 'First Lady of the Jazz Keyboard', *The Black Perspective in Music*, vol. 8, no. 2 (1980), pp. 195–214.
3. Quoted in 'Lovie Austin: The Hidden Blues Queen Who Inspired Swing Kingmakers', *Syncopated Times*, 26 August 2019, https://syncopatedtimes.com/lovie-austin-the-hidden-blues-queen-who-inspired-swing-kingmakers.
4. Quoted in Phil Patras, *Dead Man Blues: Jelly Roll Morton Way out West* (Berkeley, CA: University of California Press, 2001), p. 16.
5. Quoted in the CD booklet for *Raie da Costa: The Parlophone Girl* (Shellwood Records, 2001).
6. Quoted in Handy and Williams, 'First Lady of the Jazz Keyboard', p. 210.
7. Ibid., p. 213.
8. Quoted in Tammy Kernodle, *Soul on Soul* (Urbana, IL: University of Illinois Press, 2020).
9. Quoted in Handy and Williams, 'First Lady of the Jazz Keyboard', p. 200.
10. Quoted in Whitney Balliett, *American Musicians: 56 Portraits in Jazz* (Oxford: Oxford University Press, 1986), p. 98.

11. Quoted in Handy and Williams, 'First Lady of the Jazz Keyboard', p. 199.
12. Ibid., p. 203.
13. George McKay, 'Winifred Atwell and Her "Other Piano": 16 Hit Singles and a "Blanket of Silence", Sounding the Limits of Jazz', in Jason Toynbee et al. (eds), *Black British Jazz: Routes, Ownership and Performance* (Burlington, VT: Ashgate, 2014), pp. 153–71.
14. Ibid.
15. Ibid.
16. Quoted in Ruth Feldstein, '"I Don't Trust You Anymore": Nina Simone, Culture, and Black Activism in the 1960s', *Journal of American History*, vol. 91, no. 4 (2005), p. 1354.
17. Quoted in Martha Feldman and Judith T. Zeitlin (eds), *The Voice as Something More: Essays towards Materiality* (Chicago: University of Chicago Press, 2019), p. 195.
18. Nina Simone and Stephen Cleary, *I Put a Spell on You: The Autobiography of Nina Simone* (New York: Pantheon Books, 1991), p. 68.
19. Quoted in Feldstein, '"I Don't Trust You Anymore"', p. 1349.
20. Simone and Cleary, *I Put a Spell on You*, p. 89.

Further perspectives

1. Judith Tick, 'Women and Music: Since 1800', *Grove Music Online*, https://doi.org/10.1093/gmo/9781561592630.article.52554.
2. Eduard Hanslick, *The Beautiful in Music: A Contribution to the Revisal of Musical Aesthetics*, 7th edition, trans. Gustav Cohen (London: Novello and Co., 1891), pp. 100–1.
3. Interviewed in *Gender and Music*, programme 3, BBC Open University radio series, 1999.
4. Kae Tempest, *On Connection* (London: Faber and Faber, 2022), reviewed by Holly Williams in the *Observer*, 25 October 2020.
5. Quoted by Frank Almond, 'Röntgen Family', *A Violin's Life*, https://aviolinslife.org/rontgen-family.

Where are we now?

1. 'Gender Differences in Major Competitions and Performing Careers', *Pianists for Alternatively Sized Keyboards*, https://paskpiano.org/gender-differences-in-major-competitions-and-performing-careers.
2. Arthur Loesser, *Men, Women and Pianos: A Social History* (New York: Simon and Schuster, 1954), p. 612.
3. Ibid., p. 613.
4. Martin Bruhl, 'Music and Musicians', *Burlington Gazette*, 18 August 1916, quoted in Abelson Macleod, *Women Performing Music: The Emergence of American Women as Classical Instrumentalists and Conductors* (Jefferson, NC: McFarland, 2000), p. 93.

Coda

1. Virginia Valian, *Why So Slow? The Advancement of Women* (Cambridge, MA: MIT Press, 1999), p. 323.

FURTHER READING

We do not have an extensive literature on the subject of women pianists in history. Most of the books on female pianists focus on a specific area, such as women pianists in London, in Paris or France, in Vienna, in America, in twentieth-century literature and film, in nineteenth-century Europe or in jazz and popular music. There are books about women composers, a category that overlaps with women pianists since many composers are also good pianists. There are books about individual women such as Clara Schumann, the first woman pianist whose career made a serious impression on historians. There are memoirs by male pianists that mention their female colleagues. In a branch of memoir-writing we hear from women who studied the piano seriously and found it an enriching pursuit even if they never became professional. Then there are more general books about pianists, often written by men. Typically the main focus is male pianists, and even when women are included they are often given shorter shrift than the men, so counting the number of index entries relating to women does not tell the whole story. Happily, the balance is being redressed by a growing number of female musicologists and historians who make a point of researching and drawing attention to the achievements of women; this can include editing and publishing their compositions.

One obvious point to make is that most prominent writers on music have been men. And despite the growing number of female pianists who write, most writer-pianists have been men, from Robert Schumann through Debussy and Busoni to Rosen, Brendel, Gould, Barenboim and Hough. This is not a trivial point. As Caroline Criado Perez writes in her recent book *Invisible Women*, the assumption that the male point of view is the 'default' is built into society at a fundamental level, and music is not exempt from this.

Ammer, Christine, *Unsung: A History of Women in American Music* (Westport, CT: Greenwood Press, 1980)
Arkatov, Salome Ramras (dir.), *The Legacy of Rosina Lhévinne* (DVD)
Berlioz, Hector, *Memoirs* (1870)
Bowers, Jane, and Judith Tick, *Women Making Music: The Western Art Tradition, 1150–1950* (Urbana, IL: University of Illinois Press, 1986)
Burgan, Mary, 'Heroines at the Piano: Women and Music in Nineteenth-Century Fiction', *Victorian Studies*, vol. 30, no. 1 (1986)

FURTHER READING

Chissell, Joan, *Clara Schumann: A Dedicated Spirit* (London: Hamish Hamilton, 1983)

Citron, Marcia J., *Gender and the Musical Canon* (1993; repr. Urbana, IL: University of Illinois Press, 2000)

Clark, Linda L., *Women and Achievement in Nineteenth-Century Europe* (Cambridge: Cambridge University Press, 2008)

Criado Perez, Caroline, *Invisible Women: Exposing Data Bias in a World Designed for Men* (London: Vintage, 2020)

Dunoyer, Cecilia, *Marguerite Long: A Life in French Music, 1874–1966* (Bloomington, IN: Indiana University Press, 1993)

Ehrlich, Cyril, *The Piano: A History* (1976; rev. edn Oxford: Clarendon Press, 1990)

Eigeldinger, Jean-Jacques, *Chopin: Pianist and Teacher: As Seen by His Pupils* (Cambridge: Cambridge University Press, 1988)

Ellis, Katharine, 'Female Pianists and Their 19th Century Male Critics', *Journal of the American Musicological Society*, vol. 50, no. 2/3 (1997)

Fay, Amy, *Music-Study in Germany* (1880)

Fuller, Sophie, and Nicky Losseff (eds), *The Idea of Music in Victorian Fiction* (Farnham: Ashgate, 2004)

Grant, Elizabeth, *Memoirs of a Highland Lady*, vol. 1 (1898; repr. Edinburgh: Canongate, 1988)

Green, Lucy, *Music, Gender, Education* (Cambridge: Cambridge University Press, 1997)

Hamilton, Kenneth, *After the Golden Age: Romantic Pianism and Modern Performance* (Oxford: Oxford University Press, 2007)

Hayghe, Jennifer, 'A History of Women Pianists', unpublished doctoral thesis, Juilliard School, New York, 1997

Kennaway, James, 'The Piano Plague: The Nineteenth-Century Medical Critique of Female Musical Education', *Gesnerus*, vol. 68, no. 1 (2011)

Kline, Donna Staley, *Olga Samaroff Stokowski: An American Virtuoso on the World Stage* (College Station, TX: Texas A&M University Press, 1996)

Lancaster, Geoffrey, *The First Fleet Piano: A Musician's View*, vol. 1 (Canberra: ANU Press, 2015)

Landowska, Wanda, *Landowska on Music*, ed. Denise Restout (New York: Stein and Day, 1965)

Lebrecht, Norman, 'Spare Us the Skintight Sonata', *The Critic*, November 2021

Loesser, Arthur, *Men, Women and Pianos: A Social History* (New York: Simon and Schuster, 1954)

McCarthy, Margaret William, *Amy Fay: America's Notable Woman of Music* (Sterling Heights, MI: Harmonie Park Press, 1995)

McCarthy, S. Margaret, 'Amy Fay: The American Years', *American Music*, vol. 3, no. 1 (1985)

Messing, Scott, *Marching to the Canon: The Life of Schubert's Marche Militaire* (Rochester, NY: University of Rochester Press, 2014)

Monsaingeon, Bruno, *Sviatoslav Richter: Notebooks and Conversations* (Princeton, NJ: Princeton University Press, 2002)

Neuls-Bates, Carol (ed.), *Women in Music*, rev. edn (Boston, MA: Northeastern University Press, 1996)

Pendle, Karin (ed.), *Women and Music: A History* (Bloomington, IN: Indiana University Press, 1991)
Reich, Nancy B., 'The Power of Class: Fanny Hensel', in *Mendelssohn and His World*, ed. R. Larry Todd (Princeton, NJ: Princeton University Press, 1991)
Reich, Nancy B., *Clara Schumann: The Artist and the Woman* (Ithaca, NY: Cornell University Press, 2001)
Roberson, Steven Henry, *Lili Kraus: Hungarian Pianist, Texas Teacher, and Personality Extraordinaire* (Fort Worth, TX: TCU Press, 2000)
Roberts, Sophy, *The Lost Pianos of Siberia* (London: Penguin, 2020)
Rousseau, Jean-Jacques, *Lettre à M. d'Alembert sur les spectacles*, 1758 (Paris: Garnier-Flammarion, 1967)
Rowland, David (ed.), *The Cambridge Companion to the Piano* (Cambridge: Cambridge University Press, 1998)
Schonberg, Harold, *The Great Pianists* (New York: Simon and Schuster, 1987)
Shaffer, Karen A., and Neva Garner Greenwood, *Maud Powell, Pioneer American Violinist* (Ames, IA: Iowa State University Press, 1988)
Tempest, Kae, *On Connection* (London: Faber and Faber, 2022)
Tick, Judith, Margaret Ericson and Ellen Koskoff, 'Women in Music', *Grove Music Online*, 2001, https://doi-org.nls.idm.oclc.org/10.1093/gmo/9781561592630.article.52554
Valian, Virginia, *Why So Slow? The Advancement of Women* (Cambridge, MA: MIT Press, 1999)
Wallace, Robert K., *A Century of Music-Making: The Lives of Josef and Rosina Lhévinne* (Bloomington, IN: Indiana University Press, 1976)
A useful website mentioning other unknown women pianists: https://www.libertyparkmusic.com/greatest-women-classical-pianists
The Sophie Drinker Institut in Bremen has an excellent website devoted to research into European female instrumentalists: https://www.sophie-drinker-institut.de/startseite

ACKNOWLEDGEMENTS

I would like to thank the women pianists who generously agreed to answer my questions about their experience of being female artists in today's music world.

Thank you to: Professor Craig Clunas for advice on the history of pianists in China, Dr Maya Feile Tomes for advice on translation from several languages, Ben Tindall for telling me about his ancestor Louise Dulcken and Dr Robert Philip for advice on countless topics, as well as for compiling the index.

Thanks to the piano students, piano teachers, amateur pianists and concert-goers who told me tales of their experience as players and listeners.

Thanks to Julian Loose at Yale University Press for asking me to write this book.

INDEX

Academia Marshall, Barcelona 167
Adam, Jean-Louis
  piano studies 44
Adelaide, Queen
  Lucy Anderson, her court pianist 54
Adorno, Theodor 148
agents 138, 140, 167, 224, 226, 227, 228, 230, 237
Albéniz, Isaac 165
Albert, Eugen d' 100
Albert, Mr
  host of Mozart 8
Algiers 163
Allgemeine musikalische Zeitung 56
Altes Michaelerhaus, Vienna 34–5
Amadeus (Shaffer, Forman) 27
amateur music-making, value of 207, 219
American Civil War 97
American Revolution 25, 26
Anacreontic Society
  concert series 38–9
  welcomes Haydn 39
Anderson, George Frederick 55
Anderson (Philpot), Lucy 54–6
  charity concerts 56
  gender-specific criticism 56
  performs at Philharmonic Society 55
  performs Beethoven's concertos 55
  pupils 55, 56, 82
  repertoire 55
  royal appointments 54–5
  teaches Queen Victoria and her children 55, 56
Ángeles, Victoria de los 168
angels 11
antiquity
  images of women musicians in 5
Argerich, Martha 160, 214, 219
Armstrong, Lil Hardin 194
Armstrong, Louis 188
Arne, Thomas
  Judith 8
Arnstein, Fanny
  Bach performed in her salon 42
Arrau, Claudio 2
Artaria
  Haydn's publisher 37
L'Art musical 98
Ashkenazy, Vladimir 212
Atlantic City
  Midtown Bar 197
Atlantic Monthly 85
Atwell, Winifred 191–4
  boogie-woogie 191–4
  classical training 191
  combines classical and boogie-woogie 192, 193
  compositions
    'Let's Have Another Party!' 192
    Piarco Boogie 191
    'The Poor People of Paris' 192
  dresses 193
  honky-tonk 192
  manner 193
  marriage 191

INDEX

'other piano' 192, 193
on racism 192
record sales 191, 192
records Grieg piano concerto 192
Royal Variety Show 192
settles in Australia 193
'The Story of Three Loves'
   (Rachmaninoff) 192
success in Australia 191, 193
success in UK 191
Auenbrugger, Marianna von 37
   Haydn on 37
   Haydn dedicates sonatas to 37
   keyboard sonata 37
   pupil of Salieri 37
Auernhammer, Maria von 30–3
   compositions 32
      variations on 'Der Vogelfänger' 32
   marriage 32
   Mozart on 30–1
   Mozart's compositions for 31–2
   performs Beethoven's first piano
      concerto 33
   relationship with Mozart 30–2
      plays duets with Mozart 31–2
   as teacher 32
Austen, Jane 55
   Emma 16
   family music albums 18
   Sense and Sensibility 14
Austin, Lovie 181–5
   compositions
      'Bama Bound Blues' 183
      'Bo-Weavil Blues' 183
      'Chirping the Blues' 183
      'Downhearted Blues' (with
         Alberta Hunter) 183
   forms Blue Serenaders 183
   'masculine' style 184
   at Monogram Theater 183
   royalties 183
   session musician 183
   training 182, 183–4
   transcriptions 183
   Mary Lou Williams on 183–4
Australia 84, 100, 155, 156, 163, 164,
   191, 193
Austrian National Library 32

Bach, Anna Magdalena 7
   J.S. Bach dedicates *Kleine*
      Notenbüchlein to her 6–7
Bach, Carl Philipp Emanuel 59
   concerto for harpsichord and piano
      42
   quartets 40
   teaches Dussek and Hüllmandel 44
   works commissioned by Sara Levy
      40, 42
Bach, Johann Christian 23
   Sonatas op 5 7
Bach, Johann Sebastian 7, 62, 79, 82,
   94, 96, 128, 137, 139, 143,
   169–70, 197
   Brandenburg Concerto no 5 41
   Goldberg Variations 128, 179
   harpsichord concerto in D minor 41
   'Jesu, Joy of Man's Desiring' 139
   Kleine Notenbüchlein 6–7
   St Matthew Passion revived by
      Mendelssohn 41–2
   teacher of Johann Philipp
      Kirnberger 40
   two-part inventions 128–9
   Well-Tempered Clavier 60, 119,
      148–9, 170, 172
Bach, Wilhelm Friedmann
   128–9
   and Sara Levy 40, 42
Bachauer, Gina 210
Backhaus, Wilhelm 1, 155
Baldwin, James 196, 198
Ballets Russes 115
Baltimore 108
Barcelona 166, 167
Barenboim, Daniel
   hands 212, 233
   on Nadia Boulanger 137
Bargiel, Adolph 73
Bargiel, Woldemar 73
Barraqué, Jean
   piano sonata 173
Bartók, Béla 148
   Lili Kraus on 152
   piano concerto no. 2 233
   teaches Lili Kraus 151–2
Bartolozzi, Gaetano 38

Bartolozzi, Therese *see* Jansen Bartolozzi, Therese
Bath, England 55
Bauer, Harold 110
Bayreuth 113
BBC 186
Pot Black 192
Beach (Cheney), Amy 109, 117–21, 234
   Calvinist upbringing 118
   compositions
      Dreaming 120
      Gaelic Symphony 120
      Grandmother's Garden 120
      Hermit Thrush at Eve, at Morn 120
      neglect and rediscovery 117
      piano concerto 120 –1
         Beach on 120–1
         dedicated to Carreño 121
      piano quintet 120
      Scottish Legend 120
      self-taught composer 119
      sonata for violin and piano 120
      songs 121
   early success as pianist 118
   on her isolation 119
   on the joy of performing 121
   marriage 118–19
   performing and teaching restricted 118–19
   portrait 119
   returns to concert platform 120
   studies in USA 117, 118
   tours Europe 120, 121
Beach, Dr Henry 118
Beatles, the 196
Beauvoir, Simone de
   The Second Sex 4
bebop 189
Beecham, Sir Thomas 138
Beethoven, Ludwig van 59, 62, 94, 137, 146, 197, 202, 204
   compared with Maria Martines 36
   complete sonatas performed by Marie Jaëll 91
   concertos performed by Lucy Anderson 55
   description by Baron de Trémont 44
   piano concerto no. 1
      played by M. von Auernhammer 32
   piano concerto no. 3 162
   piano concerto no. 4 138
   piano concerto no. 5 157
   piano sonatas 172, 207–8
      recorded by Maria Ginsberg 150
      recorded by Annie Fischer 161
   piano sonata in C opus 53 'Waldstein' 81, 109, 161
   piano sonata in F minor opus 57 'Appassionata'
      played by Wilhelmine Clauss-Szarvady 79
      played by Louise Dulcken 66
      played by Myra Hess 139
      played by Clara Schumann 73
   piano sonata in B flat opus 106 'Hammerklavier'
      played by Annie Fischer 162
      played by Arabella Goddard 82
      played by Clara Schumann 78
   piano sonata in E opus 109 94
   piano trio in B flat opus 97 'Archduke' 213
   string quartet in C sharp minor opus 131 113
Belgiojoso, Countess Cristina
   salon 50
Bendixen, Louise 67
Berger, Ludwig
   teaches Fanny Mendelssohn 60
Berlin 40–1, 42, 59, 60, 62, 73, 95, 99–100, 107, 109, 110, 125, 129, 153, 162, 203
   Hochschule 126
   Philharmonic Orchestra 100
   Sing-Akademie 41, 42, 60, 73, 99
      Bach manuscripts 42
      concert hall built 41
Berlioz, Hector 59, 79
   engaged to Marie Pleyel 69
   Euphonia 69
   Memoirs
      on Marie Pleyel 68–9

INDEX

on Wilhelmine Clauss-Szarvady 79–80
Soirées dans l'orchestre 69
Bernhardt, Sarah 111
Bible, the 5
Bielitz, Silesia 110
Bigot, Marie
   teaches Fanny Mendelssohn 60
Billet, Alexandre 83
Birmingham, Alabama 199
Bizet, Georges 102, 103
   Carmen 102
Black composers 157, 175, 181–5, 187–91, 191–4, 196–200, 236
Black pianists 157–9, 174–8, 181–5, 187–91, 191–4, 194–6, 196–200, 235–6
Black Renaissance 236
Blackwell, Alice Stone 239
Blanchard, Henri
   on Marie Pleyel 70
Bliss, Arthur
   piano concerto 156
Bloomfield Zeisler, Fannie 110–13
   career supported by husband 110–11
   declines invitation to the White House 112
   on the female performer 112–13, 219, 227
   frailty and determination 110, 112
   image as housewife 110, 111–12
   pupil of Leschetitzky 110, 111
   reviews 111–12
   tours 111
Blumhofer, Jonathan
   on Amy Beach's *Gaelic Symphony* 120
Boccherini, Luigi 24
   Sonatas for piano and violin 24
   on Brillon de Jouy 24
Bolívar, Simón 96, 99
   Youth Orchestra of Venezuela 96
Bologna
   Conservatoire 57
Bonds, Margaret 157–9, 235, 236
   and Langston Hughes 158, 159
   at Northwestern University 158
   compositions
      Ballad of the Brown King 159
      Credo 159
      Marquette Street Blues 157
      'Sea Ghost' 158
      Spiritual Suite 159
      'Troubled Water' 159
   encounters racism 158
   Margaret Bonds Chamber Society 159
   pioneering Black musician 157, 158, 159
   pupil of Roy Harris 158
   pupil of Florence Price 158
boogie-woogie 191–4, 195
Borgatti, Renata 115
Boston, USA 87, 96, 109, 111, 117, 118, 121, 179
   New England Conservatory 179
   Symphony Orchestra 109, 117
Boston Globe 142
Botsford, George
   Black and White Rag 192
Boulanger, Ernest 132–3
Boulanger, Lili 133, 134
   death 134
   wins *Prix de Rome* 134
Boulanger, Nadia 116, 123, 132–7, 220
   as composer 133–4
   as conductor 132, 134, 136
   devotion to sister Lili 133, 134
   at French School for Americans 135
   on Gershwin 135
   influence of father 132–3
   manner 135–6
   at Paris Conservatoire
      denied teaching post 134
      fails to win *Prix de Rome* 133–4
      l'affaire fugue 133–4
      pupil of Fauré 133
   as pianist 132, 133, 135
      records with Lipatti 135
      tours with Pugno 133
   prejudices 136
   pupils 135, 137
      Daniel Barenboim
      Donald Byrd
      Elliot Carter

INDEX

Aaron Copland
George Gershwin
Egberto Gismonti
Philip Glass
Quincy Jones
Dinu Lipatti
Astor Piazzolla
recordings
  Brahms *Liebeslieder Waltzes* 135
  Monteverdi madrigals 135
as teacher 132, 134–5, 136–7
  Barenboim on 137
  Glass on 137
  Lipatti on 135
Boulder City, Australia 155
Boulez, Pierre 148
  second piano sonata 173
  Structures II 173
  on value of music training 207
Boyer, Isabella 113
Brahms, Johannes 93, 94, 202
  compared with Montgeroult 46
  friendship with the Schumanns 78
  piano concerto no. 2 107
  piano quintet 213
Brain, Dennis 139
Breitkopf and Härtel 52
Brickler, Mrs 8
Brief Encounter (film) 155, 156
Brillon de Jouy, Aldegonde 24
Brillon de Jouy, Anne-Louise 23–6
  Boccherini writes sonatas for 24
  compositions 25–6
    Marche des Insurgents 25
    sonatas 25–6
  friendship with Benjamin Franklin 25–6
  portrait 24
Brillon de Jouy, Cunégonde 24
broadcasting 3
Broadwood, John 7–8
  Arabella Goddard tours with piano 84
  pianos admired by Haydn and Beethoven 8
  piano acquired by Szymanowska 53
  piano liked by Fanny Mendelssohn 59

Brontë, Charlotte 10
Brooks, Romaine 115
Brower, Harriette
  on Guiomar Novaes 142–3
Brussels 147, 163
  Conservatoire 57, 71
  Ysaÿe Competition 163
Bucharest 144
Budapest 150, 151, 160
  Franz Liszt Academy 151, 160
Bülow, Hans von
  Beethoven sonata cycle 130–1
Burgoyne, Lt-General John 25
Burney, Charles
  on Brillon de Jouy 25
  on Maria Martines 35
Burton, Robert
  Anatomy of Melancholy 14
Busoni, Feruccio 112, 144–5, 151, 202
Butt, Clara 103
Byrd, Donald 135

Caballé, Montserrat 168
cadenza 39, 67, 224
Cairngorm Mountains 15
Cairo 163
Cambridge
  University of 157
Canada 84
Canals, Maria 210
Cannabich, Rosa 33
  father concertmaster of Mannheim Court Orchestra 33
  performs Mozart's concerto in B flat K238 33
  'portrait' of her in Mozart's sonata in C K309 33
  pupil of Mozart 33
Cape Town 185
  Municipal Orchestra 185
Caracas 99, 101
Carpenter, John Alden 158
Carreño, Teresa 96–101, 121, 234
  child prodigy 96–8
  compositions
    Himno a Bolívar 99
    Un Bal en rêve 100

honours 101
improvises 98
marriage 99, 100
'masculine' playing 101
opera company in Caracas 99
Paderewski on 100–1
plays at White House 96–8, 101
portrait 97
pupil of Gottschalk 96
pupil of Anton Rubinstein and G. Matthias 99
recommended by Rossini 98
reviews 98, 100
settles in Berlin 100
singer 99
tours 98–100
Henry Wood on 101
Carter, Elliot 135
Casals, Pablo 94, 146
Cassadó, Gaspar 168
Certain, Marie-Françoise 6
praised by La Fontaine 6
Cézanne, Paul 12
Chabrier, Emmanuel 103
Chaminade, Cécile 102–6
admired by Liszt 103
appearance 104–5
awarded Légion d'Honneur 102
Chaminade Clubs 104
compositions 102–4, 106
Air de ballet 105
Automne 103
concertino for piano 103
cover designs 105
earnings from 104
for amateurs 103, 106
Guitare 103
'L'Anneau d'argent' 102
Les Amazones 106
liked by Queen Victoria 105
piano sonata 103
piano trios 103
prelude for organ 104
reviews 104, 106
Scarf Dance 102
on Debussy 106
marriage 105
merchandise 104
plays at White House 106
portrait 105
pupil of Benjamin Godard 103
studies at home 102
success in USA 106
tours 103–4, 106
Charlotte, Queen 40
Chattanooga, Tennessee 182
Cherubini, Luigi 51
Chicago 87, 111, 112
Monogram Theater 183
Symphony Orchestra 112, 157, 158, 175
Women's Symphony Orchestra 158
China
Cultural Revolution 178–9
rise of piano and pianists in 178
cholera 54, 62, 99, 108
Chopin, Frédéric 78, 112, 118, 125, 143, 185, 197, 202
'Funeral March' sonata 109
hands 233
imitates Liszt 86
piano concerto no. 1 in E minor 157
piano concerto no. 2 in F minor 64, 112
relationship with Liszt 69
reputation as pianist 49
'Revolutionary' Study inspired by Montgeroult 46–7
and Maria Szymanowska 53, 54
teaching fees 18
cithara 5, 6
civil rights 157, 177, 196, 198, 199, 209
Civil Rights Act 209
March on Washington 196, 199
Clark, Kenneth 138
Clauss-Szarvardy, Wilhelmine 79–82
Berlioz on 79–80
compared with Chopin 79
duets with Clara Schumann 79, 81
Liszt dedicates works to 79
Liszt's mother on 81
marriage 81
performs J.S. Bach 9, 80
performs Baroque music 79
performs chamber music 79, 81–2
performs with Joachim 81

INDEX

plays to Queen Victoria 81
portrait 80
reviews 79, 80, 81, 82
salon 79, 81–2
Robert Schumann on 79
Clara Schumann cedes concert to 79
tours 79–81
clavichord 7, 9, 50
  mechanism 6
  in Mendelssohn home 59
  rise of 6
  Silbermann 59
Clementi, Muzio 39
  sonatas opus 33 for Therese Jansen 37
  teaches Therese Jansen 37
  teaches Hélène de Montgeroult 43
  teaching fees 18
Clifford Barney, Natalie 127
Coates, Albert 155
Cocteau, Jean 115
Cohen, Harriet 137
Colette 115
coloratura
  evoked in piano music 53
competitions, piano 209–15
  ARD International, Munich 210
  and careers 210–11
  chamber music in 213
  Clara Haskil, Vevey 210
  and equality legislation 209–10
  Gina Bachauer, Salt Lake City 210
  as gladiatorial contests 211
  and hand size 212–13
  International Chopin, Warsaw 210, 214
  Leeds 210, 211, 214
  Maria Canals International, Barcelona 210
  men usually win 214–15
  Moscow Tchaikovsky 210, 214
  repertoire 213
  Van Cliburn International, Texas 210, 214
  women at disadvantage 211–15
  women jurors 213–14
composers, women 3, 6, 11, 28, 29, 30, 32, 35–6, 37, 39, 44, 45–7, 57, 58–9, 61–4, 89, 91, 92, 96–8, 100, 102–4, 106, 117–21, 183, 185–6, 188–90, 191–2, 199–200
  discouraged from large-scale works 203–4
  Dvořák on 117
  eclipsed by male composers 47, 54, 60–1, 201–5
  excluded from composition classes 57, 119–20, 202
  excluded from networking 202–3
  Hanslick on 'lack of aptitude' 204
  Nicola LeFanu on 'gentlemen's club' 204
  write for domestic market 18
  write for own public concerts 50
Concert Spirituel, Paris
  Maria von Paradis plays in 29
concerts
  advantage of piano in 7
  early use of piano in 8
  rise of public 48–50
  dominated by male pianists 48–50
Concours Marguerite Long-Jacques Thibaud 124
conductors
  no women until 20th century 204
  women pianists' treatment by 224
Copenhagen 89
Copland, Aaron 135
Corder, Amy Freeman 162
Cortot, Alfred 1
  appointed by Fauré at Paris Conservatoire 122
  teaches Clara Haskil 144
Costa, Rae da 185–7, 191
  appearance 186, 187
  combines classical and popular 186, 187
  duets with Billy Mayerl 186
  earnings 186
  Faries' Gavotte 186
  love of 'syncopated' music 185
  Modernistic Pieces for the Piano 186
  Pathé newsreels 186
  pupil of Matthay 185, 186

INDEX

recordings 186, 187
   Liszt *Rigoletto Paraphrase* 186
   success in popular music 185–7
   virtuoso arrangements 185–6
Couperin, François 81, 128
Covent Garden Theatre 8
Cox, Ida 183
Cramer, Johann Baptist
   pupil of Hélène de Montgeroult 44
   studies eclipse Montgeroult's 47
Craxton, Harold
   teaches Nancy Weir 163
Cristofori, Bartolomeo
   invents piano 7
Crown and Anchor tavern, London 39
Cultural Revolution 178–9
Curie, Marie 201
Curzon, Clifford 2, 137
Czerny, Carl 55

Damrosch, Walter 130
dancing 12, 38
   fashion in Britain 38
   masters 11, 17, 38
   schools 38
   women play for 13
David, Ferdinand 64
David, Louise *see* Dulcken, Louise
Davis, Miles 188–9
Davison, James W, 83, 84
Death of Stalin, The (film) 147–8
Debussy, Claude 102, 103, 115, 146, 179
   Chaminade on 106
   on *Douze Études* 123
   and Marguerite Long 121, 123
   on Guiomar Novaes 141
   Prélude à l'après-midi d'un faune 172
Delbos, Claire 172
Depp, Ludwig
   teaches Amy Fay 85
Detroit News 111–12
Detroit Symphony Orchestra 175
Diaghilev, Sergei 115
Dibden, Charles 8
doctors
   on effects of music on women's health 18–19

Dohnányi, Ernst von
   teaches Annie Fischer 160
Donohoe, Peter 160
Dorival, Jérôme 47
Dorsey, Jack 188
drawing 12
Dresden 32, 79
duets, piano 12, 13
Dukas, Paul
   teaches Messiaen 173
Duke University, North Carolina 191
dulcimer 5
   piano a keyed dulcimer 6
Dulcken (David), Louise 64–8
   Academy for Young Pianoforte Players 67
   and anti-Semitism 68
   compared with Moscheles 65
   concert reviews 65, 66
   converts from Judaism to Protestantism 64
   death 68
   English premieres of Chopin and Mendelssohn 64, 65
   linguist 64–5
   marries Theobald Dulcken 64
   performs Beethoven's 'Appassionata' Sonata 66
   performs Hummel concerto age 10 64
   performs with Felix Mendelssohn 66–7
   portrait 67
   sister of Ferdinand David 64
   teaches Queen Victoria 65
   tours 66
Dulcken, Theobald Augustus 64–5
   family of harpsichord and piano makers 64
Dunot, Edouard, Comte de Charnage
   marries Hélène de Montgeroult 44
Dushkin, Samuel
   composed *Sicilienne* 'by M. von Paradis'? 30
Dussek, Jan Ladislav
   and position of piano on stage 37
   pupil of C.P.E. Bach 44

sonatas for Therese Jansen 37
teaches Hélène de Montgeroult 43
Dvořák, Antonin
　on women composers 117
dynamic markings
　Boccherini adds 24

Edinburgh 1, 99, 160
Einaudi, Ludovico 220
Einstein, Albert 201
Eisenberger, Severin
　teaches Lili Kraus 152
Elizabeth II, Queen 192
Ellis, Katharine
　on Marie Pleyel 71
embroidery 12
Enescu, George 146
Erard piano 59
Esquire magazine 191
Essex, John 11–12
Essipoff, Annette 110
Esterházy family
　and Haydn 34–5, 36, 38
Étude (magazine) 104
Evanston 158
Evening Post 142
Evers, Medgar 199

Fairbank, N.K. 99
Falla, Manuel de 165
　El retablo de maese Pedro 115, 127
　harpsichord concerto 127
Farrenc, Aristide
　sets up Éditions Farrenc 57
　supports wife Louise 57
　Le Trésor des pianistes 58
Farrenc (Dumont), Louise 56–9
　compositions 57, 58–9
　　compared with Hummel 58–9
　　Nonet 58
　family of artists 56
　fights for equal pay 56, 57–8
　performs own compositions 57
　professor at Paris Conservatoire 57–8
　pupil of Cécile Soria, Hummel and Moscheles 56
　pupil of Reicha 57

supported by husband 57
Le Trésor des pianistes 58
Farrenc, Victorine 58
Fauré, Gabriel 141, 144
　and Marguerite Long 122–3
　ballade for piano and orchestra 122–3, 125
　songs 115
Fay, Amy 85–7, 118
　on Adele aus der Ohe 107
　fights for women's rights 87
　on Joachim 86
　on Liszt 86
　Music-Study in Germany 85–6
　'piano conversations' 87
　president of New York Women's Philharmonic Society 87
　pupil of Liszt, Kullak and Deppe 85
　as teacher 85
Fay, Melusina 85, 87
February Revolution 57
Ferguson, Howard
　and National Gallery concerts 139
Fétis, Joseph
　Biographie universelle des musiciens
　on Marie Pleyel 68
Field, John
　attends Szymanowska's salon 54
　helps Szymanowska 53
Fischer, Annie 2, 160–2
　appearance and style 160–1
　child prodigy 160
　compared with Schnabel 160
　experiences anti-Semitism 160
　marriage 160
　pupil of Dohnányi and Székely 160
　recordings 161
　　Beethoven sonatas 161
　in USA 161
Fleischer, Leon 220
Florence 45
Florestan Trio 75
flute 11
Fodor, Eugene
　on Lili Kraus 151
Fontaine, Jean de la
　Fables 6
　on Marie-Françoise Certain 6

INDEX

Forman, Miklos
   Amadeus 27
Fragonard, Jean-Honoré 24
Françaix, Jean 116
Franck, César
   teachers Marie Jaëll 92
Frankfurt 81
Franklin, Benjamin
   friendship with Brillon de Jouy 25–6
Franz Liszt piano competition 160
French Revolution 26
   Arabella Goddard and 1848 82
   Hélène de Montgeroult and 43
Fricsay, Ferenc
   on Clara Haskil 147

Gambarini, Elisabetta 6
Gazette musicale, La 69
Genzinger, Marianne von 36
   Haydn's sonata in E flat Hob XVI:49 composed for her 36
   relationship with Haydn 36
George III, King 28
Gerhardt, Elena
   at National Gallery concerts 140
Gershwin, George 135, 186
Gieseking, Walter 1
Gilels, Emil 2, 170
Gillespie, Dizzy 188, 190, 196
Gismonti, Egberto 135
Gladwell, Malcolm
   Outliers: The Story of Success 16
Glass, Philip
   on Nadia Boulanger 137
Glazunov, Alexander
   piano concerto no. 2 in B 170
Glinka, Mikhail
   attends Szymanowska's salon 54
Godard, Benjamin
   teaches Cécile Chaminade 103
Goddard, Arabella 82–5
   George Bernard Shaw on 85
   and James W. Davison 83, 84
      marriage 84
   'masculine' appearance 83
   Moscheles on 83
   performs Beethoven's 'Hammerklavier' Sonata 82
   professor at Royal College of Music 84
   pupil of Anderson, Kalkbrenner and Thalberg 82
   pupil of Lucy Anderson 56, 82
   reviews 83, 84
   tours 83, 84
   with own piano 84
Goethe, Johann Wolfgang von 62
   'Aussöhnung' 53
   and the Mendelssohns 60
   relationship with Maria Szymanowska 53
Goldberg, Szymon
   duo with Lili Kraus 153
Gottschalk, Louis Moreau
   The Last Hope 118
   Marche de nuit 96
   teaches Teresa Carreño 96
Goodman, Benny 188
Google Doodle
   in honour of Teresa Carreño 101
Gounod, Charles
   on Fanny Mendelssohn 62
Grainger, Percy
   on Eileen Joyce 155
Gramophone 154
gramophone 206, 215
Granados, Enrique 103, 165, 166
Grant of Rothiemurchus, Elizabeth
   Memoirs of a Highland Lady 14–15
gravicembalo col piano e forte 7
Grenfell, Joyce 139
Grieg, Edvard 125
   piano concerto 99–100, 156
Griller Quartet 139, 140
Grinberg, Maria 150
   conflict with Soviet authorities 150
   father and husband executed 150
   records Beethoven piano sonatas 150
   relationship with Maria Yudina 150
Grove, George
   Dictionary of Music and Musicians 68
Gunn, Anita 139–40

Hamburg 64
Hammershøi, Vilhelm 12
Handel, George Frideric
   Montgeroult evokes 46
hand size 165–6, 212–13, 215, 233–4
Hansberry, Lorraine 198
Hanslick, Eduard 205
   on Clara Schumann 78
   on women composers 204
harp 5, 15
harpsichord 7, 9, 11, 64
   co-exists with piano 16, 23, 24, 25
   decline 7
   mechanism 6, 25, 127
   players 6–7, 125–9
   Pleyel 127
   revival 125–9
   rise of 6
   suitable for ladies 12
Harris, Roy
   teaches Margaret Bonds 158
Harry, Prince 30
Hartnell, Norman 157
Haskil, Clara 115, 144–7, 210
   Busoni offers to teach 145
   chamber musician 146
   character 147
   child prodigy 144
   Clara Haskill Piano Competition 144
   duo partners 146
   family 144
   and Grumiaux 146
   illness 144, 145, 156
   and Lipatti 145
   at Paris Conservatoire
      Premier Prix 144
      pupil of Cortot 144
   pupil of Richard Robert 144
   recordings
      Mozart violin sonatas with Grumiaux 146
      Scarlatti sonatas 146
      Schumann piano concerto 146
   repertoire 146
   settles in Switzerland 146
   studies violin 144
   tone 147
   tours Europe and America 146
   at Winnaretta Singer's salon 145
Haskil, Jeanne 144
Haskil, Lili 144, 146
Haydn, Joseph
   on Auenbrugger sisters 37
   and Esterházy family 34–5, 36, 38
   expelled from Vienna cathedral choir 34
   friend of Mesmer 27
   and Marianne von Genzinger 39
   and Therese Jansen 37, 38–9
   in London 36
   and Maria Martines 34, 35, 36
   piano trios Hob XV:27–9 for Therese Jansen 37
   piano trios Hob XV:24–6 for Rebecca Schroeter 40
   and Barbara Ployer 33
   pupil of Porpora 34
   and Rebecca Schroeter 40
   sonata Hob XVI:49 for Marianne von Genzinger 36
   sonatas Hob XVI:50 and 52 for Therese Jansen 37, 38
   sonatas dedicated to Auenbrugger sisters 37
   on teaching fees 17
   variations in F minor 33, 36
   visits London 38–9
health
   effect of music on women's 18–19
Heine, Heinrich 62
Hensel, Fanny *see* Mendelssohn, Fanny
Hensel, Sebastian 62
Hensel, Wilhelm 62
   illustrations for Fanny Mendelssohn 62
Herz, Henri 57, 65
Hess, Myra 131, 137–41
   character 140–1
   earnings 138
   Ford Sunday Evening Hour 138
   National Gallery Concerts 137, 138–40
   pupil of Matthay 137
   recordings 140
   review 138

INDEX

success in USA 138
touring 140
Hickenlooper, Lucy Ann *see* Samaroff, Olga
Hindemith, Paul 148
Hoffmann, E.T.A. 41
Hoffmann, Josef 212
Hohenzollern, Prince von
  appoints Sophie Menter 88
Holroyd, Maria Josepha 16
Hong Kong 84
Horowitz, Vladimir 1, 114, 115, 220
Horszowski, Mieczyław 220
Howard, Jack 187
Howells, Herbert
  piano concertos 156
Hughes, Langston 198
  and Margaret Bonds 158, 159
  'The Negro Speaks of Rivers' 158
Hüllmandel, Nicolaus Joseph
  pupil of C.P.E. Bach 44
  teaches Hélène de Montgeroult 43
Hummel, Johann Nepomuk 55, 56, 64, 65
  teaches Louise Farrenc 57
  teaches Fanny Mendelssohn 60
Huneker, James
  on Fannie Bloomfield Zeisler 111
  on Guiomar Novaes 142
Hunter, Alberta 183
  'Downhearted Blues' (with Lovie Austin) 183
  on Lovie Austin 184

Iannucci, Armando
  The Death of Stalin 147–8
improvisation
  Teresa Carreño 97
  in public 49
  Jacquet de la Guerre 6
  jazz 181–2, 189
  Brillon de Jouy 25–6
  Hélène de Montgeroult with Viotti 43
Independent 171
India 23, 84, 156

interviews with women pianists 221–38
  reasons for anonymity 223
Ireland, John
  piano concerto 156, 157
Isouard, Nicolo
  Joconde 53
Itzig family
  Bella 40, 41
  Daniel 40
  devotion to Bach family 40–2
  Hanna 40
  Mariane 40
  Sara (Levy) 40–2

Jackson, Mississippi 199
Jacquet de la Guerre, Elisabeth 6
  improvises 6
Jaëll, Alfred 91
  duets with Marie Jaëll 91
  pupil of Chopin 91
Jaëll, Marie 91–3
  compositions 91, 92
  cycles of Beethoven, Liszt and Schumann 91, 92
  duets with Alfred Jaëll 91
  joins Société des Compositeurs 91
  Le Toucher 93
  and Liszt 91, 92
  Liszt on 92
  marriage 91
  at Paris Conservatoire 91
  plays to Queen Victoria 91
  pupil of Franck and Saint-Saëns 92
  salon 91, 92
  teaches Albert Schweitzer 93
  teaching ideas 92–3
Jansen, Louis 38, 39
Jansen Bartolozzi, Therese 37–40
  Clementi dedicates sonatas opus 33 to 37
  compositions 39
  Dussek dedicates sonatas to 37
  father's dancing school 38
  Haydn dedicates sonatas and piano trios to 37
  pupil of Clementi 37

Java 153
jazz
  'A Great Day in Harlem'
      (photograph) 190–1
  audience 182
  bebop 189
  comparison with classical 181–2
  'cutting competitions' 49
  improvisation 181–2
  origins 181
  pianists 181–5, 187–91, 194–200
    earnings 182, 186
    'masculine' and 'feminine'
      associations 184–5
    royalties 183
    technique compared with classical 189
Jews 40–1, 42, 51, 59–60, 68, 125, 137, 144, 146, 148, 150, 152, 160, 172
  anti-Semitism 68, 136, 153, 160, 172
  assimilation/conversion 42, 59–60, 64, 148, 152
Joachim, Joseph 58, 81, 94, 144
  Amy Fay on 86
Johnson, James
  on effect of music on women's health 18
Jones, Quincy 135
Joseph II, Emperor 35
Josephite movement 148
Journal de Paris
  on Maria von Paradis 29
Joyce, Eileen 155–7
  Brief Encounter 155, 156
  champions British music 156
  concert dress 155, 156
    designed by Hartnell 157
  concerto repertoire 155–6
  illness 157
  international touring 156
  at National Gallery concerts 156
  Percy Grainger on 155
  plays harpsichord 157
  pupil of Pauer and Teichmüller 155
  The Seventh Veil 156
  stamina 156–7
  studies sponsored locally 155
  success in Britain 155–6
  subject of newsreel 156
  wartime touring 156
Juncker, Carl Ludwig
  Musikalische und Künstler Almanach
    on Rosa Cannabich 32

Kalkbrenner, Friedrich 69
  teaches Arabella Goddard 82
Kane, Art 191
Kansas City swing 188
Kassel 79
Katchen, Julius 2
Kelly, Michael
  on Maria Martines 35
  Reminiscences 35
Kempff, Wilhelm 2
Kent, Duchess of
  appoints Louise Dulcken 65
Kern, Jerome 186
keyboard
  early history of 5–6
  suitable for ladies 12
  women and keyboard instruments in paintings 11
King, Martin Luther 159, 196, 198, 199
King's Theatre, London 39
Kirk, Andy
  Clouds of Joy 188
Kirnberger, Johann Philipp 40
Klimt, Gustav 93
Kneisel Quartet 109
Kodály, Zoltán
  teaches Lili Kraus 150, 151
Koželuch, Leopold
  teacher of Maria von Paradis 27, 29
Krafft-Ebing, Richard
  on music and women's mental health 17–18
Kraus, Lili 150–4
  appearance 151, 152, 154
  on Bartók 152
  conversion to Catholicism 152
  Eugene Fodor on 151
  at Franz Liszt Academy 151
    admitted aged 8 151

INDEX

pupil of Kodály, Székely, Weiner 151
and Szymon Goldberg 153
  recordings of Beethoven and Mozart 153
imprisoned by Japanese 150, 153
marriage 152–3
Mozart cycles 154
pupil of Bartók 150, 151–2
pupil of Eisenberger 152
pupil of Schnabel 150, 153
teaching style 154, 218
touring 154
treatment by mother 150–1
at Vienna Konservatorium 152
Kreisler, Fritz 30, 59, 131
Krenek, Ernst 148, 202
Kullak, Theodor
  teaches Adele aus der Ohe 107
  teaches Amy Fay 85, 107
Kyiv 42

LaGuardia, Mayor 175
Landowska, Wanda 125–9
  as composer 125
  concertos by Falla and Poulenc written for 127
  controversy about historical approach 127–8
  École de Musique Ancienne 127
  escapes to USA 128
  on historical 'progress' 128–9
  marriage 126
  Nazis confiscate instruments and library 128
  plays Bach's *Goldberg Variations* in New York 128
  Pleyel designs harpsichord for 127
  and revival of harpsichord 125–7
  as teacher 126, 127
  tours 126
  training as pianist 125
Lane, Richard James
  lithograph of Louise Dulcken 68
Lang Lang 178
Laotzi (Lao Tzu) 180

Larrocha, Alicia de 165–9
  advocacy of Spanish music 165, 166–7
  chamber music 168
  child prodigy 166
  directs Academia Marshall 167
  hands 165–6, 212
  lack of ambition 168–9
  marriage 167
  performs with Poulenc 167
  recordings 167
  repertoire 168
  Harold C. Schonberg on 167
  style 167–8
  taught by Frank Marshall 166
  touring 167, 168
Larsson, Carl 12
Las Vegas 192
Latvia 66
Lausanne 167
Le Corbusier 116
Lean, David 155
Lebrun, Sophie 64
LeFanu, Nicola 204
Leipzig 69, 73, 81, 155, 170, 206
  Bach competition 169
  Gewandhaus 66, 79
Leschetitzky, Theodor 152
  on female students 110
  teaches Fannie Bloomfield Zeigler 110
Levisohn, Lew 191
Levy, Salomon 40
Levy (Itzig), Sara 40–2
  collects Bach family manuscripts 42
  commissions works from C.P.E. Bach 42
  devotion to Bach family 40–2, 59
  Itzig family 40
  Jewish faith 40, 41, 42
    assimilation 42
  and Felix Mendelssohn 40, 41–2
  performs J.S. Bach 41
  pupil of W.F. Bach 40
  salon 40–1, 42
  support of W.F. Bach 42
Lew, Henri 126
Lhévinne, Josef 201
Lhévinne, Rosina 201

Lincoln, President
   Teresa Carreño plays to 96–8
Lipatti, Dinu 115, 135
Lisbon 128
Lisitsa, Valentina 238
Liszt, Franz 62, 78, 79, 81, 93, 103,
     185, 202, 224
   complete works performed by Marie
     Jaëll 91, 92
   Concerto pathétique 88
   'duel' with Thalberg 49–50
   Amy Fay on 55–6
   on Marie Jaëll 92
   and Sophie Menter 88, 89
   piano concerto no. 1 in E flat 88, 107
   piano concerto no. 2 in A 90
   plays from memory 53
   public concerts 49
   pupils
     Adele aus der Ohe 107–10
     Amy Fay 85–7
     Marie Jaëll 91–3
     Carl Tausig 88
   relationship with Chopin 69
   relationship with Louise Pleyel 69
   Réminiscences de Don Juan 109
   Spanish Rhapsody 108
   Ungarische Zigeunerweisen (by
     Sophie Menter?) 89
   Wagner's *Tannhaüser* overture
     arranged 89
Lockhart, New South Wales 162
Loder, Kate 67
   pupil of Lucy Anderson 56
Loesser, Arthur
   Men, Women and Pianos 215
London 6, 7, 17, 23, 28, 36, 37, 38–40,
     50, 53, 55–6, 61, 64, 65, 66,
     69–70, 71, 81, 82, 83, 84, 98,
     104, 105, 113, 137, 152, 155,
     161, 163, 170, 185, 221, 222,
     223, 224,
   Aeolian Hall 138
   Argyll Rooms 65
   Hanover Concert Society 38
   King's Theatre 65
   London Philharmonic Orchestra
     192
   National Gallery concerts 137,
     138–40
   National Portrait Gallery 68
   Promenade Concerts 101, 155, 237
   Queen's Hall Orchestra
     admits women 203
   Royal Academy of Music 56, 163, 191
   Royal College of Music 84
   (Royal) Philharmonic Society 55,
     65, 89
   salons 50
   Savoy Hotel 185
   Trinity College of Music 186
   Wigmore Hall 163
Long, Claire 121
Long, Marguerite 121–5
   Concours Marguerite Long-Jacques
     Thibaud 124
   and Debussy 121, 123
   At the Piano with Debussy 121
   premieres *Douze Études* 123
   and Fauré 121, 122
   At the Piano with Fauré 121
   denied promotion at
     Conservatoire 122, 123
   on her studies with 122
   husband Joseph de Marliave 121–2,
     123, 124
     killed in World War I 123
     Ravel dedicates toccata to 123
   on importance of work 123, 125
   opens music school with Jacques
     Thibaud 124
   at Paris Conservatoire 121, 122, 123,
     124
   precision of touch 124
   and Ravel 121, 123–4
   At the Piano With Ravel 121
   premieres and records piano
     concerto 123–4
   Ravel on Long's performance
     124
   premieres *Le Tombeau de Couperin*
     123
   Ravel on Long's tempo 124
   Variations sur le nom de Marguerite
     Long 125
Lorengar, Pilar 168

Loriot, Yvonne 172–4
  composition pupil of Milhaud 173
  and Messiaen 172–4
  edits Messiaen 174
  marries Messiaen 173
  at Paris Conservatoire 172
  premieres difficult new works 173
  works composed by Messiaen for 172–3
Los Angeles Philharmonic Orchestra 159
Louis XIV 6
Lugansky, Nikolai
  on Tatiana Nikolayeva 171
Lunceford, Jimmy 188
lute 11
Luther, Mrs 7
  portrait by Reynolds 7
Lympany, Moura 137
lyre 5

McCormack, John 103
McDowell, Edward 100
McKay, Belinda
  on Nancy Weir 163
Maconchy, Elizabeth 204
Madrid Symphony Orchestra 166
Mahler, Gustav 94
Majors, Monroe Alpheus 157
Mandelstam, Osip 148
Mandl, Otto 152
Mandl, William
  on Lili Kraus 152
Mannheim 33
  Court Orchestra 33
Margaret, Princess 192
Maria Fedorovna, tsarina of Russia
  appoints Maria Szymanowska 53
Maria Theresa, Empress
  supports Marianna Martines 35
  supports Maria von Paradis 26, 27
Marić, Mileva 201
Marie Antoinette, Queen 28
Markle, Meghan 30
Marliave, Joseph de 121–2, 123
Martines, Marianna 34–7
  Charles Burney on 35
  compositions 35–6
  compared with Beethoven 36
  Michael Kelly on 35
  Mozart plays duets with 35
  plays and sings for Empress and Emperor 35
  pupil of Haydn and Porpora 34
  salon 35
  supported by Metastasio 34–5
Martines, Nicolò 34
Massart, Joseph Lambert 59
Massart, Louise-Aglaé 59
  devotion to chamber music 59
  salon 59
Matthay, Tobias 93, 137
  teaches Raie da Costa 185, 186
  teaches Harriet Cohen, Clifford Curzon, Myra Hess, Moura Lympany 137
  teaches Eileen Joyce 155
  teaches Irene Scharrer 140
  teaches Nancy Weir 163
Matisse, Henri 12
Matthias, Georges
  teaches Teresa Carreño 99
Mao, Chairman 178
Mayerl, Billy 185–6, 191
Mehta, Zubin 159
Melbourne Symphony Orchestra 162
memory, playing from 3, 132
  Adele aus der Ohe 108
  Wilhelmine Clauss-Szarvady 80
  Arabella Goddard 83
  Fanny Mendelssohn 60
  Guiomar Novaes 143
  Maria von Paradis 28
  Clara Schumann 72
  Maria Szymanowska 53
  Mary Lou Williams 187
Mendelssohn, Abraham 60
Mendelssohn (Hensel), Fanny 59–64
  Bartholdy added to family name 60
  compositions 61–4
    Abschied von Rom 62
    Choleramusik 62
    Das Jahr 63
    Easter Sonata 63

'Italien' 61
  piano trio 63
  songs opus 1 63
  death 63
  discouraged from music career 42, 60
  Gounod on 62
  growing reputation 63, 64
  Jewish family 59
    assimilation 59–60
  marries Wilhelm Hensel 61
  memorises J.S. Bach 60
  relationship with Felix 60–1, 63–4
  songs published under Felix's name 61, 205
  Sonntagsmusiken 62
  visits Rome 62–3
  Zelter on 60
Mendelssohn, Felix 55, 59, 78, 82, 118, 202
  compared with Montgeroult 46
  death 64
  family's devotion to Bach 41–2, 59
  piano concerto in D minor 64, 66–7, 83
  plans to publish Fanny's music 63
  plays for Queen Victoria 61
  pupil of M. Bigot, L. Berger, Hummel, Moscheles 60
  relationship with Fanny 60–1, 63–4
  revival of J.S. Bach's *St Matthew Passion* 41–2
    enabled by women of the family 41–2
  songs opus 8 & 9 include some by Fanny 61, 205
  violin concerto 64
Mendelssohn, Moses 59
Mendelssohn Museum, Fanny and Felix 64
Menter, Sophie 88–91
  Arrau on 90–1
  beauty 90–1
  compared with Paderewski 90
  Liszt on 88
  and David Popper 88
  portrait 90
  practising 89
  protégée of Liszt 88
  pupil of Tausig 88
  reviews 89–90
  touring 89
  Ungarische Zigeunerweisen (by Liszt?) 89
Menuhin, Yehudi 146
Mercure de France
  on Maria von Paradis 29
Mercure Galant
  on Jacquet de la Guerre 5
Mesmer, Franz Anton
  treats Maria von Paradis 27–8
Messiaen, Olivier
  Catalogue d'oiseaux 173
  interest in birdsong 173
  Loriod on 172
  and Yvonne Loriod 172–4
  Oiseaux exotiques 173
  organist 172
  pupil of Dukas 173
  Réveil des oiseaux 173
  St François d'Assise 174
  Traité de rhythme, de couleur, et de l'ornithologie 174
  Trois Petites Liturgies de la présence divine 173
  Vingt Regards sur l'Enfant-Jésus 173
  Visions de l'amen 172
Metastasio (Antonio Trapassi) 34, 35, 36
  supports Maria Martines 35
Meyer, Baroness Olga de 115
Meyerbeer, Giacomo
  Les Huguenots 99
Miami 101
Michelangeli, Arturo Benedetti 2
Mickiewicz, Adam
  attends Szymanowska's salon 54
Milhaud, Darius
  Les Malheurs d'Orphée 115
  teaches Yvonne Loriod 173
Mingus, Charles 196
Mocking Bird, The 97–8
Moiseiwitsch, Benno 2
Moke, Camille *see* Pleyel, Marie
Mompou, Frederic 165
Monde musical, Le 70

INDEX

Monet, Claude 115
Monk, Thelonius 189
Montgeroult, Hélène de 43–7, 57, 234
    compositions 44, 45
        Thirty Studies 57
    Cours complet (studies) 44, 45–7
        eclipsed by Cramer's studies 47
        inspires later composers 46–7
        compared with Chopin et al 46–7
    and French Revolution 43
    improvises with Viotti 43
    marries Edouard Dunot 44
    plays with Viotti 43
    portrait 45
    professor at Paris Conservatoire 44
    promotes music of J.S. Bach 44
    pupil of Hüllmandel, Clementi and Dussek 43
    relationship with Baron de Trémont 44
    rivalry with Jean-Louis Adam 44
    on separation of hands (rubato) 46
    teaches Johann Baptist Cramer 44
    Mme Vigée-Lebrun on 43
Montgeroult, Marquis de 43
More, Hannah
    Strictures on the Modern System of Female Education 15–16
Morning Post 9
Morny
    'Chaminade' soap and perfume 105
Morris, Gareth 139
Mort de Staline, La 147
Morton, Jelly Roll 184–5
Moscheles, Ignaz 65, 91, 118
    teaches Louise Farrenc 57
    teaches Fanny Mendelssohn 60
Moscow 150, 169–70
    Conservatory 149, 169–70
    Gnessin Institute 149
    Tchaikovsky Competition 210, 214
Mother John Moore 155
Motown 196
Mozart, Constanze 28
Mozart, Leopold 28–9
Mozart, Maria Anna ('Nannerl') 10–11, 29

Mozart, Wolfgang Amadeus 37, 43, 55, 59, 72, 79, 112, 137, 143, 146, 148, 163, 202
    in *Amadeus* 27
    and Rosa Cannabich 33
    composes piano concerto for M. von Paradis 29
    compositions for Maria von Auernhammer 31–2
    compositions for Barbara Ployer 33
    concerto for two pianos K242 31
    concerto for two pianos K365 31
    first encounters piano 8
    friend of Mesmer 27
    letters 30–1
        on Maria von Auernhammer 30–1, 32
        plays duets with her 31–2
    and Maria Martines 35
    pianists associated with 33
    piano concertos 140, 172, 173
    piano concerto in B flat K238 33
    piano concerto in E flat K449 33
    piano concerto in G K453 33
    piano concerto in B flat K456 29
    piano concerto in D K537 'Coronation' 166
    piano sonata in C K309 33
    and Barbara Ployer 33
    sonata for piano duet K358 31
    sonata for piano duet K448 31
    tours with sister 10–11
Munich 8, 64, 88, 91
    ARD International Competition 210, 214
    Neue Pinakothek 93
Musical America 121
Musical Courier 112
Mychetskaya, Raïssa 132

Naples 34
Nash, Ogden
    'Come On In, the Senility Is Fine' 221
Nashville
    Roger Williams University 182
National Youth Orchestra of Great Britain 207

Nazis 128, 146, 152, 163, 172
Neue Zeitschrift für Musik 56
   on Wilhelmine Clauss-Szarvady 82
   on Arabella Goddard and Clara Schumann 84
New Orleans
   Storyville 182
Newport Jazz Festival 190
New Symphony Orchestra 138
New York 87, 96, 107–8, 111, 113, 138, 158–9, 161, 188, 191, 196
   Aeolian Hall 142
   Café Society 188, 194
   Carnegie Hall 106, 108, 112, 129, 161, 198
   Harlem 191, 194
   Juilliard School 131, 194, 197
   Philharmonic Orchestra 175, 189
   Statue of Liberty 107, 113
   Steinway Hall 108
   Symphony Orchestra 130
   Vassar College 202
   Women's Philharmonic Society 87
   World's Fair 175
New York Herald Tribune 128
New York Sun 111
New York Times 108, 142, 161, 167
New Zealand 84, 154, 156
Nikolayeva, Tatiana 169–71
   Bach playing 169–70
   compositions
      Twenty-Four Concert Studies 170
      piano concerto 170
      piano quintet 170
      piano sonata 170
   at Moscow Conservatory 169, 170
   Nikolai Lugansky on 171
   portrait 171
   pupil of Alexander Goldenweiser 169
   and Shostakovich 169–70, 171
      Twenty-Four Preludes and Fugues 169–70, 171
   success in London and USA 170–1
Nîmes 121
Novaes, Guiomar 141–4
   compared with Paderewski 142
   Debussy on 141
   marriage 142
   on memorising 143
   on modern music 143
   on modern pianists 143
   at Paris Conservatoire
      pupil of Isidor Philipp 141
      wins entrance audition 141
      wins Premier Prix 141
   on pianos 143
   recordings 141
   reviews 142
   tone 142, 143
   US debut 142
Novello (publisher) 55–6

oboe 11
Ohe, Adele aus der 107–10
   child prodigy 107
   compositions 109
      Melodie 109
      Pastorale 109
   Amy Fay on 107
   love of chamber music 109
   plays J.S. Bach and *clavecinistes* 109
   plays from memory 108
   plays new music 109
   pupil of Kullak 107
   pupil of Liszt 107, 109
   Rachmaninoff supports 109
   repertoire 108–9
   reviews 107–8
   settles in Berlin 109–10
   success in USA 107–8
   and Tchaikovsky 108
   Tchaikovsky on 108
   as teacher 109
   tours 107–8
Ohe, Mathilde aus der 107
orchestras
   founded in 19th century 48
organ
   portative in paintings 11
Ormond Trio 164
Orthodox Church 148
O'Shea, Paloma 210
Otter, Anne Sofie von 103
Otto-Peters, Louise 242

INDEX

Pachmann, Marguerite de 201
Pachmann, Vladimir de 201
Paderewski, Ignacy 1
   on Teresa Carreño 100–1
Pagin, André-Noël 24
Paignton, Devon 113
painting
   as an accomplishment 12
paintings
   of women playing keyboard instruments 11, 12
Paradis, Maria Theresia von 26–30
   blindness 26–9
      treated by Mesmer and others 27
   compositions 30
      compared with Schubert 30
      Sicilienne (spurious) 30
   inventions for blind people 29
   Mozart composes concerto for 28–9
   notation system 28
   opens music school for the blind 29–30
   review 29
   subject of novels, plays and films 26, 27
   supported by Empress 26, 27
   studies with Koželuch, Righini and Salieri 27, 29
   tours 28–9
Paramount Records 183
Paris 6, 23, 28, 29, 43–4, 50, 51, 56, 69, 73, 79, 80, 81, 82, 88, 91, 92, 98, 99, 102, 113, 126, 127, 128, 144–6
   Boeuf sur le Toit, Le 189–90
   Concert Spirituel 29
   Conservatoire 43–4, 51, 56–9, 91, 98, 102, 121, 129, 133–4, 144
      composition classes exclude women 57, 133
      Prix de Rome 123, 133–4
   Foch Hospital 116
   Opéra 115
   Orchestre Symphonique 115
   Salle Pleyel 121
   salons 50, 51
   Schola Cantorum 126
   Tuileries 29

Parker, Charlie 189
Parlophone Records 153, 186
Passy, Paris 23, 25, 31
Pasternak, Boris 148, 149
Pathé newsreels 156, 186
Pauer, Max
   teaches Eileen Joyce 155
Pearl Harbor 128
Pergolesi, Giovanni Battista 81
Perry, Edward Baxter
   on Cécile Chaminade 104
   on Sophie Menter 89
Perth, Australia 155
   Loreto Convent 155
Philadelphia 108
   Conservatory 131
   Curtis Institute 197
piano
   art of playing 205–6
   becomes more affordable 13
   boogie-woogie 191–4
   Broadwood 7–8
   co-exists with harpsichord 16, 23, 25
   competitions 209–15
   Cristofori 7
   descendant of dulcimer 5, 6
   digital 207, 215–16
   domestic use 9–19, 206–7, 219
      decline of 206
   dominated in concert by men 9, 48–9 201
   duets 12, 13
   ease of learning at first 14
   early use in concert 8
   English 23, 25, 39
   frames 13
   future of 215
   German 23, 25
   honky-tonk 192
   invention of 7
   jazz 181–5, 187–91, 194–200
   lessons 12
   names for 7
   'novelty' 185–7, 191–4
   as permanent furniture 13
   pianists undervalued compared to composers 205–6

playing as 'accomplishment' 12, 13
  to attract husband 14
position on stage 37–8
power of expression 7, 29
rise of 6, 7–8, 9, 23, 64
rubato 46
square 7
as status symbol 13
Steinway 180
'stride' 186, 187
suitable for ladies 12, 151
'syncopated' 185–7
teachers
  author's experience of 1
  earning 17–18
  lineages 4
  masterclasses 217–18
  men dominate at advanced level 216–17
  and posture 16
  women at disadvantage 217–18
  women piano teachers 16, 53, 87, 216–17
'unsuitable' for men 9, 184–5
upright 182, 192, 193, 206, 21
Piazzolla, Astor 135
Picasso, Pablo 12
Pinto, Octavio 142
Pittsburgh 111
Plato
  Laws 5
  on music suitable for women 5
playing cards 12
Pleyel (piano manufacturer) 81
Pleyel, Camille 69
Pleyel (Moke), Marie 68–71
  Berlioz on 68–9
  Henri Blanchard on 70, 71
  engaged to Berlioz 69
  Fétis on 68
  influenced by Thalberg 69
  'manliness' 71
  married to Camille Pleyel 69
  Le Monde musical on 70
  Liszt on her classes 71
  music dedicated to 69
  performs Weber's *Konzertstück* 69–70
  relationship with Liszt 69
  Clara Schumann on 70–1
  Robert Schumann on 70
  Edouard Silas on her smoking 71
  tours 69
Ployer, Barbara 33
  Haydn composes variations in F minor for her 33
  Mozart composes concertos and a duet for her 33
  plays duet with Mozart 33
  premieres Mozart's concerto K453 33
  pupil of Mozart 33
Polignac, Eduard Prince de 114
Polignac, Princesse de *see* Singer, Winnaretta
Pollini, Maurizio 160
Popper, David
  and Sophie Menter 88
Porpora, Nicola
  teaches Haydn and Maria Martines 34
Porter, Cole 186
Postnikova, Viktoria 211
Poulenc, Francis 102
  concerto for two pianos 115, 167
  organ concerto 115
Powell, Bud 189
Poznań 53
practising 14–16, 89, 95
Prague 79, 81
  Sophien-Akademie 81
Pressler, Menahem 220
Price, Florence 236
  piano concerto 158
  teaches Margaret Bonds 158
Prokofiev, Sergei 202
  Peter and the Wolf 170
  piano concerto no. 3 155
Proust, Marcel
  À la Recherche du temps perdu 115–16
psaltery 5, 6
Pugno, Raoul
  duets with Nadia Boulanger 134
Pushkin, Alexander
  attends Szymanowska's salon 54

INDEX

Queensland Conservatorium 164

Rachmaninoff, Sergei 109, 202
   piano concerto no. 2 155, 156, 157
   Rhapsody on a Theme of Paganini 192
racism 158, 182, 193, 197
radio 138, 147, 168, 178, 189, 194, 199, 206, 215
RAF orchestra 139
Raff, Joachim 82
Ráfols, Albert
   on Alicia de Larrocha 168
railways 48, 108, 147, 165
Rainey, Ma 183
Rameau, Jean-Philippe 81, 128
Ravel, Maurice 102, 103
   Le Tombeau de Couperin 124
      on Marguerite Long's tempo 124
   and Marguerite Long 121, 123–4
   piano concerto 123–4
      on Marguerite Long's performance 124
   Pavane pour une Infante défunte 115
Rawsthorne, Alan
   piano concertos 156
reading
   aloud 13
recordings 3
   men dominate 1, 239
Reicha, Anton
   teaches Louise Farrenc 57
Renaissance
   paintings of women musicians 11
Renoir, Pierre-Auguste 12
Restout, Denise 128
reviews
   self-reviewing 222–3
   unsatisfactory 221–2
Reynolds, Joshua
   portrait of Mrs Luther 7
Richter, Sviatoslav 1, 160, 170
   on Maria Yudina 149, 150
Ries, Ferdinand 55
Righini, Vincenzo
   teacher of Maria von Paradis 27
Roach, Max 196
Robert, Richard 144

Robeson, Paul 163
Roebsaet, Victor-Nicolas 113
Rome 62–3, 69, 107, 134, 163
   Villa Medici 62
Röntgen family 206–7
Roosevelt, Edith 112
Roosevelt, President Theodore 106, 112
Rossini, Gioachino 98
Royal Variety Show 192
rubato
   spreading chords 166
Rubinstein, Anton
   piano concerto no. 4 in D minor 111
   teaches Teresa Carreño 99
Rubinstein, Arthur 1, 114, 115, 163, 166, 220
Russia
   Red Army 42

St Cecilia 11
Saint Paul, Minnesota
   Schubert Club 108
St Petersburg (Petrograd, Leningrad) 48, 53, 54, 66, 69, 89, 108, 170
   Conservatory 148, 149
Saint-Saëns, Camille 134
   teaches Marie Jaëll 92
Salieri, Antonio
   in *Amadeus* 27
   at Maria Martines's salon 35
   teacher of Marianna von Auenbrugger 37
   teacher of Maria von Paradis 27
salons 37, 43
   in 19th century 50–1
   Countess Belgijoso 50
   Natalie Clifford Bartley 127
   Marianne von Genzinger 36
   Brillon de Jouy 23–6
   Sara Levy 40–1, 42, 50
   Mrs Luther 7
   Maria Martines 35, 50
   Louise-Aglaé and Joseph Massart 59
   Hélène de Montgeroult 50
   Hazel Scott 196

Winnaretta Singer 113, 114–17, 127, 145
Maria Szymanowska 54
Mme Vigée-Lebrun 43
Leopoldine Wittgenstein 93, 94
Salvation Army 116
Salzburg 28, 31
Samaroff, Olga (Lucy Ann Hickenlooper) 129–32
   Beethoven sonata cycle forgotten 131
   changes name 130
   debut at Carnegie Hall 129
   on discriminatory reviews 131
   marriage 129
      to Stokowski 130–1
   at Paris Conservatoire 129
   on 'slick pianists' 131
   as teacher 131–2
   on unequal fees 130
San Antonio, Texas 129
San Francisco 171
   Symphony Orchestra 175
São Paulo 141
Saratoga, New York 25
Sarette, Bernard
   founder of Paris Conservatoire 43–4
Satie, Erik 92, 102
   Socrate 115
scales 15, 32, 186
Scarlatti, Domenico 81, 128, 139, 146
Scey-Montbéliard, Prince de 114
Scharrer, Irene 140
Schenker, Otto 94
Schiff, András 160
Schnabel, Artur 1, 153
   Beethoven sonata cycle 131
   Annie Fischer compared with 160, 161
   teaches Lili Kraus 153
   teaches Nancy Weir 162–3
   teaching methods 153, 162–3
Schoenberg, Arnold 94, 106
Schonberg, Harold C. 161
   on Alicia de Larrocha 167
   on Guiomar Novaes 142
Schroeter, Johann Samuel 40
   protégé of J.C. Bach 40

Schroeter, Rebecca 39–40
   Haydn on 40
   Haydn piano trios dedicated to 40
   relationship with Haydn 40
Schubert, Franz 55, 59, 146, 197
   impromptus 162
Schumann (Wieck), Clara 2, 62, 71, 72–8, 80
   child prodigy 72
   children 72, 74, 75
   compared with Arabella Goddard 84
   compared with Liszt, Thalberg and Pleyel 73
   compositions 74–5
      piano concerto 74
      piano trio 75–6
      three romances opus 22 77
      variations opus 20 77
   discouraged from composing 74–5
   duets with Wilhelmine Clauss-Szarvady 79
   father Friedrich Wieck 72, 73
   friendship with Brahms 72, 78
   hand size 213, 234
   Hanslick on 78
   income 72, 78
   joint diary with Robert 74–5
   mother Marianne Wieck 72–3
   on own piano trio 76–7
   performs Beethoven's 'Hammerklavier' Sonata 78
   plays from memory 53
   on Marie Pleyel 70–1
   portraits 72, 76
   relationship with Robert Schumann 73–8
   repertoire 73, 75, 77–8
      'early music' 72
   reputation 78
   as teacher 72, 78
   tours 72, 75, 227
Schumann, Robert 41, 59, 62, 79, 137, 143, 146, 202
   admires Szymanowska's music 52
   Andante and Variations opus 46 79
   on Clara's compositions 74
   compared with Montgeroult 46

INDEX

complete works performed by Marie Jaëll 91
death 77
Études symphoniques 100
Fantasie in C 109, 161
Faschingsschwank aus Wien 81
joint diary with Clara 74–5
mental health 77
piano concerto 112
piano quartet 75, 82
piano quintet 80
piano trio 75
on Marie Pleyel 70
pupil of Friedrich Wieck 73–4
quotes Clara's themes 74
relationship with Clara 73–8
Schuyler, Philippa 174–8
   Carnegie Hall debut 177
   child prodigy 174
   coercive upbringing 174–5
   compared with young Mozart 175
   compositions 175
      Fairy Tale Symphony 175
   explores 'black' and 'white' identities 175–6
   inspires Black community 174
   Philippa Schuyler School for the Gifted 177
   portrait 176
   quality of playing 177–8
   reacts against upbringing 175–6
   right-wing views 177
   touring 176
   in Vietnam 177
Schweitzer, Albert
   pupil of Marie Jaëll 93
   translates Jaëll's *Le Toucher* 93
Scott, Alma Long 194
Scott, Hazel 190, 194–6
   boogie-woogie classics 195
   at Café Society 194
   child prodigy 194
   civil rights activism 196
   classical training 194
   earnings 195
   films 195
   House Un-American Activities Committee 194, 195
   marriage 195, 196
   mental health 196
   radio 194
   recordings
      Bach to Boogie 195
      'Black and White Are Beautiful' 196
      'It's Gonna Be a Great Day' 196
      Relaxed Piano Sounds 196
   refuses segregated audiences 194
   salon 196
   TV show 194, 195
Scottish National Orchestra 161
Scruggs, Mary Alfrieda *see* Williams, Mary Lou
Seventh Veil, The (film) 156
sewing 12
Sex Discrimination Act 209
Shudi, Burkhart 7–8
Shaffer, Peter
   Amadeus 27
Shanghai 84, 178
   Conservatory 178–9
Shaw, George Bernard
   on Arabella Goddard 85
   on Sophie Menter 90
Sherman, Bob 168
Shostakovich, Dmitri 148
   denounced by Soviets 169–70
   and Tatiana Nikolayeva 169–70, 171
   piano concertos 156
   Twenty-Four Preludes and Fugues 169–70, 171
   on Maria Yudina 149
sight-reading 131
   Lovie Austin 182
   Brillon de Jouy 25
Signale
   on Wilhelmine Clauss-Szarvady 79, 80, 82
Signoret, Simone 198
Silas, Edouard
   on Marie Pleyel 71
Simone, Nina 196–200, 235
   adopts new name 198
   Black activism and civil rights movement 198–9
   Carnegie Hall concert 198

on her style 198
influence of Bach 199–200
Langston Hughes poem on 199
love of classical music 197
marriage 198
mental health 199
'Mississippi Goddam' 199
portrait 200
pupil of Muriel Mazzanovich 197
recordings
   'Aint Got No/I Got Life' 199
   'For All We Know' 200
   Gershwin 'I Love You, Porgy' 198
   'Love Me or Leave Me' 200
   'My Baby Just Cares For Me' 199–200
   Nuff Said 199
rejected by Curtis Institute 197
as singer 197
on singing 197–8
stands against racism 197
Singer, Isaac 113
Singer, Winnaretta, Princesse de Polignac 113–17
affairs 115
commissions
   Falla *El retablo de maese Pedro* 115
   Fauré songs 115
   Milhaud *Les Malheurs d'Orphée* 115
   Poulenc organ concerto and 2 piano concerto 115
   Satie *Socrate* 115
   Stravinsky *Persephone* and *Renard* 115
   Tailleferre piano concerto no. 1 115
   Weill symphony no. 2 115
Fondation Polignac 116
hosts Toscanini, Arthur Rubinstein and Horowitz 114
inheritance 114
marriages 114
philanthropic work 116
portrait 116
salons 113, 114–17
   model for Proust 115–16
   sponsors pianists 115
   supports ballet, opera and orchestras 115
singing 12
   women accompany 13
Smart, Sir George 55
Smyth, Ethel 115
   on Röntgen family 206–7
Société des Compositeurs 91
Solomon (pianist) 2
Soloviev, Nikolai Feopemptovich
   on Teresa Carreño 100
Soria, Cécile
   pupil of Clementi 56
   teacher of Louise Farrenc 56
Southey, Robert
   discourages Charlotte Brontë 10
Spohr, Louis 79
spreading chords 166
Stadler, Abbé
   on Barbara Ployer 33
Stalin, Joseph 147–8, 150, 169, 170
Star, The 14
steamships 84, 85, 98
Stephens, Ward
   on Cécile Chaminade 104
Stern, Isaac 146
Stockhausen, Karlheinz 148
Stokowski, Leopold
   marriage to Olga Samaroff 130–1
Strauss, Richard 94
Stravinsky, Igor 106
   Les Noces 115
   Persephone 115
   Renard 115
Stroud, Andrew 198
Süddeutsche Musik-Zeitung
   on Wilhelmine Clauss-Szarvady 80
Suffragettes 107
Sydney Opera House 192
Szarvady, Frigyes 81
Székely, Arnold
   teaches Annie Fischer 160
   teaches Lili Kraus 151
Szeryng, Henryk 146
Szigeti, Joseph 146

INDEX

Szymanowska (Wołowska), Maria
    51–4, 234
  and Chopin 53, 54
  compositions 51–2
    Caprice on the Romance of Joconde
      53
    displaced by Chopin 54
    evoke coloratura singing 53
    influence Chopin 54
    Twenty Exercises and Preludes
      51–2
  death 54
  early success in Paris 51
  income 54
  Jewish family 51
  marriage 51
  music dedicated to her 51
  plays from memory 53
  portrait 52
  relationship with Goethe 53
  royal appointment in St Petersburg
    53, 54
  salon 53
  Schumann admires 52
  teaching 53
  tours 52–3
Szymanowski, Jósef 51

Tailleferre, Germaine
  piano concerto no. 1 115
Tait, Lawson
  The Economy of Health 18
Tartini, Giuseppe 24
Tasmania 155
Tatum, Art 28
Tausig, Carl 49
  teaches Sophie Menter 88
Tchaikovsky, Pyotr Ilyich 112
  on Adele aus der Ohe 107
  death 108
  piano concerto no. 1 107, 108, 156
  symphony no. 6, *Pathéthique* 108
teachers
  author's experience of 1
  earning 17–18
  lineages 4
  masterclasses 217–18
    women at disadvantage 217–18
  and posture 16
  women piano teachers 16, 53, 87,
    216–17
  men dominate at advanced level
    216–17
Teichmüller, Robert
  teaches Eileen Joyce 155
television 3, 178, 179, 192, 193, 195,
  196, 211, 215
Tempest, Kae 206
Teresa Carreño Cultural Complex
  101
Teresa Carreño Youth Orchestra
  101
Texan Christian University, Fort
  Worth 154
Thalberg, Sigismond
  'duel' with Liszt 50
  influences Louise Pleyel 69
  public concerts 49
  teaches Arabella Goddard 82, 83
Theatre Owners' Booking Association
  182
Thomson, Virgil
  on Landowska's *Goldberg Variations*
    128
  on Philippa Schuyler 175
Times, The 67, 83, 84
  on Louise Dulcken 65
  on Clara Schumann 78
Tolstoy, Leo 126
Tolstoy, Sonia 126
Tomes, Susan
  and 1966 Leeds Piano Competition
    211
  ignorance of women pianists 1–2,
    239
  interviews women pianists 221–38
  in National Youth Orchestra of
    Great Britain 207
  The Piano: A History in 100 Pieces
    194
  'self-reviewing' project 222–3
Torra, Juan 167
Toscanini, Arturo 114
Toth, Aladár 160
trains 89, 109, 147
Trefusis, Violet 115

Trémont, Louis, Baron de
    description of Beethoven 44
    relationship with Hélène de Montgeroult 44
Tribune 138
Trinidad 191, 194
Tryon, North Carolina 196
Tyler, Anne
    Redhead by the Side of the Road 4

Valian, Virginia
    Why So Slow? The Advancement of Women 242
Van Cliburn Competition 154
Van Gogh, Vincent 12
Variations sur le nom de Marguerite Long 125
Venezuela
    Bank of 96
    Teresa Carreño 96–101
    Simón Bolívar Youth Orchestra 96
Venice 113
    Palazzo Contarini Polignac 114
Vermeer, Johannes
    paintings of women at virginals 11, 12
Victoria, Queen
    Wilhelmine Clauss-Szarvady plays to 81
    Marie Jaëll plays to 91
    likes Chaminade's music 104
    pupil of Lucy Anderson 54–5
    pupil of Louise Dulcken 65
    visited by Felix Mendelssohn 61
Vienna 17, 34, 35, 36, 42, 69, 73, 93, 144, 152
    artistic life in 34–5, 42
    Kohlmarkt 34
    Konservatorium 152
    Michaelerkirche 36
    salons 50
Vigée-Lebrun, Mme
    on Hélène de Montgeroult 43
    salon 43
violin 11
Viotti, Giovanni Battista
    plays with Hélène de Montgeroult 43

virginal(s) 11, 12
Volkonskaya, Princess Maria 50

Wagner, Paul 194
Wagner, Richard 113
    Tannhaüser overture, arr. Liszt 89
Walter, Bruno 94, 131
Wang, Yuja 178, 232–3
war
    American Civil 98
    Vietnam 177
    World War I 95, 106, 109, 116, 123, 126, 134, 142, 152
    World War II 42, 127, 129, 134, 135, 137, 138–40, 149, 150, 152, 156, 157, 160, 163, 172, 184, 196, 209
        National Gallery concerts 138–40
Washington, D.C.
    White House 96, 101, 106, 112, 195
Warsaw 51, 52, 53, 125, 210, 214
    National Theatre 53
Waterman, Fanny 210
Waters, Ethel 183
Waymon, Eunice *see* Simone, Nina
Weber, Carl Maria von
    Konzertstück in F minor 69–70, 88
    Violin Sonata basis of *Sicilienne* 'by M. von Paradis' 30
Weill, Kurt
    symphony no. 2 115
Weimar 53, 86, 92, 107
Weiner, Leo
    teaches Lili Kraus 151
Weir, Nancy 162–5
    Bangor Trio 163
    career choices 163
    community work 164–5
    compared with Mozart 163
    early acclaim 162
    earnings 164
    portrait 164
    pupil of Amy Freeman Corder 162
    pupil of Craxton and Matthay 163
    at Queensland Conservatorium 164
    on Schnabel 162–3

INDEX

teaching 164
wartime intelligence work 163
youngest pupil of Schnabel 162
Wieck, Clara *see* Schumann, Clara
Wieck, Friedrich 72–4
Wieniawski, Henryk 59
Williams, John 188
Williams, Mary Lou 187–91, 196
   arrangements 188
   on Lovie Austin 183–4
   Black Christ of the Andes 190
   compositions 188
      Masses 190
      'Roll 'Em' 188
      'St Martin de Porres' 190
      'What's Your Story Morning Glory' 188
      Zodiac Suite 189
   at Duke University 191
   on experimentation 189
   on her childhood 187–8
   influence on bebop 189
   and Andy Kirk 188
   learns notation 188
   leaves jazz scene 189–90
   marriage 188
   Mary Lou Williams Piano Workshop 189
   'masculine' style 188
   portrait 190
   on practising 191
   radio 189, 191
   religion 190
   rejects classical training 189
   and Art Tatum 188
   teaching 191
Wilson, President Woodrow 101
Windrush generation 192
Wittgenstein, Hans 94
Wittgenstein, Hermine 95–6
Wittgenstein, Karl 94
Wittgenstein, Kurt 95
Wittgenstein, Leopoldine 93–6
   collection of manuscripts 94
   salon 93, 94
Wittgenstein, Ludwig 95
   Tractatus Logico-Philosophicus 95
Wittgenstein, Paul 95
   Ravel's *Concerto for the Left Hand* composed for 95
Wittgenstein, Rudi 95
Wolff, Christoff 42
women
   and 'accomplishment' 10, 16, 36
   composers 3, 6, 11, 28, 29, 30, 32, 35–6, 37, 39, 44, 45–7, 54, 61–4, 89, 91, 92, 96–8, 100, 102–4, 183, 185–6, 188–90, 191–2, 199–200
   discouraged from large-scale works 203–4
   eclipsed by male composers 47, 54, 59, 60–1, 201–5, 239
   excluded from composition classes 57, 119–20, 202
   excluded from networking 202–3
   Hanslick on 'lack of aptitude' 204
   Nicola LeFanu on 'gentlemen's club' 204
   conductors unknown before 20th century 204
   determined to perform 10, 55
   at disadvantage in piano competitions 211–15
   discouraged from concert career 9–11, 48–50, 55, 60, 110, 118–19, 211
   education 15, 25–6, 56, 102, 131, 176, 177, 179, 180, 216, 239
   empowered by music 19
   equal pay 57–8, 87, 130, 163
   excluded from orchestras 203
   gender-specific criticism 56, 131, 138, 154
   hand size 165–6, 212–13, 215, 233–4
   health affected by music 18–19
   institutional sexism 122, 240
   instruments suitable for 11–12
   and 'masculine' playing 71, 83, 101, 111, 131, 161, 182, 185, 188, 208, 211, 230, 240–1

paintings of at keyboard instruments 11, 12
pianists
  ageism 219–21, 234–5
  appearance 30–1, 80, 83, 90–1, 104, 175–6, 187, 231–3
  champion women composers 236
  concert dress 131, 136, 147, 149, 155, 156, 157, 160, 192, 193, 231–2
  difficulty sustaining career 218–19
  fees 227, 228, 229, 230
  forgotten by historians 1–4, 36, 131, 239
  and 'gatekeepers' 237–8
  interviewed 221–38
    reasons for anonymity 223
    and 'men's repertoire' 69, 73, 101, 111, 213, 215, 232–4, 240
    and parenthood 227–8, 229–30
  public perception 219–20
  racism 235–6
  in shadow of husbands 201
  and social media 238
  success harder for women 224–7
  touring
    difficult for women 48–9, 228–9
    male pianists dominate 48–9
  treatment by agents 224
  treatment by conductors 224, 226
  treatment by male colleagues 225–6
  undervalued compared to composers 205–6
piano teachers 16, 53, 87, 216–17
  men dominate at advanced level 216–17
  women at disadvantage in masterclasses 217–18
Plato on music suitable for 5
play duets 13
play for dancing 13
play keyboard instruments in paintings 11

play solo 13
play the piano at home 9–19
prejudice against 136, 188, 204, 224
stringed instruments suitable for 5
Women's Auxiliary Air Force 163
Women's Journal, The 239
Wood, Henry 155
  on Teresa Carreño 101
Woolf, Virginia 115
Wordsworth, Dorothy 201
Wordsworth, William 201

Young, Lester 196
Ysaÿe, Eugène 59, 146
  Ysaÿe Competition 163
Yudina, Maria 147–50
  banned from performing 149
  conflict with Soviet authorities 147–8, 149
  champions modern music 148
  dismissed from teaching posts 149
  eccentricity 149–50
  performs J.S. Bach's *Well-Tempered Clavier* 148–9
  at Petrograde Conservatoire 148
  as portrayed in *The Death of Stalin* 147–8
  records Mozart piano concerto in A K488 148
  relationship with Maria Grinberg 150
  religious beliefs 148, 149
  repertoire 148–9
  Shostakovich on 149
  Sviatoslav Richter on 149, 150

Zeisler, Fannie Bloomfield *see* Bloomfield Zeisler, Fannie
Zeisler, Sigmund 110–11
Zelter, Carl
  on Fanny Mendelssohn 60
  runs Berlin Sing-Akademie 60
Zhdanov doctrine 169
Zhu Xiao-Mei 178–80
  on Bach *Goldberg Variations* 180
  child prodigy 178
  helped by Isaac Stern 179
  helps young musicians 180

love of Bach 179
manual labour during Cultural
    Revolution 179
recordings 179
    Bach *Goldberg Variations* 179–80
repertoire 179
return to China 180

study in Boston 179
success in Paris 179
Zieritz, Grete von 109
zither 5, 6
Zumpe, Johannes 7
Zürich 144